BEYOND THE BOUNDARIES

Travels on England Cricket Tours

BY SCYLD BERRY

fairfield books

First published by Fairfield Books in 2021

fairfield books

Fairfield Books
Wildfire Sport
Bedser Stand
Kia Oval
London
SE11 5SS

Typeset in Garamond
Typesetting and illustrations by Rob Whitehouse
Photography by Getty Images unless stated

This book is printed on paper certified
by the Forest Stewardship Council

© 2021 Scyld Berry
ISBN 978-1-909811-60-7

A CIP catalogue record for is available from the British Library

Printed by CPI Group (UK) Ltd

CONTENTS

To
my Godmother
and unpaid consultant
Madeleine

ACKNOWLEDGEMENTS

"He was adept at generalisation, an essential aspect of the travelling art." Thus Jan Morris, finest of travel writers, wrote about Ibn Battuta, finest of travellers. Labouring in their wake, I would like to generalise by expressing my gratitude to my colleagues in the written media in the press box, my teammates in effect. Cricket writing is a collective effort. Each of us offers something, an item of knowledge, a second opinion, a different view of an incident, a statistic, a piece of wit: "This is the first time since 1886 that England's top six batsmen have all been LBW for nought." Well, I did not know that. Yet, by pooling our resources during a day's play, we can each bake our cake – a solid and substantial cake – upon which we squirt our individual icing. Thank you, fellas, which does not exclude females.

Individually, I would again like to thank my godmother Madeleine Riley for being the best of sounding boards, having read every book in English – this is another generalisation – and several translations of books that are not. Dr Richard Leach, in addition to reading several chapters, has been kind when tempering my wilder enthusiasms. David Luxton continues to be the literary agent of all cricket literary agents, and it was he who recommended Richard Whitehead to be editor of this book. He enlisted Walter Gammie to double-check all the statistics. Richard has been absolutely wonderful, a dream to work with – and I am writing these words last to minimise the opportunity he has to cut them out.

INTRODUCTION

In the good old days, when Covid-19 could have been confined to forests around Wuhan, my England cricket tours used to begin in the dentist's chair. While he or she probed like Shane Warne or Anil Kumble on an awkward length, I looked out of the window at plummeting leaves and visualised Caribbean beaches, or Table Mountain, or Australian wine and women – if not song – or the mountains of northern India and Pakistan.

"Are you're going somewhere nice?" the dentist would ask mid-probe.

What can you say? You cannot take that tube out of your mouth which prevents, or promotes, gagging.

"Aaaagh-a" would be the closest I could get to a reply.

"Oh, America?"

"Uh, uh. Aaaaaaagh-a."

"Oh, Australia! I've always wanted to go to Australia. How long are you going for?"

"Uh, uh. Aaaagha!"

"Oh, you mean Austria!"

This is not working. I have to take that sucking tube out. "Antigua! I'm going on the England cricket tour of the West Indies."

Predictable follow-up: "Oooh, do you want someone to carry your suitcase?" Whereupon the high-pitched whining of the drill resumed and drove away all happy thoughts.

It was like being in the office and the editor declaring loudly: "You know you've got the best job in journalism, don't you?"

Yes, of course I did. This is precisely why I applied to be a cricket correspondent in 1976. What better way to earn a living than being paid to avoid the English winter and visit warm countries, containing about a quarter of our planet's population, and to watch cricket, on expenses?

English cricketers began touring in the autumn of 1859 in order to earn a livelihood, when otherwise they would have been unpaid for their skills. These first cricket tourists sailed to Canada and the USA. Australia became the popular destination once the Suez Canal had opened and Americans chose to disport by themselves, breeding a regrettable insularity. India, New Zealand, South Africa and the West Indies were further destinations by the end of the 19th century, both for professionals bent on money and amateurs on hedonism.

Starting in 1977, when I began to cover England at home and abroad, I mostly worked for a Sunday newspaper. The Sunday journalist is a lone wolf – otherwise he ends up on a Saturday morning with nothing new to write – and, like the wolf in Britain, extinct. Daily journalists hunt in a pack. The Sunday writer thinks about what he is going to do; the daily one does it. Both roles I have enjoyed immensely. Often I have got out of bed thinking: "Even if I wasn't being paid, what I most want to do today is exactly what I'm going to do."

When Thomas Cook set up his business in the 1840s, he employed the word "tour" (but never moved into cricket tours, perhaps because he was a member of the Temperance movement). England's touring schedule used to allow time for excursions up-country or off-piste, especially for the Sunday correspondent. An England cricket tour gradually became more of a business trip, every day allocated either to playing or travelling or practising. Still, it wasn't half fun; it was almost entirely fun.

The one drawback has been less family life. While my children were growing up, it was hard to go away (for me, that is – they carried on blithely with their mother at home). In a distant hotel room of an evening, the chocolate left by a maid on the pillow was not much of a substitute. My being away for weeks or months on end was of course vastly more arduous for my wife, Sunita: I could not have done my job had she not been the strongest person I have met, among other superlatives.

It has been an existence I have tried to justify on these grounds: I have consumed far too much of the Earth's resources, flown too many air miles, wasted piles of plastic, and it is only by communicating happy or interesting experiences to others that I can justify this parasitism. Besides, I could not have done much else.

This book, I hope, will therefore serve as a taste of those Test-playing countries where England toured before the curtain of Covid-19 came down. Those were the days, and nights, when anybody could accompany England on a cricket tour, meeting the players at a hotel or ground, travelling around the country, free to go almost anywhere and meet local people, often with the same interest of cricket in common, and without social distancing.

Not any more.

But for those who have not visited these countries, for those who never will, and for those who have fond memories of them, I have tried to distil the essence of each country and its cricket. The secret of living, I have slowly learnt, is to make the most and best of wherever one is.

AUSTRALIA

Cairns
Paradise Waterhole
Townsville

Brisbane
Toowoomba

Perth
Bunbury

Adelaide

Sydney
Canberra

Melbourne

Hobart

CHAPTER ONE

AUSTRALIA

Even in a first-class cabin, the voyage could be rough on the ship transporting the first two cricket teams to Australia. Dining tables had a rail along all four sides so the soup bowls would not fly into laps. In a storm, waves could wash through every deck of SS *Great Britain* from first class down to the bilges. Brunel's design for the first ocean-going ship made of iron was revolutionary, but she did not have the buoyancy tanks which made subsequent voyages to Australia such a luxurious pleasure for England's cricketers.

The first of all cricket tours had gone from England to Canada and the United States in 1859. That journey took ten days, but voyaging to Australia took a lot longer, not least because the Suez Canal had yet to be constructed. The first team of 1861/62 had stopped in Cape Town for coal; the second, in 1863/64, sailed to Melbourne without stopping, but still took 61 days because most of the time they did exactly that: they sailed, using 16,000 square yards of canvas. Only when the wind was contrary, or becalmed, were boilers stoked and the enormous propeller lowered into the sea.

Conditions on SS *Great Britain* were cramped apart from in first class, with 865 passengers on board, minus a five-year-old boy who died of dysentery and was thrown overboard in a sack tied to a cannonball. Port Out Starboard Home was the way to go, but as the *Great Britain* was made of iron, you could be gently fried in your cabin on either side of the ship. Even in first class, there was just one porthole to ventilate your cabin. When the propeller was revolving, the cabins throbbed, and the deck turned black with smuts from the funnel if the wind was wrong. Anything but POSH.

The days of *Great Britain* as the most famous ship afloat were already numbered. By the 1880s she was a mere windjammer, stripped of her engines, carrying coal not cricketers. She was dumped in the Falkland Islands and left to rot, before the hulk was hauled back to Bristol, where she had been built, and renovated. Her heyday was brief; yet one of the city's more renowned sons, Edward Grace, who celebrated his 22nd birthday during the 1863/64 voyage, left a diary describing what it was like for cricket's pioneers sailing to the other side of the world.

Being the most popular of English novelists, Charles Dickens had been the first celebrity to go on an international tour to make money, in his case to the United States. Cricketers were the next commercial proposition, touring North America initially, then Australia after the gold rushes in Ballarat and Bendigo. An agent from the Melbourne Cricket Club, which aspired to be the MCC of the Southern Hemisphere, signed up a dozen of the best English cricketers to tour Australia in the winter of 1863/64 under the captaincy of George Parr, paying each of them £250 (around £30,000 today) and their first-class fare of £78-15-0.

"But for the accident that his own brother proved greater than himself, E.M. Grace would have lived in cricket history as perhaps the most remarkable player the game has produced," according to Edward's obituary in *Wisden*. "Barring W.G., it would be hard indeed to name a man who was a stronger force on a side or a more remarkable match winner." E.M. was the sole amateur in this party, but not so very different from the professionals. They all ate and drank prodigiously, and gambled on everything that moved, starting with the distance the ship travelled per day. At the end of their tour, Roger Iddison of Yorkshire spoke for them all when he declared, with a belch that is audible down the ages, that Australians were not good at cricket (they were all amateurs in that period) but "a wonderful lot of drinking men".

E.M. was shorter, smaller, less hirsute than his younger brother: more mutton-chop whiskers than beard. He was known as "the Coroner", which he became, whereas W.G. was nothing less than "the Champion". In the family orchard at Downend, E.M. grew up to be a hitter, as his bat was so big he slogged to leg, while W.G. revolutionised batting by playing straighter. Wherever they were, E.M. and W.G. competed and squabbled.

In the absence of younger brother on SS *Great Britain*, E.M.'s rivalry was directed at the passenger who had bagged the upper berth in their cabin before Grace arrived at Liverpool docks. "There is a young fellow, the name of John Sutcliffe, going out with us," he wrote in his diary. "I think he goes to enjoy himself." Halfway through the voyage Sutcliffe is "always drinking and a very nasty fellow";

and by the time the ship had reached Australian waters, E.M. had seized him "by the shoulders, opened the door and bundled him out, flinging his clothes after him, and I would not let him in again so he had to sleep in the passage … He has warning that unless he is in by 11 o'clock he shall not come in at all.

"I can lick them all at pitching the quoits on the board," E.M. added gleefully. He tried to find male passengers to play whist so he could place bets and clean up; he tried to find female ones too, only "there is not one sufficiently to my liking as far as looks go for me to care about". Cricketers on subsequent tours of Australia, it is fair to say, have not been quite so particular. One woman, who had better remain nameless, is "most awfully ugly, squints all over the place and has a chin like an elephant." As minor compensation, E.M. concedes that "she sings very fairly".

Pursuing his medical studies was difficult when passengers pounded the deck above his cabin, but E.M. was called upon when one of the professionals, George Tarrant, had toothache. "It was the last but one on the upper jaw left hand side. It was tremendously right in and required all my force to pull it out, but fortunately it came out and that quite clean too at the first pull with 4 fangs to it." No anaesthetic, of course, other than alcohol. Of the other cricketers, George Anderson was always seasick, and Julius Caesar stricken with gout, while William Caffyn was skilled at the cornet.

E.M. records the sighting of whales, dolphins and albatrosses – some "as large as 20 or 24 feet across" – and how every empty bottle was thrown into the sea; he has a boil inside his nose which eventually bursts; meets several members of the Melbourne Cricket Club on their way home after visiting England; complains the fare is poor, even though live cows, pigs and chickens are kept on deck; and when finally they reach Melbourne Heads shortly before Christmas, a storm is raging, their coal is almost exhausted, and not a pilot in sight. The ship's captain gambled by steering the *Great Britain* through the Heads himself. "It was most awfully nervous work, the waves at times being 20 or 30 feet above us. One most fortunately burst just behind us or most likely it would have washed some of us overboard," E.M. wrote.

They landed to a grand reception and the sight of "a great many of the streets under water" – flooding which made practice impossible.

After a few days, Grace recorded "the weather seems quite settled now into something beautifully fine. About 80 in the shade and a little over 100 in the sun but really delightful." He goes to the MCG, where a stand for 3,000 spectators is being built, and considers it "a most beautiful ground". He encounters mosquitoes and nets of a different kind; and the first ball he faces in Australia, in practice at Richmond, "took my middle stump flying".

Parr's team went through their tour, including a visit to New Zealand, unbeaten. E.M. went on to open the batting in the inaugural Test match in England at The Oval in 1880. He hit the first boundary with his trademark pull, and scored 36 in an opening stand of 91 with his younger brother, who went on to 152. The youngest brother, Fred, made three Graces in one England team.

A song was composed on board the *Great Britain* by a Mr Moore. He did not go on to become Master of the Queen's Music or Poet Laureate:

> There's the cricketers bred, the Eleven of All England
> A fine set of fellows as ere crossed the sea
> I hope soon to see them with bat and ball in hand
> Astonishing the natives of proud Austra-lee...

On the whole, in fact, it has proved to be the other way round. In Australia, Australian cricketers have performed much better than English cricketers: the hosts have won 95 Tests in Australia to England's 57. Where the lyricist was right was in noting that the natives – the white ones – were proud. He thereby identified the source of their future superiority on the cricket field.

* * *

"We've chummed up."

With its slightly alarming connotation, it was not a phrase which I had heard before the first of my 11 tours of Australia in 1978/79.

The man who said it, however, fulfilled exactly my expectations of what an Australian cricketer – or a typical Australian bloke – should look like: shortish, stocky, powerful of forearm, blotched a bit by skin cancer, and friendly. His name was Neil Dansie, and he learnt so much from batting once with Sir Donald Bradman that he opened for South Australia long enough to become one of the state's top ten first-class run-scorers.

It was the eve of my first state game in Australia, at Adelaide Oval, but already a – if not the – fundamental difference between Australian and English cricket was apparent. In Australia, you practised hard before a game, because you only had one per week or fortnight, and a job besides. In England you turned up on the morning of the game and played, because it was one match out of many, and energy had to be conserved over a long season in order to sustain your livelihood. Another novelty: clustered around the nets were former South Australian cricketers, not bitter about being forced to retire and find another job, because playing cricket had never been their living, just ready to talk about the past and pass on knowledge to the next generation. The nets at Adelaide Oval were streets ahead of anything in England, spread out behind the main pavilion, their surfaces fast and true, the run-ups as long as you liked, and open for inspection by spectators.

John Woodcock of *The Times*, who had been touring Australia since 1950/51, kindly introduced this whipper-snapper to the veterans, who were occasionally giving "the Aussie salute" by swatting flies. This left me the tricky task of explaining the name Scyld. Any stuck-up Pom in Australia was going to be bracketed with Douglas Jardine, still a national hate-figure for devising Bodyline to beat Bradman.

"Hi, I was born in Yorkshire, in Sheffield," I said brightly, then with a surge of inspiration, "So I'm Sheffield Scyld!" Cricket's strongest domestic competition was still called the Sheffield Shield. Every state played the others home and away, flat out over four days, before administrators who knew the cost of everything and the value of nothing sold the family silver and renamed it "the Pura Milk Cup."

"G'day, mate! How are yer?"

The ice was broken. I was a Pom but … hey, Sheffield Scyld. My bloody oath, good as gold!

Dansie showed me the press box, which was side-on then, towards the bottom of the main stand, where Sir Donald Bradman would sit in state. In the club match in Adelaide when Dansie had batted with the Don, the second new ball was approaching when

Bradman   drove past the opening bowler, who was fielding at mid-on; he did so twice, for three runs a time. Bradman told young Dansie he was not trying to hit a four, but tire the bowler before he took the new ball.

Dansie and I chummed up, even though this was not North Africa, Gallipoli or Palestine, and we were not in the armed forces. What united us – though he was a former Australian player of distinction who had made 18 first-class centuries – then seemed more significant than what divided us. Australia's attitude to playing England at cricket, in the years building up to the infamous ball-tampering affair of Sandpapergate in 2018, was "beat the Poms at all costs". Before the 1990s, the dynamic was different. By the end of the 1950/51 Ashes series, Australian crowds were supporting England because the Poms had not won a Test, let alone a series, since 1938. Both World Wars had debilitated English cricket vastly more than Australia's, so the Aussie in the street had a sympathy for the Mother Country as the underdog who deserved "a break" – as if we were all miners or diggers together, or troops in the trenches.

* * *

The first month or more of an England tour of Australia was a mobile holiday camp, one bumper Butlin's. Ashes tours subsequently evolved into a set pattern of five Tests – in Brisbane, Adelaide, Perth, Melbourne at Christmas, then Sydney at New Year, all in the space of six weeks. When I started, the warming-up alone took six weeks, and then the Test series was far less condensed, with practice games and a trip to Tasmania in between. What a warming-up too, by day and by night, as England toured the main cities to play the states and also visited some up-country venues, without a mention of the word "curfew".

Australia, like touring itself, was much more relaxed. During my baptismal week in Adelaide, when England played South Australia, Geoffrey Boycott bought drinks in the hotel bar – or, at any rate, he nodded to the journalist ghosting his tour book to pay for a round. Players and press were one party, I saw, bound by the code that what happened on tour stayed there; and not a few of the japes were merry.

16

When we attended – and it was "we" – the Governor-General's reception in Canberra, the wine flowed. Nowadays at British High Commission parties the trays of drinks and canapes disappear promptly half-an-hour before the scheduled close, and branded on officialdom's forehead is "Time to go". Not in Australia, not then. White, as opposed to indigenous Australia, was in its late teens in the 1970s, not highly sensitive but zestful, fun-loving, always ready for a good time and a laugh. Strangers were received hospitably and entertained, even if the underlying assumption was that they should come from Britain and go home after visiting Australia. Compared to the English national character, the Australian of the Dansie generation was more generous of spirit after returning from the World Wars, ready to live and let live.

I was 24, on my first Ashes tour, unattached, so what do you expect: sobriety, self-restraint? After a few glasses, I was engaging the Governor-General's daughter in flirtatious conversation as we sauntered around lawns heady with spring blossom. Kate gave me her address, and after the game in Canberra – of which I have not the slightest recollection – I bought a silk handkerchief in Perth. I found a shop that did sewing, and had stitched upon it the name of the Shakespeare play which contained the phrase "kiss me, Kate", along with the number of the act, scene and line.

Not until the package had been delivered did I realise there are several editions of Shakespeare's plays. Lo and behold, the edition of *The Taming of the Shrew* in Perth City Library was not the same as in the Governor-General's library. Worse still, instead of the phrase to which I wanted to refer, Kate had found the corresponding line in their edition, which expressed the completely opposite sentiment – something to the tune of "Out, damned spot! O shrew most vile! Thou most evil strumpet!" I could have been expelled from Australia in a diplomatic incident had her kind, and most knowledgeable, father not advised his daughter that my edition might have been different to theirs.

* * *

It was not only England who had a chastening first state game in 1978, losing to South Australia for the first time since 1925. It was also a crash course for me in the first law of journalism. If you don't like the heat, stay out of the kitchen.

Day one at Adelaide Oval was unremarkable as South Australia scored 281 for nine. Day two was a Saturday, my big day for *The Observer*. I had already written and filed my feature, about Australia's still-decent stock of pace bowlers even after Kerry Packer had creamed off Dennis Lillee, Jeff Thomson and over a dozen more of Australia's finest players for his World Series Cricket matches. Here was cricket's biggest existential crisis: would the international game be eclipsed by Packer's private circus – consisting of an Australian team, a West Indian team and a third composed of the best from the rest of the world – trotting round the globe? The forthcoming Ashes series had to be big and competitive for the traditional order to survive.

Feature articles had to be filed during the week – only reports of live events could wait until Saturday – because *The Observer* was literally set in stone. Under the editorial floors in Blackfriars were the printing works, where a compositor would take a metal letter "t" then an "h" then an "e" and put them together to start a paragraph. It was Gutenberg souped up, and only slightly speeded up, hence all features had to be set before Saturday.

Within a few hours my first feature from Australia was completely out of date, overtaken by events on day two at Adelaide Oval. A fast bowler who had transferred from Victoria was quicker than anyone England had: he soon hit England's No.3 batsman, Clive Radley, on his unhelmeted head and effectively ruled him out of the Tests. Sir Donald Bradman, watching side-on from the committee stand, was reported to rate this new Rodney Hogg a good 'un. And what was I supposed to do, now that Hogg was Australia's fastest and brightest prospect and my feature redundant? Adelaide was ten-and-a-half hours ahead of London: by the time the sports editor was at the end of a phone in the office it would be 9pm in Adelaide.

In retrospect, I should probably have written an extra-long match report and told the office to bin my feature; but that would mean leaving a big hole in the feature pages, not something to be decided unilaterally on my second tour. There was only one course of action as I saw it: to downplay Hogg as much as possible in my match report, so the reader would have to move on to my feature about

Australia's other fast bowling prospects. Not much could be said against Hogg's vivid pace, and skiddy bouncers like the one which skulled Radley, and he jagged the ball back sharply enough to trap Boycott leg-before in both innings … but, hey, what did Bradman know about cricket? So I clutched at the straw that Hogg had walked off in mid-session, and was asthmatic, and did not like long spells – not surprisingly given that Australians were still bowling eight-ball overs – to downplay Hogg, if not quite write him off.

Imagine my ever-increasing horror over the next two months as Hogg became renowned as "the Rocket" and broke one Ashes bowling record after another. Every wicket he took was another blow to the vitals and my career. What I did not know then, and made my position still more embarrassing, was that the Australian board had introduced a new type of ball for this Ashes series: still a Kookaburra but, for the first time, stitched by machine not hand. Its seam was prouder, and more prominent – and so was Hogg. England found him a horrendous handful as he swung these new balls away then jagged them back off that extra-large seam. Good old Hoggy took seven wickets in the first Test at Brisbane, ten in the second at Perth, and ten more – for only 66 runs! – as Australia won in Melbourne to drag the series back to 2-1. Hogg did leave the field occasionally, at inconvenient moments for his captain Graham Yallop, but that was all that could be said against him. There were six Tests too, all low-scoring, and seamers dominated as never before in Australia since the 19th century. By the end of the 1978/79 series, Hogg had taken 41 wickets at the ridiculous average of 12. So much for my chances of becoming the cricket correspondent of *The Observer*. I had painted – or printed – myself into a corner in Adelaide. Grin and bear it, or stay out of the kitchen's heat?

* * *

Still, there were compensations. In Australia there always are. Players on old-time tours of Australia did not have panic attacks or bouts of depression, according to the official record: no England cricketer went home in mid-tour for anything other than physical injury until the 21st century. Sir Leonard Hutton shook his head when I ghosted him for *The Observer* and he recalled Denis Compton and

Bill Edrich on England's 1946/47 Ashes trip: "Compo and Bill," he said with an almost audible tut. "They should have been sent home." For players let off the leash of rationing which Britain had endured in the Second World War, temptations were not easily eschewed.

Fruit was a manifestation of Australia's plenitude. In the England of my childhood, fresh fruit consisted of apples, oranges, bananas and, for an exotic luxury, melon, often half ripe. To the press box at the Gabba in Brisbane, farmers would bring presents of their juiciest pineapples, watermelons, cherries – dark ripe cherries, not tasteless red ones. In Perth, at the WACA, Ruby presided over roast lunches every match-day that were fit for Christmas Day, and washed down by all the wine you could drink from vineyards a few miles up the Swan River.

One Christmas Day morning in Melbourne, the correspondents had drinks with the players before they went off in fancy dress to a festive lunch with their families. The rest of us congregated in the lobby of the MCG Hilton. It was an inversion of the original Christmas: plenty of room at the inn, nobody in town. The city streets were deserted; not a tram moved; it could have been the final scene in Nevil Shute's *On The Beach* about the ending of the world after a nuclear war. Alex Bannister of the *Daily Mail* announced with wry wit: "I don't know whether to go to bed, or go to bed, or go to bed."

Brian Bearshaw of the *Manchester Evening News* (local and regional newspapers would send their own correspondent on tour if their county had a strong representation) had some friends from Lancashire who had emigrated to Melbourne. He made a phone call, came back a few minutes later, said we had all been invited to Christmas lunch at their place, so we all piled into a couple of taxis. A lucky family in a far from affluent part of the city suddenly had a visit not from three wise men but ten journalists. Hospitality, specifically towards strangers, has been regarded as the supreme virtue in several cultures; and so it was then in Australia.

* * *

The Gabba, or strictly the 'Gabba as an abbreviation of Woolloongabba, replaced Kensington Oval in Barbados as the biggest barrier in the minds of England cricketers, and their least successful Test venue. The Gabba's pitches have been bouncier than any in England, except Old Trafford in the 1990s, and therefore more favourable to leg-spin as well as pace. But surely it has been more a matter of acclimatisation, or the failure to do so. Whereas Australia's other state capitals are not so different from British cities, Brisbane is more like the southern United States: hot, humid, sub-tropical and probably the city I would choose if I had to live in a mainland state capital. Many Queenslanders live in a "Queenslander" – a wooden, single-storey house on stilts that allow air, snakes and scorpions to pass underneath.

Whenever England have played a game in Queensland before the Brisbane Test, they have not fared too badly at the Gabba, considering it has usually been the first Test. When they have approached Brisbane from the south, and turned up in Queensland three days before the Test, they have been wiped out. A classic case was 2006/07, when they were supposed to defend the Ashes, and flew in from Adelaide on the Monday evening at the same time their wives, girlfriends and children were arriving from the UK. The players practised on the Tuesday, then had to focus their minds while wide-awake wives or jet-lagged girlfriends looked after crying kids. Everyone needs a week to adjust to Queensland, where the sun shines brightly before 5am. Joh Bjelke-Petersen, Queensland's premier when it was known as "the Banana Republic", liked being re-elected, so everyone in Brisbane had to wake up early, and time was adjusted to suit the working hours of farmers out west, who were his vote-bank.

When England did play a first-class game in Queensland outside Brisbane – Toowoomba in 1994/95, Cairns in 1998/99, and Townsville in 2017/18 (I missed the Carrara game in 1990/91 when David Gower flew his plane over the Gold Coast) – it was a privilege to see the outback. In Toowoomba, my wife wanted to go riding, so we found a farm out of town that had horses – and the owners informed us they had not had any rain for three years. What had been their garden was grey powder in which the carcasses of their plants lay buried. I tried to imagine being in England in 1994 and saying it had not rained since 1991.

So inaccessible is the Australian outback that inhabitants of coastal cities can go a lifetime without seeing it except from the air.

You cannot jump into a car and go into the desert: you need two four-wheel-drives in case one breaks down. On your own, you are limited to where Greyhound buses stop and trains go. Even then, on the air-conditioned Ghan from Adelaide to Darwin, or the train to Perth across the Nullarbor, you can look out the window, but your other senses are as detached from what goes on outside as in a modern press box.

After England's 1982/83 tour, while writing my book *Train to Julia Creek*, I rode in the guard's van of a goods train from Cairns to Forsayth; and in the single rail-car from Croydon to Normanton on the Gulf of Carpentaria, which ran once a week for a handful of passengers. Another train in Queensland went only once a month. Thanks to Bjelke-Petersen, farmers out west still wanted the trains to be subsidised heavily, even if they used lorries, and not to feel neglected by politicians in Brisbane.

Townsville was the right place to acclimatise for the Gabba Test of 2017/18, being tropical rather than sub-tropical so even hotter and more humid. If the cricket-cum-footie stadium was typical, so was the municipal swimming pool next door, open to all and free. That's Australia for you, at its best. I heard someone in the changing-room saying it was the best swimming pool he had ever been in. It was outdoors, and unheated; the UV reading was "Extreme" and the "burn time" six minutes.

This Townsville game was the first match in 40 years of touring Australia in which I saw indigenous spectators. Most were schoolchildren bussed in for a weekday morning, playing around in the stands, but a few adults sat beside and chatted with white Australians. This was some progress, because not until 1971 did Queensland's government permit indigenous people to live outside reservations, and then they made it difficult. There had been Aborigine cricketers, in addition to the first Australian team to tour England in 1868: the fastest bowler Sir Donald Bradman ever faced, so he wrote, was Eddie Gilbert bowling for Queensland on a damp pitch at the Gabba in the early 1930s. Then around 2010, having ignored the indigenes so long, Australian cricket's governing body swung to the opposite extreme and became a model of encouragement.

After this game I drove north from Townsville on the Bruce Highway, over Cassowary Creek, and Leichhardt Creek: Leichhardt, the German explorer, was the historical basis for *Voss*, the famous Australian novel by Patrick White. Leichhardt crossed the Great Dividing Range in the 1840s and walked on into the interior, never to return. In late afternoon, when the bush is glowing, I arrived at Paradise Waterhole. The only swimmer said there were "no salties" – no crocodiles, who swim up creeks from the Coral Sea. It must have been something else then above the surface that winked reassuringly.

In the hour before sunset the rainforest turns from light green to dark green to grey. I walked upstream to listen to the birdsong: this is what I miss most when staying in high-rise hotels with windows sealed, in a world besotted with air conditioning. I heard fresh water trickling over stones, the rarest of sounds in the driest of continents.

Back in the Paradise car park a few campers slapped sausages and steaks on the electric barbecues provided for a few coins. I made do with a couple of mangoes from Bowen down the coast before driving back to Townsville for the flight south to Brisbane in the morning and the first Test. I feel happier if I have seen a city from the outside, so to speak, in its geographical context. I like to think that I know where I am.

* * *

I'm not fussy, honestly. All I ask is a seat behind the bowler's arm, and not in an air-conditioned press box (unless England are playing in Sri Lanka), where you can not only see the game but feel what is going on in the middle and in the crowd. Lord's had a brand-new media centre in 2000 when England, for the first time in a generation, bossed West Indies and dismissed them for 54. Next day I heard the ground had been Bedlam, so excited was the crowd at the tables being turned and West Indies being blown away by England's fast bowlers. In the press box, sealed and air conditioned, silence had reigned, broken by the odd murmur. A grand view, but one might as well have been watching in the Hampstead Odeon.

The old Gabba ticked more boxes than any other press box in Australia: natural warmth and windows that opened, fresh fruit at intervals, a perfect view, and always something in the pitch for bowlers. An umpire or player on the field is obviously closer to the action, but the spectator watching closely is in a better position to sense which way a game is going, who is winning.

From such a position at the Vulture Street End, I watched England win the first Tests of 1978/79 and 1986/87. They had not won there since the 1930s; and no country won there from 1988, when West Indies did, to January 2021 when India pulled off an historic run-chase. Before both of their victories England had already played a first-class match against Queensland, at the Gabba too. So nothing was strange; England were familiar with, if not their enemy, at least their battleground.

No lack of audience participation either. The Gabba had a hill, a grass bank without any fixed seats where spectators could sit or lie down or stand as they pleased. Late November was the end of the student year; they had done their exams and were in party mood, as they used to be at Edgbaston when the first Test of a series was staged there in June; and how better to party than go to the Gabba with a few crates and abuse the Poms? In 1982 they brought along a live pig because England's off-spinner Eddie Hemmings was considered rotund.

Australia's team in 1978/79 was in effect their second XI, except for good old Rodney Hogg, fit and firing in the form of his life. In 1986/87 the balance was tipped England's way by the unchallenged accuracy of England's two finger-spinners, Phil Edmonds and John Emburey, and by the last hurrah of Ian Botham. In his 14th and final Test century, he not only trashed Australia's bowlers but dominated their whole team mentally, for the rest of this series, as he had in 1981 and 1985. Even with a damaged intercostal muscle, Botham had only to amble in and turn his arm over to take five wickets in Australia's first innings in the fourth Test at Melbourne, his last five-wicket Test haul. He was just 31. He did not play his last Test until 1992, yet no more barnstorming hundreds, no more match-winning spells. Had he lived in a later era of fitness regimes and diets, Botham would have been more productive after the age of 30; but I do not think he would have been quite so dominant as he was before 30, so uninhibited and inspiring. His lifestyle – play hard by day, and no less hard by night – relaxed him by taking away the stresses he would otherwise have experienced alone in his room.

For the modernised Gabba, not much can be said other than it is a serviceable stadium; the first in Australian cricket to install multi-coloured seats, so there appears to be a crowd even when there is not. The old Gabba was a cricket ground; the new one is a stadium, for Aussie Rules, and rugby if needs be, so that Queensland play few first-class games there any longer. It is a bowl which has not been designed specifically for those who bowl.

* * *

Adelaide is often rated the world's fifth most liveable city, or thereabouts. I have not researched the top four, but assume they are Boston, Venice, Vancouver and Stoke-on-Trent, in some such order.

With what pride Adelaide's city fathers must have laid out their new settlement in the 1830s. They were free settlers, not bloody convicts like in Sydney; and what a natural resource they had, especially after building a weir on the meandering river and re-naming it the Torrens. Until then it had made a fertile feeding ground for the original inhabitants, who were packed off to an institution in town to be taught English and the Bible, if they survived the relocation.

Beauty is not only in the eye of the beholder, it also depends on the beholder's position. If you sit on the old Hill at Adelaide Oval almost behind the bowler's arm, and look down the ground, the red roofs of the stands to either side are agreeable, so too the skyline of the city's few tall buildings. It is not, however, the picture postcard which makes Adelaide most scenic Test venue in Australia and, debatably, the world.

It is from the River Torrens End that the view is beautiful, up there with Sabina Park in Kingston, Queen's Park Oval in Port-of-Spain and Newlands in Cape Town. You might no longer be able to see the Adelaide Hills to your right, because the new stand soars far higher than the few rows of seats which were situated in front of the Victor Richardson Gates (when Australia's batsmen were hit by Bodyline, the spectators standing on this side of the ground were reported to protest the loudest.) They are lovely hills too, especially towards evening when not too harsh a light is thrown on the sparseness of their vegetation, and hint at the villages where German immigrants planted vineyards. The bush beyond has been immortalised by

Hans Heysen, whose paintings hang in the art gallery less than a mile up the road from the Oval. Adelaide never seems to have much work to do – beyond government and retail – but, in the age before lorries and road trains, drovers and their dogs had to drive cattle down from southwest Queensland to ship the meat. Heysen perceives this scene through rose-tinted spectacles: not a single fly in sight, instead of a mass of black dots around the cattle. The work of Albert Namatjira also hangs in the gallery – he was so famous that in 1957 he was the first indigenous Australian allowed to become a citizen of his own country – and his outback is not exotic or "other", but what is, and always has been.

The handsome stone of St Peter's Cathedral serves as an immutable backdrop to the Oval, for all its modernisations, as do the remaining Moreton Bay fig trees on the Hill, offering their shade, and the scoreboard. The same letters that spelled out Hobbs and Rhodes for the 1911/12 Test, then Bradman and O'Reilly, have subsequently spelled Lillee and Thomson, Cook and Anderson, or Ponting and Warne, in the same continuous calligraphy. In my childhood I would see photographs in the papers of Australian scoreboards that carried England's bowling figures at close of play: Trueman 1 for 83, Statham 1 for 64, Dexter 0 for 54, Titmus 2 for 116 and so on. No hiding in Australia: the board told you and the world exactly how good or inadequate you were. If you are dismissed for a duck in England, your name and 0 are taken down at the fall of the next wicket, and a veil politely drawn.

Inside, the Adelaide scoreboard is not so much a building as an old wooden sailing ship, far less modern than the SS *Great Britain*. Timbers expand when the hot wind comes from the north out of the Simpson Desert, and creak again when contracting in the cold. The rear is corrugated iron, which makes the scoreboard an oven, like E.M. Grace's cabin. Inside, the scoreboard crew climb ladders at the end of an innings, when all the names of the batting side have to be taken down and moved to the other side of the board. Ten minutes barely suffice for swarming up the masts to unfurl the sails and rig them again.

Behind the main stand at Adelaide Oval, Jane Austen would have had a ball. This spacious area, normally given over to cricket nets and grass tennis courts, is covered in marquees, deck chairs and

26

champagne stalls. The finest produce of the Riverina, and of South Australia's wineries and seas, is laid on white tablecloths: the size of the portions of prawns and lobsters, steaks and racks of lamb, cherries and strawberries, are beyond British ken. Young men take a glass of wine or beer into the stand when a South Australian player is performing well – Clem Hill, or Don Bradman after he had moved from New South Wales, or the Chappell brothers or Jason Gillespie – and if the socialising should lull, young women would walk down the tunnel under the main stand, then turn towards it – as if their purpose were to be seen rather than see – before tossing back their hair and returning to the marquees.

The Fourth Estate were allowed a taste of this sumptuousness before the 1980s when every Test included a rest day, and Adelaide offered the most enjoyable of them. Both teams, and the media, were invited to the winery owned by the Hill-Smith family. Part of the family dates back to Clem Hill, the first left-handed batsman in the world who could be called great: even today only nine batsmen have scored more Ashes runs than Hill's 2,660; even today nobody has made a higher score in the Sheffield Shield for South Australia than his 365 not out against New South Wales in 1900/01. But he rebelled against the Australian Board which was wresting control from the players who had promoted all the early tours of England themselves, a rebellion which culminated in Hill and five other leading cricketers being banned from the 1912 Triangular tournament in England. Mrs Hill-Smith told me of a fascinating exchange of letters between the Board and Clem; and that Sir Donald Bradman had borrowed them, and never returned them.

Adelaide Tests used to be very high-scoring and often end in draws. From 2015 they have been played under floodlights with a pink ball and became low-scoring, culminating in India being rolled for 36 in 2020. In between, though, when Les Burdett was head curator, he devised the perfect formula whereby almost every Test ended conclusively in the final session – as in 2006/07, when it ended in heartbreak for England after they had declared with 551 on the famous scoreboard.

* * *

England's cricketers visited Perth only once before the First World War, when the town was smaller than the port of Fremantle. This was in 1907/08, when they beat the locals so emphatically that they did not stop off again until 1920. What occurred then, if not the harbinger of Covid-19, was the nearest precedent to a century later.

A passenger on England's ship from Naples had contracted TB, and was removed at Colombo for treatment. On reaching Australia, the whole England party was ferried down the coast from Fremantle to Woodman's Point and kept in quarantine for a week. One of the players, Percy Fender, wrote that going to bed and getting up early, with healthy walks and basic food, was better acclimatisation than practising in the nets and socialising. The players practised their dancing, too, with each other, before expanding their repertoire later in the tour.

The former England all-rounder Trevor Bailey told me the two best coaches in cricket are sunshine and space; and boy, does West Australia have space. In the 1880s, when the four cricket clubs in Perth and Fremantle formed themselves into the Western Australia Cricket Association (WACA) and asked the state government for some land, they were granted hundreds of acres beside the Swan River. It was pretty swampy, but there was room to breathe, and play, and expand. In the earliest photographs a little grandstand is the sole building, with dressing-rooms on the ground floor and seats for spectators above; the quaint wooden pontoon bridge across the river is now a multi-lane flyover which leads to the new Perth Stadium, built at enormous government expense, for various sports.

To make decent pitches in this drained swamp, a clayey soil was brought from south of Perth and Abracadabra, the Perth ground, or the WACA to rhyme with Packer, was the fastest pitch on the planet – so fast it gave birth to the Carmody field, named after the WA captain who placed every fielder in the slips. England's first real taste was in 1928/29 when their all-rounder George Geary opened the batting in England's second innings and was hit flush in the face and carted off to hospital. Geary had to miss the train across the Nullarbor to Adelaide, and only just recovered to be a member of the four-man attack that won the series 4-1, England's joint-best performance in Australia. Even friendly fire can be lethal at the WACA: before England's triumph of 2010/11 Graeme Swann, batting in the nets against Tim Bresnan, was hit on his right finger which needed a protective stall when he fielded for the rest of the series, though he had to remove it when bowling. Without Swann's off-spinning spell that won the second Test in Adelaide – before England were swept aside as usual in the third at the WACA – Andrew Strauss's team would not have achieved the finest Ashes win of this century.

Not until Perth had grown during the Second World War was first-class status granted to Western Australia, so that it joined the other mainland states in the Sheffield Shield in 1947/48; even then, such were the distances that the WA players had to fly to the east coast and Adelaide to play their matches and had no home fixtures. Not until 1970/71 did Perth stage a Test, whereupon the WACA soon became the world capital of cricket at its most macho, as if the sport was being staged in the Wild West of America not Australia. Wyatt Earp and Kit Carson would have slotted seamlessly into Ian Chappell's team of the early 1970s, behind the moustached Dennis Lillee as he thundered in and scared more than daylight out of the Poms. (It shouldn't be so funny, but it is: the YouTube clip of David Lloyd, alias Bumble, being struck amidships by Lillee's opening partner, Jeff Thomson, and ever so slowly keeling over.) You weren't a man if you didn't drink 20 cold glasses of Swan Lager during a day's play, chanted "Lillee, Lillee!" and threw bottles – filled with some liquid or other – at Poms fielding on the boundary.

Subsequently the WACA reversed direction and became the opposite of what it was. When England visited in 2017/18, the ground's sponsor was the WA Health department, and during their two-day tour-opener the only advertisements in the whole ground read: "Alcohol: think again".

The WACA's chief executive, Christina Matthews, was at the forefront of the campaign to make cricket's language gender neutral and, therefore, the sport more inclusive. Batter, not batsman; and why not? The terms were interchangeable in the 19th century. It was only formally, in newspapers in Britain, that "batter" was edited out. It has always been part of the players' vernacular.

Fielder, instead of fieldsman, yes. Not so sure about how to modify "nightwatchman" without being too cumbersome. And third man should now become "third", Matthews said, but that can be confused with third slip. It was a debate which needed to be had, in any event, and it illustrated how much the WACA had changed.

"A young country, and a lucky country: so Australia styles herself." So said Shirley Hazzard, who grew up in Sydney and lived abroad as the daughter of an Australian diplomat working for the United Nations, before becoming a diplomat herself. In the Australian Broadcasting Corporation's annual Boyer Lecture of 1984 (p41) she went on: "But youth gives place to maturity; and luck is a basis, only, for achievement." To world civilisation, Hazzard argued: "Australia's contribution is distinguished, but as yet small. It might even be thought disproportionately small, given the relative ease and liberty, the endless opportunities which many Australians enjoy. It is emphasis on quality that sometimes seems lacking from the discussion of Australia's identity. Quality has been pursued, instead, in physical activity and sport.

"Elsewhere in the world, knowledge was esteemed," Hazzard went on. "In Australia, it was not. As far as I can recall, I never heard a man refer to a good or a great book. I knew no one who had mastered, or even studied, another language from choice. And our articulate, conscious life proceeded without acknowledgement of the preceding civilisations which had produced it … The Australian ethos was, as it still largely is, gregarious. The enforced loneliness of Australia's early decades (to which I would add the severity of the bush and climate) had produced a need to do things in clusters." So men huddled together, or joined clubs, to combat loneliness, and to drink and talk about sport, and bet, both in war and peacetime.

Western Australia had so much space, and money (from all the mining up north), that a new 60,000-seater stadium was built for A$1.5 billion a mile upstream from the WACA. Perth has plenty of high-rise buildings, but they are office blocks, and hotels for overseas visitors and employees of mining companies who fly from the interior for a weekend of R&R. Nobody lives in this city centre, apart from in a few old terraces or if sleeping on the streets. Perth is the most suburban city in the cricket world, and therefore highly conducive to the pursuit of "physical activity".

According to a recent state census, only 6% of the population live in apartments (most would overlook the Swan River or Indian Ocean); 16% in terraced or semi-detached homes (eg older houses in the des-res area of Guildford); while 77% live in a completely detached house with its own piece of land, meaning space for a garage, patio, barbeque and backyard where the kids can play cricket. Perth, in consequence, has a footprint twice the size of Tokyo with a small fraction of the population, extending 150km along the coast and up to 50km inland.

Nowhere better to "cluster" and play cricket than the suburbs of Perth, as dozens of English county cricketers have discovered every winter for decades. Go to a suburb and you will find a park, a spacious one, with artificial cricket nets waiting to be used by anyone, and grass pitches maintained by the local council. You can practise and play all day with your mates. Provided you top that up with hard practice sessions on Tuesday and Thursday evenings at your grade club, you might get a game for one of the elevens on Saturday. The saying that you are only six centuries away from playing for Australia might still hold true: that is, you only have to make three hundreds for the first team of your grade club to get picked for your state team, and three hundreds for your state team to get picked for Australia – while withstanding, of course, the sledging along the way.

* * *

It was a quiet Sunday morning in West Australia. I had the weekend off before the Perth Test and took the train to Bunbury, halfway down the coast to Margaret River, hired a bicycle and stayed in an Airbnb on the very edge of the bush.

On the Sunday morning, I cycled along completely empty roads. In several miles I passed five or six bungalows and another plot waiting to be "developed". I did not see any human being, or car, or other vehicle. As the bush was falling silent in the mid-morning heat, I heard at last the sound of a car coming behind.

"Use the bloody bike-path!!!" roared a man leaning out of the passenger window.

I swerved at the next opportunity on to the cycleway. The man had a point: strictly speaking, a cycle path had started a few yards earlier. Nevertheless, I was a little shocked by the vehemence of this greeting, especially on the Sabbath. And there was enough space to go round.

"Ouch!"

A few miles further on during this Sunday morning ride, after joining the main road into Bunbury, something hit my cycling helmet, which had to be worn under Australian law. A few seconds later, it happened again, a sudden thud, and more painful as something was trying to rip the hair off the part of my head not covered by the helmet.

I cycled on while the traffic from an out-of-town shopping mall roared past into Bunbury. "Ouch!" – for a third time came an aerial strike. Something was dive-bombing my head and making me wobble on the main road.

The owner of the Airbnb where I was staying was a conservation officer for the Western Australian government. Top bloke, like his missus. By the time I had cycled into central Bunbury, on the sturdy and heavy bike I had hired from the Tourist Information centre, the temperature had hit 40°C, and I was starting to feel dizzy from dehydration. Even dolphins were feeling the heat: it was the first day that season they had not come into the shallower waters of Bunbury harbour, because the ultraviolet can give them skin cancer. So the conservation officer generously collected me, put the bike in the back of his utility truck, and on the way back to his place said it must have been a magpie that attacked me: not an ordinary British magpie that targets eggs, but an Australian magpie. When they spot a cycling helmet, he said, they think the hair underneath would be useful to line their nests.

In Australia, both man and nature are more aggressive than their English equivalents. If you get sledged when cycling on a deserted road on a Sunday morning, imagine what it is like if you hang around in the middle for a few overs.

* * *

It is a loss that Tasmania has been deleted from England's itinerary for a Test tour, and limited to a one-day international. Tasmania is Australia at its most English; gentle in parts and green, if windy; where skin does not burn so quickly as on the mainland; where England's cricketers of the 19th and 20th centuries were accustomed to lick their wounds.

Being a small island, Tasmania found its cricket dogged by politics. Hobart was the seat of the Tasmanian Cricket Association, while Launceston was the seat of the Northern Tasmanian Cricket Association, and Burnie the seat of the North West Tasmanian Cricket Association. Not until 1977/78 did the island join the Sheffield Shield, mainly thanks to an Englishman. On the old TCA ground on a hill above Hobart, akin to Queen's Park in Chesterfield, Jack Simmons had paved the way by beating mainland states in the domestic 50-over competition, captaining amateurs with sideburns and bucolic surnames like Cowmeadow.

It was usually too far, and too costly, for mainland newspapers to send a correspondent to Tasmania – besides, the Poms were usually losing by Christmas – so for a week or more in mid-December England's players could rest and play in peace. Hobart, around its harbour on the Derwent River, is the most English of Australia's state capitals, with warehouses and terraced cottages of thick enough stone to withstand the winds. Not so remote and romantic as Strahan on Tasmania's west coast, where you can look out at Hells Gates in Macquarie Harbour, where unruly convicts were chained to a rock to be lashed by the Roaring Forties. But Hobart offers therapeutic respite, like a walk up Kunanyi, or Mount Wellington to give it its more recent name; while Tasmania's north coast, with its rolling hills, small fields and place-names such as Launceston, echoes Devon and Cornwall. English cricketers did not fly home with mental stress when a Test series included an interlude in Tasmania.

* * *

"Wish I had your job!" Not on Christmas Day you don't; not when you have to cover the press conference at 9.30am by an England captain who is already 3-0 down in the series and looks as though he has spent the night agonising over whether he should resign after the fourth Test or the fifth.

Melbournians celebrate Christmas at home, whereupon they take the plane north to Queensland for the rest of their summer holiday, which comes at the end of their academic and calendar year. Plane after plane leaves Tullamarine airport full, bound for the Gold Coast or Brisbane, and returns empty for another load. Hence the crowd for the MCG Test decreases, from 85,000 to 50,000 to 30,000 to 20,000. If you are still in Melbourne on day five of the MCG Test, you are probably an England supporter.

The highlight of an MCG Test is when Australia's captain reaches his century. Assuming Australia have won the toss and batted, their captain – normally batting at No.3 or No.4 – will reach his hundred between tea and the close. It is a significant moment in Australian life. Until recently cricket was the one sport that all Australian males played at some time, and followed to some degree. I imagine a farm so far into the outback of Queensland that doors are left unlocked even when everyone is away, while farm workers are still out in the paddocks as mum prepares tea. She is tuned to ABC radio for a bit of company, maybe still out of range of satellite TV; and when the Australian captain on 97 plays a back-cut and the ball runs away to the third-man boundary, she murmurs: "Good on yer, Ricky!" or "Smithy, you beauty!" Out in the Kimberleys, at Ayers Rock, at gas stations between Adelaide and Darwin, on Kangaroo Island if the wind stops blowing long enough for those outside to hear the radio, and from millions of bungalows in the suburbs, the same approbation is heard. It is a reaffirmation that Australia is good as gold, and that we or our forefathers were right to come and live here.

Melbourne was the first cricket ground to cater for large crowds. By the inaugural Test in 1877 it had an even bigger stand than the one which E.M. saw being built, and a pavilion. But the two best bowlers in New South Wales had failed to take the ship to Melbourne, and Victoria's best bowler Frank Allan (a bibulous soul) had written to say he preferred to attend the carnival in the town of Warrnambool where he was working. So a couple of bowlers from Melbourne grade clubs were summoned to fill the gaps left by Allan, Edwin Evans and Fred Spofforth. Neither Tom Kendall nor John Hodges had played a first-class match, for Victoria or anyone else; both were making their first-class as well as Test debuts. Yet in Australia's second innings, Kendall and Hodges shared a last-wicket stand of 29, which turned England's target into 154, then took nine of England's second-innings wickets. It is hard to imagine the equivalent: of England, before playing their inaugural home Test at The Oval in 1880, being forced to pick a couple of London club players, who turn out to be match-winners. Australia's suburbs had saved the day.

Fast-forward 140 years to a Melbourne first-grade match at Junction Oval. Much has changed, much has stayed the same. St Kilda are the home team, one of the main grade clubs, then and now; the scoring is similarly low. On a cloudy and drizzly morning, St Kilda have stuck Dandenong in and reduced them to 15 for five before a slight recovery to 90 all out. The ball is still moving around when St Kilda reply, and lose wickets in their turn. It is looking as though there will be an outright result, which now happens about one game in ten – provided day two, next Saturday, is dry.

The intensity of this grade game is greater than county cricket. Fielders fling themselves, even when they do not have to, because they have energy to burn, unlike county cricketers who play five or six days a week. Batsmen do not dawdle between wickets; even if it is an easy single, they sprint. What gives the game away that this is essentially amateur cricket is that the mannerisms are not quite so polished and, above all, there is not the same economy of movement.

St Kilda, like every big club, train on Tuesday evening and Thursday evening. They do not have an overseas player this season owing to expensive developments to the ground and funding issues; but the club captain – injured for today's game – is Rob Quiney, who played a couple of Tests for Australia and a decade for Victoria. Another former Test player in the St Kilda team is Max Beer, a left-arm spinner who is not needed as the pace bowlers run through Dandenong. Peter Handscomb, another of St Kilda's Test players, is away playing for Victoria. A couple of weeks earlier, he represented the Prime Minister's XI against England in a T20 on the Friday evening in Canberra, jumped on a plane next morning, and turned up to make 40-odd for St Kilda.

It is mind-boggling for anyone bred in English cricket that the Victorian government have invested A$40m in Junction Oval. Yet so much tradition sits alongside the new infrastructure. The only bowler to have taken two hat-tricks in one Test played for St Kilda, and he was a leg-spinner, though his name was Jimmy Matthews, not Shane Warne, another St Kilda player. It was also the grade club of Bill Ponsford, John the Baptist to the Messiah who was Don Bradman: Bradman eclipsed Ponsford's 429 against Tasmania and 437 against Queensland but his 452, also against Queensland, was The Don's only quadruple-century. A couple of other St Kildan spinners who represented Australia between the World Wars, Don Blackie and Bert Ironmonger, have one of the two old grandstands, both listed buildings, named after them.

The present is too pressing, though, to allow St Kilda to wallow in the past. Cricket Victoria have been muscled out of the MCG, after not far short of 200 years, by Aussie Rules, and relocated to Junction Oval. The inducements were state-of-the-art nets, indoor and outdoor; office space and meeting-rooms; the ground levelled and fenced; and two more grounds across the road. Victoria are still committed to play at the MCG in the first half of the season, but from the beginning of every March they play at Junction Oval. The MCG has become a misnomer, because it mainly stages the Australian Football League.

Dandenong's professional is Darren Pattinson, who played a Test match, though not for Australia but, by accident of his birth in Grimsby, for England in 2008. Pattinson is resting for this grade game though, because Dandenong are confident they will finish in the last eight in the table of 18 clubs, and qualify for the quarter-finals. Dandenong have a strong link with Nottinghamshire, as Darren and James Pattinson, Stuart Broad and Alex Hales, have represented both teams.

"There are no more hairy quicks in grade cricket," lamented Shaun Graf, the CEO of Cricket Victoria, and another St Kilda player who represented Australia. "Same reason that a lot of them don't want to play two-day cricket – the better ones do, but the more marginal players have got so much else on, like socialising. They don't want to commit as much as they used to."

On one side of the ground, across the road, are two more cricket grounds: St Kilda's 3rd XI are using one, while the final of the Melbourne women's T20 has drawn a bit of a crowd on the other. T20 is boosting the number of participants, male and female, as never before. Graf says: "Young players still want to wear the baggy green and play Test cricket for Australia, and if they make a career out of that, then fine, they will stay with it. But when they lose their Test place they are not going to hang around playing state cricket for Victoria – they'll go on the T20 circuit and play round the world and make big dollars. So the turnover of Test players in future is going to quicken up, for better and worse."

Both Blackie and Ironmonger were 46 when they made their Test debut for Australia against England in 1928/29. Ironmonger went on to take 74 Test wickets at only 17.9 each. But it is ever more a game for young bucks, not veterans. Whatever generation they belong to, however, St Kilda's players work in the high-rise offices or educational institutions or eateries around Junction Oval and live in St Kilda, so commuting time to the club for practices and matches is minimised. No country has such a strong social and economic foundation for cricket as suburban Australia.

* * *

What do you think this is, Bondi Beach? So the British child is asked by indignant parents if he or she brings sand indoors and dumps it on the carpet. Bondi, in the British imagination, epitomises Australia.

When the writer and poet Alan Ross covered England's tour of Australia in 1954/55, he wrote: "The ocean is the moving axis of Australian happiness. In the dry, exhausting, empty interior, Australians find a historic pride of conquest; in the raising of cattle, a reason for existence. But in the surf they come to terms with beauty in their unique context." Sydney sometimes staged two Tests in a home series, before Perth joined the rota in 1970/71; and Ross had plenty of time to study the beach at Bondi and write about its lifeguards, as the second of his Sydney Tests was largely rained off.

Let us savour the birdsong on our way to Bondi soon after sunrise. Australian birdsong is so strange to the European ear, like a barrel organ played backwards. The galah is reputed to mock but it speaks a different, rather raucous, language. Strangeness is not what westerners expect from birds and trees. Have Australians tried to make their land so similar to Europe – roads, traffic lights, bungalows, department stores – precisely because the land is naturally so strange?

Bondi Beach is a kilometre of dazzling golden sand. No rocks except at the headland at each end, no pebbles; just sea, sun, sand and surf. It is almost intoxicating at any time of day, but Australia comes closest to perfection in early morning, when the slanting unharsh sun spotlights the trunks of eucalypti and polishes them into silver.

Down a few flights of steps and the tang of salt leads us to the beach. Red and yellow flags point to the stretch where a lifeguard watches over swimmers. Dump your stuff anywhere safe from the waves: this is the aquatic equivalent of the Garden of Eden and man surely does not steal. Slap on the sun cream, as Richie Benaud told us, grab that surfboard or bodyboard and charge into the water. The first few steps almost accustom you to the zingy-zing temperature before the first wave envelops.

It is not true that the best things in life are free, but once you have hired a board, some of them are. The exhilaration of catching the right wave and being borne to shore for the first time; the thrill of approaching waves taller than oneself; brilliant light, azure sky, the smell of sun cream, bronzed bodies male and female, none made pale by European winter. When Wordsworth composed his line that "Earth has not anything to show more fair", he was looking down on the Thames before the installation of sewers in London, when the river was full of rubbish. Can do better than that, mate.

Surfing is not mandatory. Walking along the shore, just dipping their toes, are tourists from China, Japan and Southeast Asia. Has anywhere on earth introduced so many people to the joys of the sea, whether they swim or surf or simply splash?

Many Australians or their parents have migrated from war zones in Europe, Asia or Africa. I would guestimate one-tenth have seen genocide or been told stories of it by their relatives. One feature of Australian life is the number of taxi drivers who arrived as refugees. A driver in Adelaide had been a child in Srebrenica as the world watched while more than 7,000 Muslims were massacred: he told me he had not slept for more than 30 minutes, without waking up, in the two decades since. Nothing will wash away those memories, but beaches like Bondi offer balm for their scars and the possibility of a new, post-trauma, beginning.

Fully alive, you walk back up the beach, before the sun makes your skin more than tingle. In Australia public amenities are excellent. You can shower, or wash your feet under taps, for free. The social contract is that there will be a minimum standard of living for all, as a share of the country's mineral wealth. This, too, is Australia at its best, clean, wholesome and generous in supplying basic needs.

At breakfast in a café you are greeted by the sheer cheerfulness of Australians, their good humour and forthrightness.

"Please can I have smashed avocado and poached eggs?"

"Too easy!"

It might be expensive by non-Australian standards, but the quantity is abundant, tap water freely available, and those working there are well-paid, with no obvious reason not to be cheerful. The shade is welcome by mid-morning; the sound of the waves still almost audible, however far your ear from the sea. Such memories should be stored. After a gorgeous New Year's Day in 2018, for the next three days it continually rained in Sydney, as it had for Alan Ross during the Test of 1954/55.

* * *

Before the end of the 20th century, Sydney had booked its place as the venue of the fifth and final Test in the first week of New Year. It makes the most appropriate Australian ground for a grand farewell. The victors are saluted not only by spectators but the ghosts of the past, who are commemorated in the names of the stands or on the honours board in the dressing-rooms in the players' old wooden pavilion. The retiring cricketer is guaranteed the applause he has earned.

Two of the greatest bowlers have taken their final bow at the SCG, Glenn McGrath and Shane Warne, simultaneously, as well as Steve Waugh and Don Bradman. The fifth Test of an Ashes series in Australia has seldom been a dramatic climax in itself – England have often lost the series by then – but the occasion is grand, whatever the scoreline. This is what Sydney deserves, for being the heart of Australian cricket from the time the first ball was bowled in the new colony circa 1800.

Sydney, more than anywhere else in the world, has set the standard for cricket through the ages. The three other global hotspots of cricket, as I see it, have been the West Riding of Yorkshire, Bombay (or Mumbai, as it is now called) and Barbados. But they have waxed and waned, whereas Sydney has been a never-failing fountain of excellence.

Intensity was inherent in cricket in Sydney from the moment British soldiers played against those transported to Australia whom they had come to guard. From the Victoria Barracks at Moore Park, on the hill above the harbour, the military kept their eyes and guns trained on everyone below. There was no rebelling against these soldiers who held all the ammunition. The single way to ruffle their plumage was to beat them at cricket – and even then the military held the advantage, because they had bats and balls brought out for them from England, while convicts and their children had to make do with whatever local equivalents they could manufacture. In the absence of shoes, many of these "Native Australians" played in bare feet. Melbourne's cricketers would be middle-class, so too Adelaide's; Sydney's were rough and ready to do anything to win, and when these elements were combined they made a potent mix. I see some ancestor of David Warner, pent-up at practice as the Native Australians prepare to play a British regiment, flinging himself to deny the soldiers every run, trying out new types of local wood for a bat, full of acerbic asides to opponents during the game and, afterwards, trenchant shouts to his mates in the tavern.

The original hotspot of cricket, the West Riding, was founded on damp pitches: so the priorities were accuracy, economy, finger-spin and sound defensive technique, personified by old masters such as Wilfred Rhodes, Herbert Sutcliffe and Len Hutton. Sydney's cricket has been based on harder and bouncier pitches: it has therefore been more aggressive, and more suited to export overseas than Yorkshire's style. England have won Ashes series in Australia only when they have had an exceptional pace bowler, such as Harold Larwood, Frank Tyson, John Snow or James Anderson.

Now Sydney leads the vanguard against the existential threat to cricket's popularity in Australia. The structure of the Australian Cricket Board never changed until the Smith-Warner ball-tampering affair; so committeemen, representing the interests of each state, sat and fiddled while the Victorian Football League spread nationwide to become the Australian Football League. In the process, this winter sport took precedence at what had been principally cricket grounds. Brisbane's Gabba was converted into a multi-purpose stadium; Adelaide's Oval had to introduce drop-in pitches because Aussie Rules chewed up the square; the WACA was superseded by Perth's multi-purpose stadium; the MCG had been first to introduce drop-in pitches because of the damage done by Aussie Rules, and the ground is packed most weekends, but not for cricket. The NSW administration has been moved out of the SCG because Aussie Rules rules. But at least in Sydney's suburbs the sport still thrives. When Warner and Smith were banned, the Australian team was carried by other Sydneysiders in Mitchell Starc and Pat Cummins, while Josh Hazlewood moved from rural New South Wales to Sydney to become, aged 19, the state's youngest pace bowler.

When England appointed the former NSW batsman Trevor Bayliss as their head coach in 2015, his template was for England to have an attacking No.3 batsman (like Charlie Macartney, Don Bradman, Ricky Ponting); positive intent both in attack and defence, because then a batsman takes up a better position than he would if merely blocking; two spin bowlers, one of them a wrist-spinner turning the ball both ways (like Bill O'Reilly or Shane Warne); excellent fielding without exception; and no practice except intense practice. Having implemented these values and practices in their 50-over side under Bayliss, England bought into them temporarily for Test matches as well. Even England adopted the eternal values of Sydney's cricket.

Provided the sport flourishes in Sydney, Australia will be strong. Those "natives of proud Austra-lee" can play cricket all right, as well as drink.

ENGLAND IN AUSTRALIA,
1876/77 — 2017/18

Overall

Played **351**   Won **110**   Lost **146**   Drawn **95**

In Australia

Played **180**   Won **57**   Lost **95**   Drawn **28**

In England

Played **171**   Won **53**   Lost **51**   Drawn **67**

England's record at each venue

Melbourne Cricket Ground

Played **56**   Won **20**   Lost **28**   Drawn **8**

Sydney Cricket Ground

Played **56**   Won **22**   Lost **27**   Drawn **7**

Adelaide Oval

Played **32**   Won **9**   Lost **18**   Drawn **5**

Brisbane Cricket Ground (the Gabba)

Played **21**   Won **4**   Lost **12**   Drawn **5**

Perth (WACA)

Played **14**   Won **1**   Lost **10**   Drawn **3**

Exhibition Ground, Brisbane

Played **1**   Won **1**   Lost **0**   Drawn **0**

Series won

Series won	Captain
1884/85	Arthur Shrewsbury
1886/87	Arthur Shrewsbury
1887/88	Walter Read*
1894/95	Andrew Stoddart
1903/04	Pelham Warner
1911/12	Johnny Douglas
1928/29	Percy Chapman
1932/33	Douglas Jardine
1954/55	Len Hutton
1970/71	Ray Illingworth
1978/79	Mike Brearley
1986/87	Mike Gatting
2010/11	Andrew Strauss

One-match series

Highest scores

287	Tip Foster	Sydney	1903/04
251	Walter Hammond	Sydney	1928/29
244*	Alastair Cook	Melbourne	2017/18
235*	Alastair Cook	Brisbane (The Gabba)	2010/11
231*	Walter Hammond	Sydney	1936/37

Best bowling

8-35	George Lohmann	Sydney	1886/87
8-58	George Lohmann	Sydney	1891/92
8-68	Wilfred Rhodes	Melbourne	1903/04
8-81	Len Braund	Melbourne	1903/04
8-94	Tom Richardson	Sydney	1897/98
8-126	Jack White	Adelaide	1928/29
7-27	Frank Tyson	Melbourne	1954/55
7-28	Billy Bates	Melbourne	1882/83
7-40	Dick Barlow	Sydney	1882-83
7-40	John Snow	Sydney	1970-71
7-56	Wilfred Rhodes	Melbourne	1903/04

BANGLADESH

Sylhet ★

★ Mirpur

★ Dhaka

Chittagong ★
Cox's Bazar ★

CHAPTER TWO

BANGLADESH

The countryside of Bengal, whether West or East, is fertility itself. If you were listening to music in 1971, you will recall the pop concerts to raise funds for the starving people of the new country of Bangladesh. As in the case of most famines, however, it was the result of the foolishness of mankind not the miserliness of nature.

Watered by the Brahmaputra and Jamuna, Bengal is the original home of more than 300 types of rice. On such profits the officials of the distinctly dishonourable East India Company waxed fat in Calcutta: they drank their champagne and several bottles of claret at dinner, before retiring to become nabobs in London and Cheltenham, like the odious Joseph Sedley in Thackeray's *Vanity Fair*. Judging by the diary of William Hickey, never have British people lived to such bibulous excess – not even in the City in the 1980s – as did these traders, before the East India Company's abolition in 1857.

But no rulers on earth, I would guess, have had such absolute authority as the Pharaohs of Egypt and emperors of China. The source of their authority was one river, in the case of the Nile, and two in the case of the Huang He and Yangtze. Control the fresh water and therefore food production, save the people from starvation annually, and they will eat out of your absolute hand.

Bangladesh has not one or two but innumerable rivers after the Himalayan snows melt, and these tributaries are constantly changing course, so that where a bridge is not required one year, it is the next. The emperor in China needed mandarins who could read and write and thereby exercise control over the two rivers: to build the canal which linked them, take drinking water into the dry north, and irrigate the land for millions. Pharaohs had their high priests, bureaucrats and slaves to devise hieroglyphics and build, in the shape of pyramids, the largest structures made by humankind. No such authority has lasted for long, however, in Bangladesh.

The Moghul emperors were imposing a bureaucracy in what is now Bangladesh when the East India Company invaded. When government took over from the Company in 1857, there was some improvement in controlling the annual inundation, but again this bureaucracy, and the knowledge it had gained, was partly lost at Partition in 1947, when West Pakistan took control of East Pakistan. The same happened in 1971, when the Pakistan army massacred the mainly Hindu elite, before withdrawing to concede independence. Thus continuity, stability and knowledge were lost yet again. Famine returned, in spite of fundraising concerts by George Harrison of the Beatles, amid the most painful birth pangs.

* * *

The train from Chittagong to Dhaka trundles past paddy fields, villages, ponds, and rivers of astonishing breadth. It no doubt passes much else besides – the windows allow only a very clouded view because they have not been cleaned. The story circulating on one England tour was that certain government ministers had sons who owned bus companies, and they did not want competition from the railways, which were deliberately run down and their rolling stock not renewed. Hickey would have been aggrieved at the lack of refreshment: nothing remotely like a well-stocked buffet car.

The films of Satyajit Ray offer a clearer view of Bengal's countryside, although they are a bit grainy after being shot in the 1950s and 1960s in black and white. The fertility of the soil, and its abundance of water, and the heat of its climate, combined to make it the bread basket, or rice bowl, of the world – until incompetent rulers bled it dry. Ray, my favourite filmmaker, captures this countryside in his *Apu* trilogy; and again in *The Chess Players* about a rural squire before the First World War in the build-up to independence. Most of these Sardars and Zamindars, being Bengali, were highly cultured. Rabindranath Tagore, the first Asian to win the Nobel Prize in Literature, wrote much of Ray's material and is unique in having his verse used in the national anthems of two countries, Bangladesh and India. Bengali, ahead of Afrikaans or Welsh, is, I would say, the second language of cricket.

Six or seven hours out of Chittagong, the express-that-never-was reaches the outskirts of Dhaka. The land remains flat but no longer fertile; or rather it sprouts buildings not vegetation. Slums reproduce amoebically. People live beside, almost in, open sewers and drains, others in shacks or under awnings on islets in the middle of mud-brown rivers. Your compassion is fresh: suppose I gave to this family a thousand pounds, what could they not do with it? Or to that family, the one with three babies? All too soon it becomes fatigued. Where to begin to alleviate this mass of poverty? Slower and slower, the train nears the end of the line in Dhaka, and when you look out the window, smudged as the glass may be, you begin to comprehend the epic scale of the population density of Bangladesh.

If you go through inner Mumbai on a train, to Victoria Terminus as was, or Chhatrapati Shivaji as it is now, or Churchgate station as it still is, the "chawls" or slums stand around four feet from the train: in other words, the walls and corrugated iron roofs of the shacks are almost within touching distance if you lean out of the window. In Dhaka, for the last few miles before Kamalapur central station, the slums have expanded and expanded until they are two touchable feet from the train.

During the Covid-19 pandemic, I wondered about the sufferings that have occurred inside these slums. At the best of times, a person could never be more than two metres away from somebody else. All the medics in the world would never be able to test, track and trace.

* * *

Extreme density of population is not in itself inimical to cricket. Mumbai is one of the sport's capitals, if not the world capital. Green spaces – parks or maidans – were built into the Raj's design of Bombay, for its own pleasure of course. But soon the Parsi community was included, then the Hindu community, then the Muslim, to be divided and ruled as Caesar had prescribed for empires. The boundaries for some of the matches played in Mumbai are no bigger than the semi-circles for a limited-overs game, but the pitch is the thing: bowlers can bowl flat out, the bounce is trustworthy, and batsmen can grow.

Bangladesh, however, has less space to spare: if land is flat and dry enough to play cricket on, it is flat and dry enough for people to build on and inhabit. In Indian cities you can probably find a street, if only at night, where you can bat and bowl for a few minutes. In Dhaka, the Pan Pacific was the hotel where "everybody" stayed, and I remember being in a taxi which drove straight to the hotel's exit and there we had to wait, with one car ahead, for ten minutes, simply to inch forward on to the main road, so densely packed was the traffic.

In the years when Bangladesh was part of British India, and when it was part of Pakistan, this land produced no Test cricketer. The nearest that people of this region came to international cricket was in 1882/83 when a tramp steamer collided at night in the middle of the Indian Ocean with the ship transporting the England team to Australia: not the SS *Great Britain* by then, but P&O's *Peshawur*. England's captain, the Honourable Ivo Bligh, recorded that the men on the tramp steamer were mostly "Lascars"; and Joseph Conrad also used the term to describe sailors from the Chittagong area. They manned the merchant steamers and sailing ships that plied the ports from Africa and Aden to India, Indonesia and China, and back to Zanzibar.

The hastiness of Bangladesh's promotion to Test status after the 1999 World Cup, and without any historical background, was not only a blot on the record of the ICC but a huge handicap for the players themselves. None of the necessary infrastructure for Test cricket existed a generation after independence. This promotion was almost entirely based on Bangladesh's victory over Pakistan at Northampton, in the most dubious circumstances, in the group stage of that year's World Cup.

Pakistan's passage into the second stage of the tournament was already certain before their group match against Bangladesh. In this context Pakistan could afford to be generous, but the donation of 40 extras to Bangladesh's total was rather excessive: what would have been a modest 183 was converted into a competitive 223 for nine. Four of Pakistan's six bowlers were world-class, yet somehow they managed to contribute 28 wides and seven no-balls. This generosity, if that is the right word, continued when Pakistan batted and none of their stellar line-up could reach 30. Three Pakistan batsmen were run out, and not even the most ardent Bangladesh supporter would claim his side had a "gun" fielder.

The only other evidence offered in support of Bangladesh's sudden promotion to Test status was a report written for the ICC by three retired Test players. When these three assessors visited Dhaka to compile their report, the main players were on strike so there was no cricket of note for them to see until reconciliation was achieved and a match against a touring MCC side was improvised. According to the second report to the ICC by the inspection team on its visit to Bangladesh in January 2000:

> *"Unfortunately the Bangladesh Cricket Board (BCB) had not advised the ICC that there had been problems between the BCB and the players' association, dating back to last November. Relations had been broken off completely when 7 top players were suspended by the BCB. The issues were still unresolved when the inspection team arrived. The BCB was forced to field a 3rd or 4th string team in the 4 day match 18-21 January against the touring MCC side, and this was disappointing and frustrating. Although the BCB had prepared an itinerary and booked internal flights for the inspection team, it was realised on arrival that a completely changed programme was necessary for us to achieve our objectives."*

It was incredible, not that Bangladesh should have been granted Test status, because it had the potential of its enormous and expanding population, but that it should have been granted Test status so quickly, when its first-class tournament had been going only one year; when the country had never won a first-class match; when Bangladesh had never beaten any country in any format except Pakistan in that game at Northampton, Scotland, earlier in the 1999 World Cup, and Kenya; and when they had not made a first-class tour anywhere. Their experience was limited to nothing bouncier than their pitches at home. The ICC inspection team recommended "a concentrated diet of overseas experience": a quick tour of South Africa and that was it.

Overnight, club cricketers – with physiques and skill-sets you would expect from weekend amateurs – were transformed, if only by administrators, into Test players. I went to see them in their first practice after landing in England for the 1999 World Cup, and was not surprised when told that the couple who had previously played club cricket in England had not been selected for the first XI of their clubs. "We are satisfied that Bangladesh has an elite group of top players who possess a high level of technique and basic skills, and are more than capable of competing with other Test teams," the ICC report concluded. "Bangladesh could be a real force in world cricket in 5-10 years."

Instead, these poor pioneers were compelled to endure humiliation. They lost 25 of their first 26 Tests, and the other was drawn when Zimbabwe were baulked by rain. In their first eight-and-a-half years of Test cricket they won one game, at home to Zimbabwe. Experience is not worth acquiring if it is the experience of losing. When they won two Tests in the West Indies in 2009 it was because all the leading home players had gone on strike, so Bangladesh beat what was tantamount to West Indies third XI. Sometimes they would compete in a Test for a couple of days, before the lack of physical and mental robustness told in another collapse. No country found it harder to adapt to Test cricket – not even New Zealand or Zimbabwe – than Bangladesh, who started at minus square one.

* * *

Bangladeshi cricket had one strength on which to build, one domestic competition of quality: the 50-over league in Dhaka, to which any talent around the country gravitated. Why? "It is still evident that the game is being run from Dhaka with Dhaka interests as their paramount concern, to the detriment of Bangladesh cricket at the present time," the ICC report noted. Another reason why promotion to Test status was granted far too prematurely, before "the appropriate decentralised structures have been put in place".

By the 1990s sufficient money was floating around Bangladesh for Dhaka's leading clubs to sign overseas players such as Neil Fairbrother, Alan Fordham, Richard Illingworth and Phillip DeFreitas from England; various Sri Lankans, including Sanath Jayasuriya and Arjuna Ranatunga; even Wasim Akram from Pakistan. And the big game, Bangladesh's derby, was the clash between Mohammedan Sporting Club and Abahani, not only in cricket but football and hockey too.

MSC was the traditional club, from the old part of Dhaka. Abahani, on the other hand, was set up after the Liberation War by a son of

Sheikh Mujibur Rahman. It has therefore come to be associated with the Awami League, one of the country's major political parties, and the long-time prime minister, Rahman's daughter Sheikh Hasina.

Bangladeshi politics are polarised, and based on your interpretation of events at independence in 1971 (as polarised as American opinion when people entered the Capitol after President Trump had disputed the general election result). Who was the hero? Sheikh Mujibur, who had won the general election but then been imprisoned by the West Pakistan army? Or the army commander who seized the radio station and declared independence, Ziaur Rahman? Rahman founded the Bangladesh National Party, and succeeded Mujibur as the country's president; his wife, Khaleda Zia, became prime minister.

For derbies between MSC and Abahani, the Bangabandhu was used: not one of Berlusconi's nightclubs in Milan, as the name might suggest, but the national stadium in central Dhaka. Its stands were packed with passionate supporters who would hurl more than insults when controversy arose on the field. "When I played, in some games it was a full house in Bangabandhu stadium – it could be 20 to 25,000 people watching the game." This is the recollection of one of the world's most remarkable cricket coaches. Universally known as "Ratan", rather than Mohammad Shahidul Alam, he was a wicketkeeper-batsman in – and briefly for – Bangladesh; then he coached Bangladesh Under-19s and Malaysia, before being appointed chief executive of the London-based charity Capital Kids Cricket. Ratan is the nearest I have to a soul-brother: both of us want every child in the world, male and female, to play cricket or at least have the option of doing so. The difference is he can coach them.

"Football was more popular in Bangladesh before 1997, because on that day of course everything changed and everybody started loving cricket. I was following Abahani from my childhood, listening to radio commentary when they were playing football – when they lose, I used to cry," Ratan recalls. "In those days there were Mohammedan and Abahani flags everywhere, all over the country.

"When we played it was a golden era for club cricket, now it is a golden era for international cricket. Even when we used to do practice [at Abahani], people used to come and stand on the fence and watch when we are training. Whichever team we played in domestic cricket, we had five or six thousand people coming and watching the game. A couple of years we had three overseas players. The future finance minister, Mustafa Kamal, he was chairman of Abahani and spent his own money on hiring these players.

"Whatever happened during the league, whatever your standing, that match [the derby against MSC] you have to win. People in the road used to give us tips about how to win the game, like you must get him out quickly tomorrow. It was tense. I could not sleep at night because I would be the first person receiving the ball, as opening batsman or wicketkeeper. The crowd will be shouting to the players and officials, 'He's no good, he's no good, Ratan is rubbish, he missed a catch today and because of him you lost the game' – it could be something like that. Fighting between the crowds, yes, throwing stones from one gallery to another: Mohammedan and Abahani had two different seating galleries at the stadium with neutrals in between. There was no salary or prize money. Maybe if we win the match we get dinner in a nice place, from the club officials or sometimes a fan."

Football was more popular, just as it was in West Bengal, until the epoch-making moment in 1997 when Bangladesh won the ICC qualifying tournament for the 1999 World Cup. In the final in Kuala Lumpur, they beat Kenya, who were on their upward trajectory to becoming semi-finalists in the 2003 World Cup. In a rain-affected final, spread over two days, Bangladesh were set 166 off 25 overs, and they won by two wickets off the final ball.

The impact of this match off the field was greater still: Bangladesh had won something for the first time and thereby raised the prestige of their people. Wherever Bangladeshis had gone in the world to find work, most were treated badly, often worse than anyone else, because their country was new and had no clout. If a company was not going to pay its workers for several months, then it was not the Americans or Europeans who went unpaid, it was the Bangladeshis. If they worked in a restaurant, they were subjected to petty restrictions, like not being allowed to talk to customers or sit down during their hours of work. They still are treated inhumanely in several countries. In their desperation to find a job outside Bangladesh, people somehow raise the money at home – up to several thousand pounds, often at exorbitant rates of interest – to pay an agent who makes big promises. Most end up sleeping many to a room abroad, working six, or more likely, seven days a week, and unpaid for months. Your PPE rubber gloves were probably made in Malaysia by Bangladeshis – yet unpaid, whose passports have been confiscated by their employers.

It has happened in Malaysia as much as anywhere. This is another reason why victory was so sweet at the Kilat club ground, which was packed, and not with Kenyan supporters. After the rain, some Bangladeshi supporters were so desperate for victory that they took off their shirts to help dry the ground: England supporters at The Oval in 1968 were ready to mop up to defeat Australia but not to that extent. Bangladesh, by winning this tournament, finally made a positive mark on the world. Cricket, therefore, took off: they could rise to the top ten in the world in the rankings of this sport, never in football.

* * *

Meantime, while Bangladesh carried on losing in those years following their too hasty promotion, a left-handed batsman was growing up in one of Chittagong's more affluent houses, close to the MA Aziz Stadium, which was the city's first Test ground. On their inaugural tour in 2004, England played their first Test at the Bangabandhu Stadium in Dhaka, the second at the Aziz Stadium in Chittagong. On England's second tour in 2010, they played on the two new grounds of Mirpur in Dhaka, and on the outskirts of Chittagong, or Chattogram as it has become known.

Tamim Iqbal was Bangladesh's first top-class cricketer, an opening batsman most countries would have accommodated. Tamim's uncle, Akram Khan, had represented and captained Bangladesh, most notably on that famous occasion in Kuala Lumpur; and his elder brother Nafees Iqbal had made a Test century. Tamim had grown up with a bat presented by his uncle, and he had used it on the driveway that adjoined his house. The driveway was made of concrete and provided a fast pitch. The one on which Virender Sehwag was raised on the outskirts of Delhi was very similar; and Tamim set out to become a left-handed version of the most attacking right-handed opener that Test cricket had seen. Not handicapped by his family contacts, Tamim was selected for the Bangladesh Under-17 and Under-19 team, and toured India more than once.

Trinidad, on March 17 2007, saw one of cricket's most consequential matches. India, by losing utterly unexpectedly to Bangladesh, were pushed to the brink of elimination from the 2007 World Cup after one game. The Indian players might have assumed that they could afford to lose to Bangladesh: they would still qualify for the next round, because all they had to do was defeat Sri Lanka, the other major team in their group of four, by a margin which made their net run-rate superior to that of either Bangladesh or Sri Lanka. All three clobbered Bermuda.

As I was following England at that stage of the World Cup, I could only watch the Bangladesh v India match on television and wonder how India's batsmen failed to cope. They start global tournaments slowly: this was one explanation, but not quite adequate. India's team contained some of the best players of spin who have ever lived, yet Bangladesh's three left-arm spinners bowled 30 overs and took six wickets for 117. Sourav Ganguly ate left-arm spin for breakfast – nobody in the world at the time was better at demolishing it – by running down the pitch to loft straight or over long-on, yet he chewed up 129 balls in scoring 66. So it went on: Sachin Tendulkar scored seven off 26 balls. M.S. Dhoni made a duck. India could set Bangladesh, who in 2007 were still almost as minor as a minnow, no more than 192 to win.

Tamim Iqbal chose this occasion to announce himself. He was only 17, he was almost entirely an offside batsman, but that was enough to blaze 51 off 53 balls. Mushfiqur Rahim and Shakib al Hasan also weighed in with fifties and saw Bangladesh to victory by five wickets. India then lost their group game against Sri Lanka, and were eliminated at the first hurdle. Pakistan meanwhile were losing to Ireland as well as West Indies. So the 2007 World Cup was reduced to anticlimax by the end of the qualifying round. The Super Eight match between Bangladesh and Ireland did not attract quite the same global audience as India v Pakistan would have done.

When Ratan coached Bangladesh Under-19s, his three outstanding players were Tamim, Mushfiqur and Shakib. To date they are the three highest run-scorers for their country in Tests and one-day internationals. Almost all the victories Bangladesh have enjoyed have stemmed from one or another. I confess to a soft spot for Mushfiqur from the moment he waddled out in his pads for his

Test debut at Lord's in 2005: he was only 17, and diminutive to put it mildly, yet he had an immaculate technique which enabled him to bat longer against Matthew Hoggard, Andrew Flintoff and Steve Harmison than any of his teammates. Shakib, according to Ratan, "was always a hard worker" on his way to becoming a world-class all-rounder, whereas Tamim, as a teenager, "was a little more casual – not now but in those days."

A couple of weeks after that historic upset in Trinidad, I interviewed Tamim in Antigua. He did not have more than a few phrases of English, so Bangladesh's media manager translated. Yet I could still sense the imperturbability of teenaged youth; not for Tamim the resigned defeatism to which his older teammates had so long been subjected. After Tamim had played a two-Test series in England in 2010 – reaching his hundred at Lord's off 94 balls by running down the pitch to Tim Bresnan and, far from aiming offside, pulling him to the square-leg boundary and hitting him over mid-on – then following up with another century on a fast pitch at Old Trafford (the England players having warned him he would struggle there), I had no hesitation in picking Tamim as the first *Wisden* Cricketer of the Year from Bangladesh.

During the Covid lockdown, I had the chance to talk again to Tamim on a TV show chaired by Ratan. Tamim kept calling him "Sir", so I could see the respect he had for his former coach. He talked about the phenomenon of roof-top cricket. Such is the lack of space on the ground in Bangladeshi cities that kids have to play in the air. Tamim said that his off-sided style had been shaped not only by his driveway but by the roof of his childhood house, where there was less space to leg; and that when he was young the Ashes were the matches they played against the kids on the neighbouring rooftop. A batsman on one roof, however, did not face up to a bowler on the next roof: the game was staged on one roof at a time. But how dangerous, as Ratan said, because any parapet around the roof would be low. Kite-fliers on the roofs of houses have been known to back-pedal and fall off.

Tamim also recalled the formative moment in his career when he was at the Bangladesh academy and omitted from their youth team to tour Pakistan. He recalled how Ratan, as head of the academy, had told him that if he worked hard he could be playing for the

Bangladesh national team in six months. Tamim did work hard and, at 17, he was knocking India out of the World Cup.

* * *

My father-in-law recalled going to Sylhet, in what is now north-eastern Bangladesh, as a young boy in the 1930s. He went in the company of his grandfather, who was – according to family folklore – the first native Indian district judge in Bengal. Sylhet, up in the hills above the floodplain, does not offer much employment. So tens of thousands have emigrated to Britain and established restaurants with names such as "Prince of India" or the "Taj Mahal", but altered their cuisine to suit British tastes. I took my parents-in-law to an "Indian restaurant" in England, and neither had ever seen anything remotely resembling the rice mixed with raisins and sultanas and covered with dry cooked meat which had then been dumped in a sauce. It was the equivalent of a Russian restaurant calling itself Café de Paris.

Malay, my father-in-law, remembered a luxurious house and garden where the district judge would reside for sessions; and two policemen stationed at the front gate when a death sentence had to be passed. Back in Calcutta, at school during the Second World War, he saw the famine when people begged, not for anything so lavish as rice, but for the water in which rice had been cooked. Three million people died of starvation in Bengal as the consequence of Britain's wartime strategy against Japan. Understandably, Malay became a medical student. After Partition, it was the job of medics, including him, to go to Howrah station when a train arrived full of passengers who had been massacred to clear up the bodies and put them in bags. Many more were to die in East Pakistan when its people, incensed at having their Bengali language banned and replaced by the foreign tongue of Urdu, rose against the army from West Pakistan.

* * *

It would be foolish to expect that a country which has seldom enjoyed stable government would soon establish a board of control to maximise Bangladesh's cricket resources, such as they were. Without any factory making bats and balls, the new country relied on imports from India and Pakistan, so that only the affluent could afford to play formally. Ratan remembers that even in the top division of the Dhaka League in the 1990s, only the national players had a bat of their own, while everyone else shared the club kit. Plenty of sunshine, the first prerequisite for cricket outdoors, but few maidans, which other cities of the subcontinent had, and therefore little space.

If the Test results were anything to go by, the Bangladesh Board got its first-class structure wrong from the start: they devised six teams, which was probably the correct number, and named them Chittagong or Sylhet or Barisal, but the matches were not staged in those places on a home-and-away basis. The main players were spread around the teams, so often they were not representing the region they came from, with the loss of rivalry that entailed. The first-class competition was merely a tournament in which six teams were posted to two or three grounds around Dhaka, without preparation and full-time coaches. Would the board have been wiser if it had granted first-class status to half-a-dozen teams in the Dhaka League, like Abahani and MSC, and built from there? Sri Lanka have had a similar geographical problem in being Colombo-centric, and giving first-class status to clubs in the capital has not worked there.

* * *

When Bangladesh was East Bengal it was famous for jute. Lascars sailing from Chittagong wrapped their belongings in hessian bags. The sandbags that brought troops in the trenches a little protection in the First World War were made of jute. Every British household until the 1970s would have had a sustainable bag of the same material to carry their shopping. Then came plastic bags, Bangladesh's economy collapsed, and plastic filled the oceans, not to mention the fish and whales swimming in them.

Clothes factories now line the Chittagong River, which is broad and deep enough for most shipping. The majority of factory workers here are female and veiled. The Chittagong Hill Tracts have been out of bounds for foreigners whenever I have visited Bangladesh. The indigenous hill-people began to resort to violent means to protect their remaining forest from being chopped down and exploited by people advancing from the plains. Overdensity of population brings out the worst in people.

Cox's Bazar sounds nice, on Bangladesh's coast, not far north of Thailand, overlooking the Bay of Bengal. A long coast of palm trees, golden sand, boutique hotels and the odd fisherman's shack serving fresh fish, unlike those in the polluted Sunderbans. And there it was on the news: blue all right, bright blue, as far as the camera's eye could see. Only it was not the sea but the blue plastic tarpaulin of the refugee camps of the Rohingya, about 750,000 of them, packed on to the hillsides above Cox's Bazar. Burma, or Myanmar, did not want them because they were Muslim; Bangladesh did not want them as the country had enough mouths to feed. Only the Rohingya girls were wanted, for abduction and sale.

Not until I visited a refugee camp for the first time did I realise that cricket could have a role in such places: to provide a form of escape for those who have escaped. I went to the Shatila camp in Beirut and saw the delight of boys and girls as they were introduced to the sport – by Ratan. The pleasure at middling a ball, even a tennis ball with a plastic bat, is universal. Most camps are located in tropical and subtropical regions, where refugees could play the game year round, if not in the middle of the day. A high proportion of refugees are Muslim, and while boys are allowed to play football, often girls are not, even if they wear scarves, veils or burqas, because it is a contact sport. Everyone can play cricket.

* * *

It was the Bangabandhu which staged Bangladesh's inaugural Test against India in November 2000. (Ratan acted as India's liaison officer, and observed how casually they took the game until Bangladesh finished almost equal on first innings, whereupon India turned it on and the home side collapsed.) It also staged their first against England, before being dedicated to football, and a new national headquarters for cricket was then constructed in the suburb of Mirpur. Every space under the Bangabandhu stands was used, mostly by shops selling sports gear or clothes or luggage, and rightly. A cricket stadium should be alive all year round, in and out of season.

Here, maybe, comes another consequence of this lack of space. Bangladesh were the tenth nation to become Full Members of the ICC – and most other styles had been already booked. You would soon recognise an Australian team in the field, from a distance, without any need for commentary: the crispness of their cricket as they hurl the ball around, their pace bowlers bowling flat out, the dedication – and noise – of their fielders, in addition to the distinctive method of the wicketkeeper taking the ball to his left side, not in front of him: this is Aussie. The West Indian style is casual, chilled, relaxed between deliveries, an explosion of energy when the bowler runs in. Pakistan? It depends on the mood: sluggish, or at any rate energy-saving in the heat of the day, then all animation when the ball starts to reverse swing, and the players swarm through the breach in a session.

Bangladesh, when made to start in Test cricket at minus square one, were defeatist: they had no chance of winning and knew it, until Tamim, Mushfiqur and Shakib changed the culture. Firstly, they began to win at home in 50-over cricket: this, after all, was the domestic format in which they grew up, the country's starting point. Soon they were winning one-day internationals away as well, as England found out in Adelaide in the qualifying stages of the 2015 World Cup: simply on grounds of enthusiasm, Bangladesh deserved to qualify ahead of England. Mashrafe Mortaza, their captain, had ruined knees so he had been forced to give up Tests, but he led with remarkable zest. This is what, I suspect, the lack of space does. It channels the enthusiasm of the Bangladeshi cricketer, who knows he is one of the fortunate few to take the field at all, into a tigerishness worthy of the inhabitants of the Sundarbans in the Brahmaputra Delta.

* * *

I first met Ratan in the course of my talent ID competition called the Wisden City Cup, which has since evolved into the ECB T20 City Cup. It began with four teams in London north of the Thames, and Ratan was the coach of London East. The three other teams all had a former first-class cricketer to captain them; London East did not, yet they still won the competition in their third year.

From Ratan I learnt there were more than 100,000 Bangladeshis in the east end of London, and not a single turf pitch. A couple of their more promising youngsters played at Wanstead CC, and that was about it. Apart from Victoria Park, which has a few artificial pitches, this community were as disadvantaged in cricket terms as if they had been back home in Dhaka, Chittagong or Sylhet, or more so. Doug Insole, the former Essex captain and England batsman, once told me that no England cricketer had come from the east end of London; and that Essex cricketers had grown up further out of the capital, with access to grounds and grass pitches. Nothing comes from nothing: no turf pitches, no cricketers.

Still, Ratan found a fine young off-spinner in the third year of the Wisden City Cup: Diyapan Paul, born in Bangladesh, who had the chipper demeanour and accent of a Cockney kid. Strong orthodox action, sound fielder, knew which way to hold a bat, promising cricketer. By then we had expanded the competition to Leicester, and at the end of that third season our combined Leicester-London XI played MCC Young Cricketers at Grace Road. After five of their 20 overs the MCC YCs were 16 for four: Paul had opened the bowling, up the slope, and taken a couple of wickets. Mark Alleyne, however, was captaining the YCs as the MCC head coach. Having led Gloucestershire to five limited-overs titles in two years, Alleyne knew how to rotate bowlers and set a field. We lost by six runs; but Paul was taken on as an MCC Young Cricketer for the following summer.

"We'll be very happy if you find us a player like him every year," said John Stephenson, the MCC Cricket Secretary. Paul took plenty of wickets in the Second XI championship – then damaged his knee. It was autumn, and he was out of contract with the YCs, so the insurance scheme of the Professional Cricketers' Association did not cover him. He had to wait for the NHS to operate, came back for a second season with MCC, then damaged his other knee. It was not going to happen.

Still, Paul brought along a friend called Aminul Islam to the trials in Victoria Park, which were conducted on an artificial surface, of course, in the nets. This spindly lad was a natural left-arm spinner: he took three or four paces to the crease, turned his whippy arm over, and every ball was almost exactly like the previous one but somehow not quite: a touch quicker maybe, or more flighted, or wider of off-stump. When the Wisden City Cup XI played the following year's final at Grace Road, Alleyne was not playing but MCC YCs had a stronger team, including Joe Root's younger brother Billy, who was already adept at reverse-sweeping. Islam took three wickets for 11 in three overs. Had he bowled his fourth, I think we would have won.

Islam was a very quiet lad. He worked, fairly predictably, as a waiter in Brick Lane; the weekends were his busiest time, so he was never able to play league cricket. He had played a bit in Bangladesh before he emigrated aged 15, but not since, and he was now in his early 20s. He had never had the chance to learn how to bat, and he fielded at mid-on, dutifully if not athletically. Yet he could bowl, superbly, and it was arranged for him to go to the Middlesex nets that winter. After England's winter tour, I got in touch to find out how Islam had fared. As he did not drive, let alone own a car, a volunteer from the charity London Tigers had taken him – midweek, when he could get time off work – to the Middlesex nets, but for only two sessions. Why? The coach had sent him away, because he couldn't speak English, and didn't understand what he was told to do. No, Aminul Islam could not speak English, but he could make a cricket ball talk; and a few years later everyone was asking why there were no left-arm spinners in England except Jack Leach, and scant if any diversity.

A country like Bangladesh is the opposite of Australia, where every talented young cricketer is given the opportunity to fulfil himself. In Bangladesh there is so much talent that never gets a chance, even to reach the first rung of the ladder and play a single game, because demand so far outstrips supply. And England comes somewhere in between, depending on your background.

Ratan tells the story of Bangladesh's district football competition for Under-15 schoolgirls, launched by the government, which was won by a team from a village near Mymensingh. The girls from this village were selected en masse to represent Bangladesh in a four-nation Under-15 tournament, and they won it, without conceding a goal, including a 14-0 victory over Pakistan Under-15s. But for a piece of enlightened administration, they would never have had the chance. In Bangladesh, only a few tigers can survive.

ENGLAND IN BANGLADESH, 2003/04 — 2016/17

Overall

Played **10**   Won **9**   Lost **1**   Drawn **0**

In Bangladesh

Played **6**   Won **5**   Lost **1**   Drawn **0**

In England

Played **4**   Won **4**   Lost **0**   Drawn **0**

England's record at each venue

Zahur Ahmed Chowdhury Stadium, Chattogram

Played **2**   Won **2**   Lost **0**   Drawn **0**

Shere Bangla National Stadium, Mirpur

Played **2**   Won **1**   Lost **1**   Drawn **0**

Bangabandhu National Stadium, Dhaka

Played **1**   Won **1**   Lost **0**   Drawn **0**

M.A. Aziz Stadium, Chattogram

Played **1**   Won **1**   Lost **0**   Drawn **0**

Series won	Captain
2003/04	Michael Vaughan
2009/10	Alastair Cook

Highest scores

173	Alastair Cook	Chattogram (Zahur Ahmed)	2009/10
145	Paul Collingwood	Chattogram (Zahur Ahmed)	2009/10
138	Ian Bell	Mirpur	2009/10
113	Marcus Trescothick	Dhaka	2003/04
109*	Alastair Cook	Mirpur	2009/10

Best bowling

5-35	Steve Harmison	Dhaka	2003/04
5-49	Richard Johnson	Chattogram (M.A. Aziz)	2003/04
5-57	Moeen Ali	Mirpur	2016/17
5-90	Graeme Swann	Chattogram (Zahur Ahmed)	2009/10
5-127	Graeme Swann	Chattogram (Zahur Ahmed)	2009/10

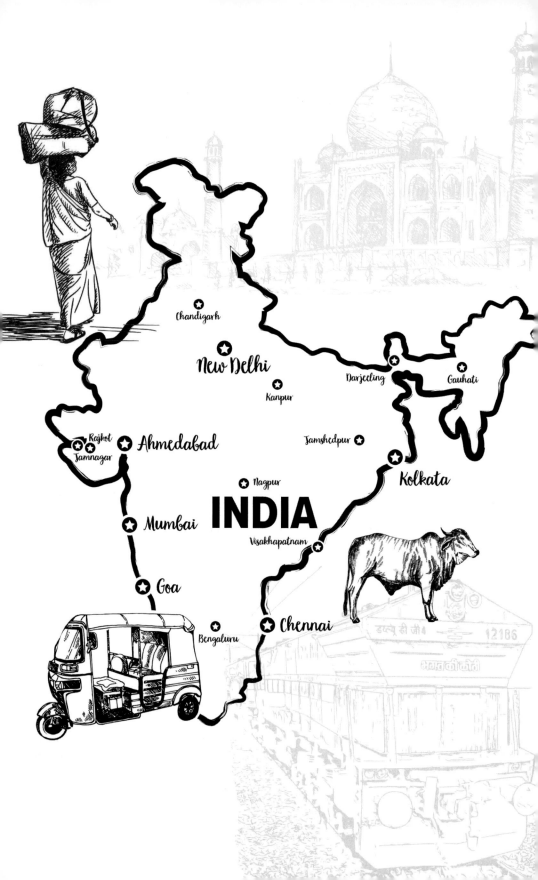

CHAPTER THREE

INDIA

A man – to all appearances a Westerner and probably British – walks up a rural road in India. His age, we can deduce, is approaching 30. Much younger would not do because then he could be a backpacker, and no country wants to encourage too many of those as they do not spend big tourist dollars. But no older, because India must be made to seem a destination for the adventurous and young at heart. And this road is not only clear of all traffic, it is clean of all rubbish, without another human being in sight, long before social distancing was invented.

He is walking towards a red pillar box beside this road in the middle of nowhere – and how reassuring its presence! For our British traveller can be confident that the pillar box will keep him in touch with civilisation – his own Western civilisation, for it was his forefathers who brought the Raj to India and with it the railways, hill stations, cricket, drinking tea and pillar boxes. Our traveller can therefore enjoy the best of both worlds: all the romance of India – its vastness, the Taj Mahal, women wearing saris and exotic food – in addition to the best of reliable British. Our traveller posts his letter or postcard, thus reconnecting with home, then – confidently, contentedly – strides on through this beautifully untouched scenery into the sunset.

"Incredible India!" this advertisement tells us in conclusion.

How potent are these images which India can stir in the British imagination. Simply say "India" and we think of the Taj Mahal, without anybody in sight, except perhaps a celebrity posing in front of one of its fountains; or of the Ganges, or the purest snows of the Himalayas, or a lagoon or beach in southern India. Some girls are named India. Never Pakistan, Bangladesh, Azerbaijan or Nagorno-Karabakh.

E.M. Forster tried to be more realistic, but he never visited the country before or after writing *A Passage to India*. Paul Scott was poignantly realistic in *Staying On*, about the British couple

– Anglo-Indians as the term was used at the time – living out their last years in a hill station in newly independent India. The film was as exquisite as the novel; yet it was Scott's trilogy, *Jewel in the Crown*, which became famous, after being romanticised into a glossy television series, one of several set in India and made in the 1980s. Thus India's image has been polished ever more brightly. Advertisements are not in the business of presenting us with reality, but this "Incredible India" ad seemed to me to be particularly remote, even before the virus.

The one letter which I posted in India, other than in a hotel, was the most important letter of my life. In several handwritten pages to my girlfriend – most fulsome in extolling her beauty and brains – I set forth the reasons I wanted to marry her. I was staying in Goa at the time (writing my first book *Cricket Wallah*), bought stamps in Panjim's central post office, and posted the letter to her in Poona (as Pune was then spelt), no more than 150 miles away.

It never arrived. As this was 1982, it was impossible to speak by telephone either: wires did not yet lead from Goa, which had been governed by Portugal until 1961, to Poona. It was not until later, and then by means of a telegram, that she learnt of my intentions. Compared with my heartfelt letter, this telegram erred necessarily on the side of cursory, or even terse ("Think u r dead fit. How about it? RSVP soonest"). Even after three decades of marriage, she still does not believe I ever wrote my long declaration of intent, but I swear that I did; and that the postal service in India was useless when I needed it most.

As for walking along a road in India alone, it is inconceivable. Kids would be all over you like mosquitoes.

"Hello, mister! Hello, mister!"

"Sir, sir, what is your name?"

"What is your good name?"

Walking along a road in rural India is the equivalent of Ravel's *Boléro*, starting with a gathering of two or three children, who multiply until hordes flock to see what is happening, amid noise like an IPL final.

"Col' drink, col' drink!"

Some urchin will soon try to sell you a bottle of warm fizz, striking the glass with his bottle opener; another will be hawking packets of crisps and snacks. Dozens of hands will be imploring you for money, the more importunate tugging your shirt. A dozen tuk-tuk drivers will see the growing crowd and rush to the scene to offer their services at ten times their normal rate. This is incredible India: incredible in the density of its population, in the material poverty of the majority, and their cheerful, imperturbable, friendliness.

My only taste of social distancing in India was emphatically not when walking down a road, but when I had to give a talk for the British Council in New Delhi. My excuse is that it was a couple of days before Christmas, and therefore everyone was busy preparing for the festivities (this narrative has to ignore the fact that most Indians are Hindu). An enormous hall had been hired at the British taxpayer's expense: an auditorium built to accommodate hundreds or even thousands of delegates for Commonwealth meetings. My name was advertised outside as one of two speakers along with the BBC's cricket correspondent.

I reckon the entire audience totalled five, maybe six.

India's image in the British imagination is akin to Somerset's. You only have to mention the word Somerset to conjure up visions of Glastonbury Tor, and villages with names like Dumpling Gurney, and cottages bathed in sunshine and honeysuckle – irrespective of the fact that it is an agricultural county in which manure is spread liberally, and that while driving to Dumpling Gurney you are bound to get stuck behind a tractor and trailer trundling down a country lane at 12mph, spreading muck in front of your car. You decide to take the first motorway out of Somerset, and move on to another place on which the romantic imagination has feasted, like Devon, Dorset or Cornwall.

* * *

If one's childhood is impressionable, as I suppose everyone's is, an arrow will hit the mark. It was the film *North West Frontier* in my case. Kenneth More played the dashing army officer who had to escort a young Indian prince – and, far more photogenically, his nanny Lauren Bacall – out of the walled town in the desert, where they had been encircled by Perfidious Tribesmen, to safety. Our hero's only resources were his own bravery, an old steam engine, a carriage so that Ms Bacall and the princeling did not have to slum it, and Gupta the faithful engine driver – all in the face of these Perfidious Tribesmen, who had cut the railway line in inconvenient, but spectacular, locations.

This film was not too romanticised. Other passengers included a dodgy Dutch arms dealer who advanced the case for Indian independence during the journey, and who was unhelpful when the train had to stop for our hero to replace some hijacked rails. The scenery was breathtaking: it was Rajasthan, I would guess, as the North-West Frontier lies in Pakistan, and Pakistan does not have the same romantic image as India. The sky was cloudless so the tribesmen could signal to each other by heliograph, their mirrors flashing in the barren hills. Heat and the silence of the desert prevailed whenever the steam engine stopped, as when our hero carried the princeling across a bridge by walking along the single remaining rail like a tightrope – the other had been blown away – above an immense drop to the bottom of the gorge.

Every year the boarding school to which I had been sent – not "went" – had a weekend when parents came to inspect their offspring and his schoolwork (or the more exhibitable parts) then take him out for a feed. My father, recently widowed, could not drive: he had depended on my mother for every practical thing, and Ampleforth was in the middle of the North Riding. On the Saturday evening the handful of boys who had nobody to take them out were treated to a film – the first film I had seen about India, at the stage of life when my imagination was ready to be fired.

On the other side of the valley from Ampleforth is Gilling. There must be something about this place. It made the national news when the prep school for Ampleforth, based at Gilling Castle, was exposed as a centre of appalling paedophilia. A century earlier, too, it had been the scene of some depravity.

The Rector of Gilling was the tutor at Trinity College, Cambridge, who took under his wing an Indian student who had been sent to England to improve his cricket. Ranjitsinhji fulfilled his side of the bargain on the field by rising through the teams of Cambridge, Sussex and England to become the finest batsman in the land, and in the world until Victor Trumper peaked in 1902. Ranji's style was all his own because he scored square or behind the wicket on both sides, using his wrists like no batsman before. W.G. Grace and other predecessors had favoured a driving game.

Ranji's glances, however, were not limited to whipping the ball to fine leg. He had also noticed the Rector's daughter, to the extent that he had a child by her, outside marriage. Ranji subsequently refused to have anything to do with his daughter, not contributing a penny to her upbringing. He left all responsibility for her to the Yorkshire and England captain Lord Hawke.

This scandal emerged long after I first walked to Gilling to meet a man in his eighties who, as a lad, had bowled at Ranji. He said Ranji would come down from the castle of an afternoon, select a patch of grass, plant three stumps and place a sixpence on top of them, then invite the village lads to bowl as fast as they liked at him – he who hit the stumps, if anyone, won the coin. This old man was rapturous as he recalled genius. Ranji took batsmanship to new heights, he invented new strokes, he was the first to score a Test century in a session; he was called, by W.G. himself, a once-in-a-century batsman. Yet here again the gap between the romantic image and the reality was enormous. Ranji manifestly had a sense of entitlement, the feeling he could do what he wished, never mind the consequences, and was notorious for leaving his bills to tradesmen unpaid.

* * *

Contradictions: India is said to be full of contradictions. I would prefer to say extremes. The country is so large – the world's seventh in size – and so populous, behind China or maybe now equal, that it contains all the sorts that make a world.

From an upper window in the old part of the Taj Mahal Hotel in Mumbai one could look out towards the Gateway from what used to be called the Sea Lounge. Here was served not simply "a buffet lunch" but a banquet that would have sated Roman emperors. What consommés (because they had the staff to boil bones for hours)! What salads! What biryanis, kormas and European dishes, then acres of dessert if you could stand up and get some. All the while a mother was standing beside the Gateway and holding a baby in one arm while pressing the fingers of her other hand to her lips.

Nothing but a siesta afterwards in the hotel garden while lying beside the swimming pool ("Guests only"). Here is an updated version of the paradise that Persians first conceived, of shade and running water on a hot afternoon, perhaps to the tune of lutes or lyres. If no damsels bear trays of sherbet, then waiters bring green tea. The noise of the world is kept at bay by solitary crows in the trees, and the odd toot of a horn muffled by high stone walls.

At the other extreme on a tour of India come those occasions when I have produced a delivery quicker through the air than anything by an England fast bowler. Projectile vomiting is a far cry from merely being sick, the operative word being "far". It does not matter how big your bathroom, or even if you have reached the washbasin, every single corner of the room will be sprayed. It is inexplicable how the contents of your stomach can be splattered on every wall, but they are. A second visit to the bathroom, or a third, and it will be completely redecorated again.

Once it happened in Kolkata after I had eaten the media lunch at Eden Gardens, in spite of having glimpsed the crumbling kitchen in which the meal was being prepared and the number of hands fingering the chicken. The second occasion – and this has only happened to me in India – was in New Delhi, on a morning when I was due to fly home: it was getting serious, because I had to leave for the airport, only every few minutes I was respraying the bathroom. ("Not to worry, sir, it is always happening," said Concierge cheerfully when he came for my suitcase.) I managed not to vomit in the taxi but could not stop – nothing can stop this projectile – at the airport entrance. I thought the security guards would prevent me travelling, but they too did not seem to think it abnormal.

Some of my colleagues carried bottles of handwash on tours of India, even before coronavirus; another never opened a door, even to his hotel room, without holding the handle in a tissue. You could see their point, when a waiter gives you a fork by holding the prongs shortly after wiping his nose. On my last England tour of 2017 I read a newspaper article – from this context you might see why I did not cut it out and keep it – which quoted a UN survey saying that half of the world's defecation outdoors is done in India. Yet, and yet, as an example of hygienic extremes, half of the world's vaccines were being made in India before and after Covid struck.

Vegetarianism is one obvious solution on a tour of India. I flew into Mumbai in the early hours for one England tour, hung round at the airport for the dawn flight to Rajkot, then took a taxi to a hotel on the outskirts. What better way than an all-night journey to work up the appetite for a cooked breakfast?

The receptionist pointed to the breakfast-room, which did not seem promising: a roof terrace with a few bare plastic tables and chairs. No sign of a menu.

"Hello, good morning, what do you have for breakfast? Please may I have bacon and eggs?"

"No, sir. Not available."

"OK, what about sausages?

"Not available."

"What about eggs then – scrambled eggs? Surely you've got some eggs?"

"Not available, sir."

A breakfast-room without bacon or sausages: perhaps it was a non-meat day in Gujarat. But why no eggs?

"What do you have available?"

"Tost."

So toast it was. The only breakfast which this four-star hotel offered was toast, butter and jam. It was a Jain hotel, and more vegetarian than vegan, because Jains do not eat anything which involves killing – not even onions or potatoes, because of the microorganisms that are disturbed when a tuber is dug out of the ground.

To drink, however, this hotel offered fresh orange juice as well as tea – and orange juice in the true sense of fresh, squeezed there and then, not the Western definition of "fresh" which means some sticky fluid stuck in a cardboard box with a heap of additives several months before. No such thing as a bad breakfast if it kicks off with real orange juice.

For dinner, the main hotel restaurant offered a menu of dozens upon dozens of dishes, all of them variations on the five themes of aubergine, lentils or dhal, okra and a couple of other non-root vegetables. Still, during England's first Test against India at Rajkot, no upset stomach let alone projectile vomiting.

An England tour of India used to consist of more than a series of five or even six Tests. They would play other first-class matches, for example against all five Zones, which would assuredly take you out of your comfort zone, because the venues did not have the same quality of hotels as the main Test centres.

On England's 1984/85 tour, the normal schedule was disrupted by the assassination of Indira Gandhi, and England found themselves warming up against an India Under-25 XI in Ahmedabad, not at the stadium which became the world's biggest cricket ground, but a modest college venue. England lost by an innings, the first game outside a Test that England on tour had lost by an innings since New South Wales beat them in 1962/63.

Some England batsmen of this period were undecided on how to play spin, caught between eras. The old technique of gliding down an uncovered pitch to drive the ball on the half-volley had disappeared, and the new skills of sweeping and reverse sweeping had not been widely adopted. E.W. Swanton's judgment of the sweep – "the bane of English batting" – still had many influential supporters. The authorities did not think much of the reverse sweep either after England's captain Mike Gatting was dismissed trying one in the World Cup final of 1987 in Kolkata. It was to be decades, rather than years, before horizontal-bat shots were accepted to be just as safe for scoring off the spinning ball, if not safer.

Before that game in Ahmedabad I was allowed a bowl in the nets against the home side. Ravi Shastri was their captain, a left-arm spinner himself, and soon to become the second batsman after Sir Garfield Sobers to hit six sixes in an over in a first-class match. He would have needed only 17 of my deliveries to make a hundred, but contented himself with one big hit then patted the rest into the side netting. I was not too surprised how his career developed, given this combination of skill, politics and diplomacy. He started as a left-arm spinner who went on to take 151 Test wickets; grew like Wilfred Rhodes into a right-handed opening batsman, hitting a double-century in Sydney and averaging 77 against Australia; became one of the two television commentators employed by the Indian board, along with Sunil Gavaskar; then head coach of the Indian team that won two consecutive Test series in Australia.

I did not realise, until Shastri told me, that English was his first language. He had grown up in south India and not learnt Hindi until he moved to Mumbai, where he had slotted into the Indian Test team by the age of 18. He lost his bowling – it happened to him while playing for Glamorgan – and told me how to recover from the yips. He advocated starting your spell of left-arm spin over the wicket: get some dot-balls and maiden overs under your belt, even if the right-handed batsman is kicking you away. Settle in first, and only then think about bowling round the wicket: because if you start round the wicket, and especially if you run between the umpire and the stumps, it is in effect a gate which can bar your way psychologically.

Joining an English county was a rarity for Indian cricketers. Farokh Engineer and Bishan Bedi adorned Lancashire and Northamptonshire respectively, Sunil Gavaskar had one season at Somerset, Kapil Dev played briefly for a couple of counties, and it was just as well for Warwickshire that their deal with Manoj Prabhakar fell through in 1994 and they replaced him with Brian Lara. There were a couple of others but still, it was a glamorous list to which Shastri added himself when he joined Glamorgan. Indian followers, indeed, were wont to say he had joined "Glamour-gun." His enjoyment of a drink after close of play might not have been crushed in Swansea and Cardiff. It all added to his qualifications when Shastri became a commentator, *the* Indian commentator along with Gavaskar.

Patting those balls back in Ahmedabad might have been reciprocal hospitality. When the Indians had toured England in 1982, I had invited them for a boat trip on the Avon at Bath. All it took in those days was a phone call to Raj Singh Dungarpur, their tour manager, and he unilaterally decided to bring the team over in their bus after a game in Bristol. Raj Singh was the éminence grise: he was to India's cricket what Gubby Allen, then Doug Insole, had been to England's. As an energetic pace bowler he had played for Rajasthan against MCC back in the 1960s, and he had stayed in administration out of love of the game not money.

Sunil Gavaskar and Kapil Dev missed the Gloucestershire game to socialise in London, but all the other players were there, such as

Shastri and Sandeep Patil. We had a lovely sunny evening on the river, and some food, then they went up the motorway to Manchester for the Old Trafford Test. Patil at least was not adversely affected: he hit six fours in one over from Bob Willis, driving like a languid Ted Dexter, and I do not recall him running after playing a single shot, not even a token jog to the non-striker's end. "He is such a lord," said Raj Singh: he would have known, as one himself. And over the subsequent decades I came to think that if one word described India's best batsmen, at and away from the crease, it would be lordly – as I suppose most of us would be, if we were adulated by tens of millions, and granted the status of semi-divine.

Again, in that Old Trafford Test of 1982, I watched Shastri walk across his stumps and glance a ball which pitched outside off stump, and which stayed on a line outside off stump, to the fine-leg boundary. This, I realised, is exactly what Ranji had invented – the stroke that dazzled Late Victorians. English coaches who spent the winter in India in the 1920s were spread thinly, a handful at any one time, employed by maharajahs such as Patiala and Cooch-Behar. They did not conduct inner-city coaching clinics; and the style they taught before the Second World War must soon have been overtaken by the vernacular.

If in eternity I have to watch batsmen from one particular country bat all day, it would be India's, ahead of Sri Lanka's. Still under the influence of their school coaches perhaps, Sri Lanka's batsmen hit a little straighter than India's. Using a little more leading elbow, Sri Lanka's whip in front of, not behind, square leg; they drive through extra cover when India's would aim square of the wicket.

It would be too emotionally draining to watch England's batsmen constantly; Australia's would be attractive, as they hit "down the ground", straighter than India's or Sri Lanka's, but almost too efficient; West Indian batsmen would be the most aerial and spectacular; but, if given a choice, I would opt for India's. My favourite left-handed batsmen have been the eclectic mix of Saeed Anwar, Brian Lara and David Gower, but my list of favourite right-handers is stacked with Indians. It starts with Sunil Gavaskar and Sachin Tendulkar – the young counterattacking Tendulkar, that is, not the older accumulator – as the most famous, and includes Gundappa Viswanath, and Mohammad Azharuddin (I was dazzled by his first three Test centuries, in his first three Tests against England, and dismayed when he was a central figure in the report into match-fixing by India's Central Bureau of Investigation); and V.V.S. Laxman, Virender Sehwag, Rahul Dravid, Rohit Sharma and Virat Kohli. And I have admired not only their style, but their desire to bat all day, apart from Sehwag in profligate mood, whereas too many of their English contemporaries had their fill after reaching 100 – a vestige of playing six or seven days a week and always having another game to follow.

What distinguishes India's best batsmen is the precision of their placement; owing to their wristwork, they find the gaps between fielders more frequently than batsmen who depend more on their forearms. The most aesthetically pleasing stroke has not only to be beautifully executed, it must also beat the fielder and go to the boundary. We feel foolish when our cry of "shot!" is uttered just as the ball is stopped by cover, or goes to the sweeper for a single.

Of all these batsmen, if there is one single innings I could watch again, it would be one by Sehwag. Not one of those coruscating hundreds or double-hundreds he used to make as an opening batsman, although I recall a day in Durban, the eve of a Test, when both captains – Graeme Smith and Andrew Strauss – kept looking at the TV in the press-conference room at yet another Sehwag century scored at a faster rate than any Test opener had attained before. (Sehwag, in Tests, averaged 82 per 100 balls; the strike-rate of old-timers went unrecorded.). The innings I will always remember was down the order, and only amounted to 66, but it was the finest display of its kind I have seen. It was the Bangalore Test in December 2001, when even southern India was a little wintry and damp. Both sides were going to be happy with a draw, as India were ahead in the three-match series and England would take losing 1-0 with an inexperienced team. So Ashley Giles bowled over the wicket outside Sachin Tendulkar's legs and was kicked away for over after over. Sehwag, alone, would have none of this negativity. In only his fourth Test, he sailed down the pitch – almost the adjacent pitch – and drove to all parts. I cannot believe more muscles are involved in the playing of a stroke than when a batsman runs down the pitch as Sehwag did and drives a left-arm spinner landing in the rough over extra cover. If any one of those muscles in his eyes, neck, shoulders, arms, hips, legs and feet is out of sync, he does not hit the ball in the middle of the bat and can be dismissed. So much in cricket remains to be discovered, like which muscles are involved in an intricate stroke, or what goes on in a great batsman's head, ball by ball, in the course of a major innings.

Manual dexterity of the highest order is seen in India not only on its cricket fields but in concert halls and streets: that vendor with a barrow selling hot *chaat* has the same dexterity when whipping out the next banana leaf and covering it with spiced potato and condiments, before serving it to you with a flourish. I speak as someone who, on Christmas Eve, takes an age to wrap up one present: I have cut the paper just too small, and where on earth has the start of the Sellotape gone? To see someone take a handful of dough, slap it a few times then place it on a hot grill or in an oven without burning his or her self – perfect hand-eye coordination – is always a pleasure to watch.

The same applies to classical Indian music. Once the artist has warmed up for a raga on the sitar, or sarod, or santoor, or veena, accompanied by tabla – here is one of this world's greatest glories.

* * *

Allegations of cheating, which ended up in accusations of racism, were like projectile vomiting in leaving a bad taste in the mouth. Anyone who has grown up since the introduction of the Decision Review System and neutral umpires might not realise how the relationship between two teams could turn so nasty.

England's tour of India in early 2021 offered a glimpse of how it was. A ball balloons off the Indian batsman's pads to be caught by England's short leg. The close-in fielders are not just trying it on, they are genuinely convinced it is out, caught bat-pad. The umpire (Indian, because this is a series played under the Covid restrictions) says not out. Joe Root appeals for a review. The third umpire watches a replay of the ball missing the bat and gives not out immediately. It does not occur to him that the ball might have then hit a glove on the way out.

This is how it often used to be before the 1990s and incremental changes in umpiring. Very few Test umpires in India have played at first-class level, or in some cases much at all. It is possible to be the best umpire in the world without having played a first-class game – Steve Bucknor of Jamaica, for instance – but the umpire who has a feel for the game from his playing days is far more liable to make the correct decision than his counterpart who does not.

After conducting the one interview I have had with an Indian Test umpire and researching the subject for *Cricket Wallah*, I concluded that theory is valued too highly in umpiring exams in India, which deters the former first-class player. From India's inaugural home Test series in 1933/34, when Douglas Jardine brought the former England batsman Joe Hardstaff senior to umpire at one end, while he tolerated the Australian Frank Tarrant at the other, India's single Test umpire who has been a Test player has been Srini Venkataraghavan. More to the point, India for years on end had no member on the ICC Elite Panel of Umpires. Given all its resources – given most of cricket's resources! – India was underperforming in this one department of the game.

It was horrible to watch relationships, like old milk, turning sour. Everybody began a series with the best intentions of winning the game for their country and their teammates, thereby securing his place in the team. An England batsman would then be given out by an Indian umpire, hounded by the home players running at him with arms aloft, and by the crowd. Swaroop Kishen, the umpire I interviewed, stressed how difficult it was in the middle of a packed Indian ground to hear an edge because of the constant crowd noise. The England batsman would stand there, registering his disbelief at the LBW verdict (no match referee then to impose a penalty), looking at the part of his bat which had hit the ball, before dragging himself from the crease as the injured victim, nay martyr.

If this series was getting tight, England would let slip to "their" media their belief that the umpires were being "blatant", their codeword for deliberately cheating; and the Indian/Pakistani/ Sri Lankan media would sense old-style colonial racism. Passions became heated; battle lines were drawn; there were no peacemakers; patriotism flared into nationalism. There was no ceiling, no limit to the anger as there is now, when the protagonists of each side are likely to have played or play in the same T20 franchise together.

* * *

My favourite up-country venue in India was Gauhati, where England met East Zone in 1984/85. It was a favourite for England's opening batsman Graeme Fowler, too. The hotel where we were staying was little more than a dak bungalow – spacious but basic – on top of a well-wooded hill outside the city. Below us lay the Brahmaputra: not only broad, being spread over several channels, but deep, immense, ever-changing, ever-watchable. Fowler told me later that it was in Gauhati he came to terms with India. Having had a poor tour, he came good in successive innings of 114 against East Zone, 49 in the third Test, 201 and two in the fourth, and 69 in the fifth – a substantial contribution in turning England's 1-0 deficit into 2-1, their last Test series victory in India until 2012.

Also on that tour, in the north-east, in a lull before Christmas, I had the chance to visit Darjeeling with she who had become my wife – and still is, in spite of that letter not being delivered. The toy train from the plains up to Darjeeling was not running owing to landslides, so we went by road from the airport to the hill station, and stayed at the Windamere Hotel, paying extra for logs so as to have a fire in our room (sorry, no alternative source of heat). When the mist cleared we beheld, awestruck, the wonder of wonders which is Kanchenjunga. You have to walk a short way from the Windamere, past the Tibetan colony trying to sell their carpets, to the lookout point – and there, across the valley extending into Sikkim, rises this tremendous triangle of white. You can also watch Mount Everest lit by dawn provided you take a taxi to a ridge above Darjeeling, though it is too distant to be breathtaking, if not too early for the senses.

Most hotels and rest houses up-country – especially when the England team occupied one hotel and journalists were consigned to the second "best" in town – made us sigh for the Taj Mahal in Mumbai, where the first Test had usually been staged. Up-country hotels would offer a large room, which is always a start, but dingy, especially if the plastic curtains had not been washed since their installation. Nothing, however, could keep out the sound of buses and lorries roaring past like British binge-drinkers and vying for the title of India's least tuneful horn – nothing could drown out that noise, not even the rattle of the air-conditioning unit, with vibrating tufts of dust above its vent. Your request to Reception for the A/C to be switched off in your room would be met by a wobble of the head.

Knock, knock.

You have caught the 6.50am flight from Trivandrum via Cuttack to Chandigarh, or rather you caught the plane that had been scheduled for 6.50, but was delayed several hours. Now, a few minutes of siesta in your new hotel room in Chandigarh, even in the company of that solid rubber pillow, would not come amiss.

Knock, knock, knock.

Who's there?

"Laundry! You have laundry, sir?"

"No, not today. Please come back tomorrow."

"Tomorrow not available, sir!"

"Why tomorrow not available?"

And once you have raised your head from that stony pillow and opened the door, it turns out that tomorrow is the start of a four-day religious festival, therefore no dhobi wallah is available for the rest of your stay. So you have to let the room boy in, and unpack your suitcase, and make out a laundry list, and fish out some rupees for a tip – by when it is time to ring the office and tell them just how restful your rest day has been.

Making out a laundry list on a tour of the subcontinent can be as time-consuming as writing a match report. Some days, on some tours as a Sunday correspondent, the nearest I came to work was filling out my laundry list.

Articles of Western clothing are listed in full, and Eastern clothing, too. The men's list often begins with "Suitings". Next: do you want to send your suit for laundry or dry cleaning or pressing only (please tick)? Subsequent categories include "Trouser" (seldom plural), and "Underpant". Does "Undershirt" mean a vest, not that I have one, or tee-shirt? Laundry is the one area where newspaper accountants have not cut back: difficult to tell your correspondent abroad to wear sweat-stained shirts. Yet if I list my shirt as "dress shirt", it will cost 30 rupees to clean, whereas if I enter it as "casual shirt", it will only cost 25. Should I try to save my employers five rupees, or uphold their ethical reputation by paying full price?

One may have to scroll down the list of Eastern garments – kurta, salwar kameez, sarong – to find "socks (pair)". Often, like shirts, long days demand two pairs. (Old hands normally put on a new shirt in the evening for dinner and wear it again next morning.) Laundry for Ladies will list much more besides, like sari and petticoat, brassiere and panty. Hey, what about ticking petticoat, just this once, to see if it is spotted when one finally takes these expenses to the office?

This list is still far from being filled out. "On hanger" – or "Folded"? A tricky one. How long till we leave this hotel? Packing is easier when slipping laundered shirts, already folded, into a suitcase; there again, it is a bore to take one out of its packet before the next journey when so many pins attach the shirt to its piece of cardboard. I have removed a dozen pins and still almost punctured my jugular when fastening the collar.

Normal Service, or Special Service, or Express Service? Normal will be returned the same evening if sent before 10am; Special will be returned the same evening, if sent after 10am, for 50% extra; Express will be done in three hours for 100% extra. In Perth, where water is scarce, laundering a pair of socks at the Normal rate is greater than buying a new pair. For the cost of sending a pair of socks at the Express rate in Perth, one could buy a whole suiting in Asia.

Knock, knock. "Housekeeping!"

The sun is setting when your laundry is returned and your shirts are hung up in the wardrobe, even though you ticked Folded. Thank you, dhobi wallahs, for making me look less dishevelled. One drawback: the amount of starch used to make the creases sharp, in addition to steam ironing, wears out your favourite shirt by the end of a tour.

Then you find your list still on your desk, in triplicate. After all that work, you forgot to include it in the laundry bag.

* * *

No need for a wake-up call in these up-country hotels, given the quality of noise insulation: the businessman in the room next door is the equal of any alarm clock once he has embarked on his ablutions and expectorations. As he clears his throat, at 6.41am, it sounds as if there is no limit to the reservoirs of spittle and polluted phlegm.

Chandigarh became one of England's more frequent venues, even though the ground in the neighbouring suburb of Mohali was one of the smaller ones, because a very influential member of the Board of Control for Cricket in India was based there: Indrajit Singh Bindra, a Sikh who had fled Lahore at Partition for the new city of Chandigarh. As Le Corbusier laid it out in a grid pattern with wide straight streets, it was far easier for security purposes to send a cricket team there and whisk them to the stadium in police and military convoys. In 2001 the security outside the England team hotel was so intense in the build-up to the game, it was almost impossible for the media to enter it, or only after every coin and key had been scanned. By the Saturday evening of the Test, the hotel had been given over to a big society wedding, attended by hundreds of guests wandering through the hotel and its grounds, the security of the England players forgotten.

Even this new model city of Chandigarh could not control its pollution. I don't think I have stayed in a better modern hotel than the one when England last played a Test in Mohali: part of an American chain, rooms palatial with a large glass bathroom in the middle, food superb, the Italian restaurant headed by a chef from Genoa. This hotel would also host society wedding receptions, where marquees were erected in the grounds along with neon lights and bunting. Yet as sunset approached, and final touches were put to the bouquets, a blanket of dust and smog would descend on the garden, the sun no longer having the strength to burn them off. It is the same in every Indian city. It was the same in London from Dickensian times until the 1950s. Whole days of first-class cricket in Delhi have been abandoned owing not to rain but smog.

It must be a real pain to be the duty manager when hotel guests offer smart-arse suggestions. "Have you thought of mending the pavements outside your excellent hotel?" I ventured. "That would reduce the amount of dust when you have a wedding in the garden..."

Outside the gate of this American-chain hotel was another world, the India of the people. Most guests never went out the gate except in their chauffeur-driven, air-conditioned car; only a strange Westerner, like a journalist, would try to cross the dual carriageway to see the shops and chai cafés on the other side where lorry drivers stopped for a break. Anyway, I tried suggesting that if this hotel mended the surrounding pavements, which had crumbled since Le Corbusier's time into dusty rubble (the municipal road budget might have gone astray), less pollution would rain down on the heads of wedding guests. There was also a roundabout right next to one corner of the hotel and it too had lapsed from its original design as a floral delight into a mound of rubble: were that to be rebuilt, grassed over, and maintained, again the pollution would be reduced. The idea might even catch on in other parts of Chandigarh that businesses could take care of their immediate environment?

The duty manager listened politely, bewildered. As my wife explains it, India has never had a civic tradition. Your loyalty extends from your family to your extended family to fellow members of your caste then possibly of your religion, not to society as a whole (maybe there are too many people for one to do something for everybody). But this was before Covid, when a new civic sense was detected.

The image of India that stays with me is not one of walking along a rural road alone, but from the opposite extreme. It happened late at night on the way to or from Mumbai airport. The road had been dug up and was being re-tarmacked. As every vehicle roared its engine to get through the pot holes, fumes from the waiting tar lorries added to the smoke from exhaust pipes and all-prevailing dust. The road was still divided into two lanes in a way, with an average speed of 2-3mph, and there in the middle between the two lanes was a pile of aggregates about 5ft high. And on top of that pile of stones, nearing midnight, in this scene Dante could never have conceived because he never saw such pollution, lay a baby, wrapped in swaddling clothes.

* * *

It only took a fortnight after first arriving in India before I worked out that ABR – Anything But Roads – was my preferred form of travel. Road accidents claim 100,000 lives per year in India. The photographer Adrian Murrell and I went to stay at Ranjitsinhji's old palace in Jamnagar at the invitation of his great-nephew Prince Shatrushalyasinhji. He was as avid in protecting wildlife in the marshy wilds of Jamnagar as previous generations of maharajahs and Jam Sahibs had been in popping it off in the company of Raj officials, and he showed us the carefully preserved study where Ranji had worked after his return from playing cricket in England. At the end of our visit Prince Sat, for short, kindly supplied a car to drive us to Baroda, where England were to play their next game, and a liveried driver to take us.

For about a mile. We had hardly gone beyond the palace gates when our driver jumped out, and a few minutes later a boy climbed into the driver's seat. Whether he had driven a car before was something neither Adrian nor I were able to deduce. The lad was definitely not liveried, but we were mildly livid when we realised what was going on. We took it in turns to sit in the passenger seat and show him certain basics, like how to use the brake or change gear. I used up one of my nine lives after it had got dark and we came to a T-junction, a phenomenon beyond the lad's experience. He did not decelerate, while I yanked the wheel hard enough to turn it most of the 90 degrees. To give him credit, no sign indicated a sharp right turn to Baroda.

* * *

It is easy to glamourise train journeys.

Once upon a time I took the Orient Express from Istanbul. The last sunlight was glittering on the Bosphorus and Sea of Marmara as we pulled out one evening, reflecting the gold braid on the cap of the attendant who conducted me to my wagon-lit. In the dining-car, corks were popping from the all-inclusive champagne. As we sped through the night towards Paris, while my luxurious berth was being turned down by a buxom maid, a five-course meal prepared by French chefs culminated in the finest crêpes I ever tasted. No, it was not like that, prosaic truth be told. The train which lurched out of Istanbul consisted of three carriages, and no dining-car, not even a refreshment trolley, nothing but basic seats on which to sleep. When we crawled into Belgrade I tried to find something hot to eat or drink at the end of the platform, and by the time I got back the compartment was overflowing with Yugoslav women and the vegetables they had bought at market, so I stood until the border. This was the less glamorous, post-Agatha Christie reality of my journey on the Orient Express.

Shashi Tharoor, in *An Era of Darkness*, has explained how the construction of railways in India resulted in enormous profits for British shareholders, but they were not built for the benefit of natives. Yet, it cannot be denied, since 1947 the railways have become thoroughly Indianised, like cricket. On England's 1981/82 tour we had a couple of rail journeys, from Jamshedpur to Calcutta as it then was, and Bombay to Poona as they then were.

Indian trains have an intensity all their own, as a result of the population density. A train in Sri Lanka is simply an eastern version of a British train, maybe of times past. You have to buy a platform ticket if you are not travelling; if you are, you present your ticket to a uniformed collector after climbing aboard a carriage that is basic but not packed to the gunwales. If you catch a train in Colombo, Kandy or Trincomalee, nobody is dying on Platform 2, nor are there a hundred homeless people asleep on Platform 7, nor are thousands braced to ram themselves through the doors and windows before the train has even stopped on Platform 19.

The instant you reach an Indian station your suitcase is seized by a porter to whom you have not been formally introduced – you may not even have had time to present him with your business card (before mobile phones India loved business cards almost as much as autographs). Fear not – provided you can see your suitcase borne aloft on the porter's head, albeit that several hundred people separate you from your luggage. You had omitted to pack that course of antimalarial tablets, which must be taken daily, in your hand luggage – it is in that suitcase which is almost visible at the end of Platform 21 – but you did exchange one word with your assiduous porter, which formed something in the nature of a contract, when you shouted "Simla!" or "Chennai!" Admittedly, you did not have the chance to tell him that you had to go to the ticket office first, before he headed straight for the appropriate platform, but your suitcase will almost certainly not be lost, let alone stolen. Nevertheless, what would have been a calm manoeuvre at a station in Scotland or Sri Lanka is turned into a drama, if not panic attack, by milling crowds. From where did they get the idea for that ad?

England cricketers were warmly welcomed when they entrained. An open invitation was issued to any member of the party who wanted to climb into the driver's cab for a leg of the journey. I accepted the offer when we stopped at a station between Jamshedpur and Kolkata. It was night, several hours after the one-day international, and more thrilling to head into darkness. It was not diluted, only heightened, when the driver stopped and pointed to a bridge ahead which looked vaguely familiar: yes, it was just like the one in *North West Frontier*, which had been blown up by Perfidious Tribesmen except for a few remaining rails. A sign in front of the bridge cautioned "Dead Slow, 5 mph". The bridge over this river was very weak, said the driver, who proceeded to take the train over at walking pace. Back in the carriages, amid the card-playing and tea-drinking, nobody had sensed anything untoward.

* * *

"They are all orphans," said Michael Brearley, who had retired the summer before as England's captain after a rather triumphant 1981 Ashes, and who was visiting friends in Calcutta as it then was. "It must be a sad place," I replied.

"Not at all, exactly the opposite," he said. "Come along tomorrow and see." He was right: this orphanage in Calcutta, run by SOS Children's Villages, was a joyful place, because nobody took anything for granted, as most of us tend to do.

Orphanages in Calcutta used to be all the rage. Anybody who was a celebrity wanted to be photographed alongside Mother Teresa. When South Africa were readmitted to world cricket after apartheid, their first tour was to India – and what public relations company could have dreamed up a better photo opportunity than the South African cricketers, all bar one white, cuddling brown babies and orphans?

My father-in-law could forgive Britain for starving three million Bengalis to death in the 1890s, and again in the 1940s: he was an army doctor so he could understand a military imperative. But he could not forgive Mother Teresa for, as a medical man in Calcutta he had heard from his contemporaries what went on behind the scenes when paparazzi were not shooting celebrities cuddling babies. What she wanted was souls for the Lord: so starving people were swept up from the streets, clothed, fed and converted to Christianity. But, he said, they were not given medical treatment. That would have delayed the moment when they could give their souls to the Lord.

The SOS Children's Village, in the part of Calcutta known as Bidhannagar or Salt Lake City, was a veritable joy: calm, organised but not overly so, almost serene. I spent an afternoon there, and when England returned in 1984/85, I went back with two players, Neil Foster and Vic Marks, who were not playing in the Test. We held a pick-up game. Fossie captained one team, including me, and Vic the other; no such thing as a pitch except the bare earth between the bungalows where every sort of game was played, and a tennis ball. Which did not stop Fossie playing very keenly because he was desperate for a run-around. The selectors finally read the signs before the next Test, in Madras, where he took 11 wickets to win the fourth Test.

Boys whizzed around; girls (for this was the era before women's cricket in India) watched from outside the bungalows, each presided over by a woman, often from equally indigent circumstances herself, who acted as mother to the ten or 12 children under her care. It was such a happy environment because every bonus was appreciated. If you were given a new shirt, or an exercise book and a biro, that made your week. A treat was a bun or biscuit which your "mother" gave secretly to you. The older kids in each house took such delight in mentoring the younger ones, to whom they were not related by blood but friendship.

Vic's team made a decent total. But Fossie, batting, was in the mood to knock off the target with a succession of lads and me for partners. Vic brought himself back for an important over: Fossie slog-swept him, or pull-drove as we said in those days, and his partner scored a few, too. One of Vic's team then bowled a more economical over of medium-pace, before Vic stepped up to bowl his next. He was an England regular in ODIs, an essential member of the 1983 World Cup team – and this orphan lad, aged about 12, doing what he thought best for his team, ran up and took the ball from Vic in order to bowl the next over himself. Proper pace, not English off-spin! Vic, slightly abashed, took it well, grinned, and retired to the covers.

The girl I sponsored at the village grew up, got married and went to live in a *chawl* – slum is a close if not precisely accurate translation – near the main road leading from the centre of the city to the airport at Dum Dum (where the bullets were manufactured).

It was not bad as *chawls* go. Her husband drank too much – his eyes spoke of nothing other than despair and alcohol – so she had to do the housework, and earn the money, and make the most of what he did not take for drink. Her hut had no fresh running water – that had to be bought in a big plastic container and carried home on her head – but there was a communal tap nearby; and the walls of corrugated iron, with a thatched roof, kept out some heat and rain except perhaps the monsoon, and a couple of drapes partitioned the hut into a couple of rooms, one a kitchen with a bottle of gas to cook their dhal and rice. She was tiny herself, having been malnourished from birth, yet full of fortitude; and she had a son, who promised to be her future.

I still cannot understand, though, never mind forgive, the scale of values which condemns tens or hundreds of millions of women in India to live in villages and urban settlements without sanitation, where they have to walk by day and night to relieve themselves at the risk of being raped.

* * *

The politics of India were so much simpler under the leadership of the Congress Party. Nehru, soon followed by his daughter Indira Gandhi, formed a quasi-royal dynasty which kept a secular lid on the country until she was assassinated by Sikh bodyguards. Once this secular, or at least pluralist, lid was removed, forces were released which culminated in the destruction of the Babri Mosque at Ayodhya and a right-wing Hindu nationalist government.

Cricket has not been exempt. Narendra Modi, as Chief Minister of Gujarat, headed the Gujarat Cricket Association when the world's biggest cricket ground was conceived for Ahmedabad. In the same state at the same time, the world's biggest statue was being built, by the same architects, as another monument to Hindu nationalism.

When Modi was elected Prime Minister, then re-elected, such was his popularity with the majority, the new president of the Gujarat Cricket Association was Amit Shah, who also became India's Minister for Home Affairs in Modi's government. *The Financial Times* on 27 February 2021 described Shah as Modi's "right-hand man". Shah's son, Jay, became secretary of the Board of Control for Cricket in India.

When the third Test between India and England ended in Ahmedabad in two days, on a pitch that was at best controversial, there seemed no chance of anyone being penalised by the ICC. Soon, no country would be so devastated by Covid as India under Modi.

The Congress lid could not stay on forever because too many forces were being contained; and the system, whereby all the jobs and favours were kept in-house, was too corrupt to last. Corruption takes many forms, however; every country is corrupt in its own way, such is human nature. In India, as my wife argues, there is something to be said for corruption: for example when you want to have electricity installed in your house quickly instead of being on the waiting list for months or years. This way everybody gets a slice of pie, from an official in the state's department of power, to the boss in a local office who gives the go-ahead, to the man who digs a hole for the cable, and the electrician who does the wiring. No doubt several others benefit along the way, most of them on very low official salaries or wages. Everyone is a winner, provided you have the money.

Britain is so subtle we seldom call it corruption. A plum job is coming up, or the chance for a gilt-edged investment: a nudge or a wink on the old boys' network is sufficient, no need for anything obvious or sordid. And the beneficiaries are those at the top who need the money least.

Take cricket in England. Your 12-year-old son is a keen batsman. What's the best way to get him selected for your county Under-13s? Nothing as blatant as bribing one of the selectors. Of course not! This is England. Well, not bribing directly as such. However, the county selectors for age-group teams are Level 3 coaches. Until recently, doing the course was by invitation only. Even if you had been a Level 2 coach for donkey's years, you could not apply for Level 3.

Your nearest Level 3 coach – who happened to be a county age-group selector – ran his own academy and charged £50 per hour for one-on-one coaching; and, lo and behold, if you happened to hire this coach on a regular basis, your son's chances of being selected for the county Under-13s were vastly increased, if not guaranteed. Who would have credited it? An amazing coincidence, for coincidence it must be, because we don't have corruption in England. Do we?

* * *

Permit me to record that one of my best bowling spells took place in Mumbai, and my worst. Unfortunately, the former occurred at a secluded ground without any spectators: it was a new one, in Bandra, where rumour had it that Sachin Tendulkar practised, with fine facilities and a variety of net surfaces. It was one of those days – oh all right, it was the only day – when the ball landed where it was intended to and the batsman reacted as I had planned. If I tossed up a wider leg-break, he duly ran down the wicket for Stephen Brenkley of *The Independent* to complete the stumping. Figures of 4-0-15-3: not bad for a 20-over game, even a media match.

And in this land of extremes came the media game in Mumbai on England's next tour. It was a few months after I had been seriously ill for the one time in my life, with septicemia; and of course it was played, not on the same secluded ground with pace and bounce, but on one of those maidans in central Mumbai where thousands walk past and watch. It was a hot and sweaty nightmare. I had lost so much muscle – a stone and a half in ten days – I could barely make the ball reach the batsman without bouncing twice. Try bowling in a T20 in front of your colleagues and many spectators in the middle of Mumbai against an Indian media team with several ringers (one batsman said he had been in the same school team as Rohit Sharma, the first to hit two double-centuries in ODIs) and with straight boundaries of 40 yards at most. Put it this way, it was the quickest 50 I have achieved.

Nevertheless, had I to be a cricket correspondent in another time and place, I would like to have been in Mumbai between the two world wars, or even during. An apartment please on Malabar Hill, where the sea breezes suffice for air conditioning; and what a tournament to cover in the Bombay Quadrangular or, as it was from 1937, the Pentangular. Matches between the various communities had such intensity, with fascinating social currents at work. Ram Guha in *A Corner of a Foreign Field* captured the drama when the Hindus were so desperate to defeat the Muslims that they selected a spin bowler from the scheduled castes, Palwankar Baloo; and so happy were they upon winning that Brahmins carried their Untouchable match-winner on their shoulders from the field.

It would have been too far to walk on a match-day morning from Malabar Hill across the Colaba peninsula to the Gymkhana Ground, so the cost of a horse-drawn gharri would have had to go on the newspaper's expenses. Once the Brabourne Stadium opened in 1937, how delightful to have walked to the ground along the Queen's Necklace in the sea air, oblivious to the clock's ticking as the Second World War approached; and back in the evening after play, perhaps drinks in armchairs on the outfield, and dinner at the Cricket Club of India.

A few more decent stories were to be told, in addition to Baloo's. In the 1928 Quadrangular, Kumar Shri Duleepsinhji, Ranji's scarcely less talented nephew, while batting for the Hindus against the Parsis, was faced with a packed off-side field. India's future Test left-arm spinner Rustomji Jamshedji bowled consistently wide of Duleep's off stump. According to Edward Docker in *History of Indian Cricket*, "suddenly the young prince twisted the blade in his hands and drove the ball in reverse direction down to third man! Kapadia [Doli Kapadia, the Parsi captain] instantly appealed to umpire Joe Birtwhistle to give the batsman out for using unfair means, but Birtwhistle turned down the appeal. He [Duleep] hadn't obstructed the field or otherwise played the ball unfairly." My interpretation is that this is the first recorded instance of the reverse sweep.

Even during the Second World War, the Pentangular was contested keenly: fewer matches, but the prestige of the Europeans was even more at stake. So much so that after being hammered in the 1942 competition, they brought in three batsmen who had scored or were to score Test centuries for England: Reg Simpson, Denis Compton and Joe Hardstaff junior. They raised not only the standard of the tournament but that of the contest between the star batsmen of the various communities. When Rusi Modi scored a double-century for the Parsis, Vijay Merchant beat that by scoring 250 for the Hindus, only to be trumped by Vijay Hazare scoring 309 for the Rest (mainly native Christians). No better cricket anywhere in the world, during the Second World War, than the Pentangular.

Being a cricket correspondent in Mumbai between the wars would not have been a year-round job, though. I would have had time to holiday in the Himalayas, taking in a game at Simla, and at Chail, which claims to be the world's highest ground, and Darjeeling.

How about a touring team to Kashmir, and staying on the lake in houseboats at Srinagar, in those years before Kashmir saw one of the most enormous manifestations of human folly?

* * *

Indian cricket can boast many superlatives: the most first-class teams; the IPL, the biggest T20 franchise tournament; the highest celebrity status for its national players; the largest media coverage, and press conferences too.

A popular TV programme might attract an audience of over ten million in Britain, but this is nothing compared with that for India's cricket captain. India has so many TV channels; and so many newspapers in so many languages because classified advertising has not evaporated, as from British newspapers, and circulations have held up.

The law of supply and demand is at work. In countries where cricket is not the number one sport, like New Zealand, the top players outnumber journalists, and need them to popularise the game. In Asia the media usually outnumber the players. In India specifically the leading cricketers are so rich they need have nothing to do with the written media. A television interview, yes, after a good performance in the IPL, but this is only a few formulae: "Yes, it was important to win this game." Players need never reveal anything in an interview on television.

India's captain is different: he has to give a press conference before a Test match in accordance with ICC regulations. Ever more cameramen pile into the back of the room, behind row upon row of journalists, as the scheduled time for the press conference passes without any sign of the demi-god. When he eventually appears, it is all too tempting for a journalist to make his mark by addressing the demi-god matily by his first name, then asking a very lengthy question, so his editor, his colleagues, and his family, including all his aunties, know that he is at the very Heart of Events.

I wish the international cricketers of India – like those of Sri Lanka, where Murali set the ethical example – had used their enormous influence more. When there is a cause célèbre, like a young woman raped and murdered on a bus in New Delhi, or students from the scheduled castes are bullied into hanging themselves at university, words from politicians only go so far, if uttered at all. A statement of condemnation from the national cricket team, and a visit by one of their players, would surely go much further in reforming societal attitudes.

* * *

I did not require prophetic powers to end *Cricket Wallah* in 1982 with the sentence: "India is destined to become the capital of cricket." All the resources were present; and all the resources have been maximised, except in one department, umpiring.

Partition was a tragedy on an epic scale, but if it had any silver lining, it is this: blend into a single eleven Pakistan's fast bowlers alongside India's batsmen, together with the best spinners from Bangladesh as well as India and Pakistan, and such a team would seldom if ever be beaten by anyone. India, if unpartitioned, would have held a monopoly in cricket. India, as it is, is cricket's one superpower.

India is not "Incredible" in the literal sense of unbelievable, and still less so in the way that PR companies and advertisements would have us think. It never ceases, however, to astonish and amaze, including its colossal contribution to the culture of cricket.

ENGLAND IN INDIA, 1933/34 — 2020/21

Overall

Played **130**   Won **49**   Lost **31**   Drawn **50**

In India

Played **64**   Won **14**   Lost **22**   Drawn **28**

In England

Played **66**   Won **35**   Lost **9**   Drawn **22**

England's record at each venue

M.A. Chidambaram Stadium, Chennai

Played **11**   Won **4**   Lost **6**   Drawn **1**

Eden Gardens, Kolkata

Played **10**   Won **2**   Lost **3**   Drawn **5**

Wankhede Stadium, Mumbai

Played **8**   Won **3**   Lost **4**   Drawn **1**

Feroz Shah Kotla, Delhi

Played **7**   Won **3**   Lost **0**   Drawn **4**

Green Park, Kanpur

Played **6**   Won **1**   Lost **0**   Drawn **5**

Narendra Modi Stadium, Ahmedabad

Played **4**   Won **0**   Lost **3**   Drawn **1**

—————————— **I.S. Bindra Stadium, Mohali** ——————————

Played **4**   Won **0**   Lost **3**   Drawn **1**

—————————— **Brabourne Stadium, Mumbai** ——————————

Played **4**   Won **0**   Lost **0**   Drawn **4**

—————————— **M. Chinnaswamy Stadium, Bengaluru** ——————————

Played **3**   Won **0**   Lost **1**   Drawn **2**

—————————— **Nehru Stadium, Chennai** ——————————

Played **2**   Won **0**   Lost **1**   Drawn **1**

—————— **Dr Y.S. Rajasekhara Reddy Stadium, Visakhapatnam** ——————

Played **1**   Won **0**   Lost **1**   Drawn **0**

—————————— **Gymkhana Ground, Mumbai** ——————————

Played **1**   Won **1**   Lost **0**   Drawn **0**

—————— **Saurashtra Cricket Association Stadium, Rajkot** ——————

Played **1**   Won **0**   Lost **0**   Drawn **1**

—————— **Vidarbha Cricket Association Ground, Nagpur** ——————

Played **1**   Won **0**   Lost **0**   Drawn **1**

—————— **Vidarbha Cricket Association Stadium, Nagpur** ——————

Played **1**   Won **0**   Lost **0**   Drawn **1**

Series won	Captain
1933/34	Douglas Jardine
1976/77	Tony Greig
1979/80	Mike Brearley[†]
1984/85	David Gower
2012/13	Alastair Cook

† *One-match series.*

Highest scores

218	Joe Root	Chennai (Chidambaram)	2020/21
207	Mike Gatting	Chennai (Chidambaram)	1984/85
201	Graeme Fowler	Chennai (Chidambaram)	1984/85
190	Alastair Cook	Kolkata	2012/13
186	Kevin Pietersen	Mumbai (Wankhede)	2012/13

Best bowling

7-46	John Lever	Delhi	1976/77
7-48	Ian Botham	Mumbai (Wankhede)	1979/80
7-49	Hedley Verity	Chennai (Chidambaram)	1933/34
6-45	Geoff Arnold	Delhi	1972/73
6-48	Roy Tattersall	Kanpur	1951/52

CHAPTER FOUR

NEW ZEALAND

Two police officers approached as I was walking along the concourse from Wellington railway station to the Westpac Stadium for a T20 international. I had just arrived from Australia, where law enforcement officers have as much sense of humour as American ones, so I immediately averted my gaze. One male, one female, this pair of police officers sought eye contact, and sought it again until I looked at them, and the woman smiled warmly, if the man less so. New Zealand, unless you are playing rugby, is not confrontational.

Fences in Australia, whether they are designed to keep out humans or other animals, are barbed. Fences in New Zealand are not barbed. Hotel rooms and apartments in Australia have a safe. Hotel rooms and apartments in New Zealand do not have safes – except in Auckland, which is by far the country's biggest city and far too pacey for other New Zealanders, slower than Melbourne or Sydney, similar to Brisbane.

Most houses in Australia are made of brick, in New Zealand of wood. Most houses in Australia are standardised bungalows; most in New Zealand are individually designed, especially when built on hills, as they are in Auckland, Wellington and Dunedin. Australians superimpose their houses on the land; New Zealanders adapt them to the contours.

Cricket in Australia is aggressive and conformist; in New Zealand it is friendlier and quirkier. Australian cricket has always celebrated the fact that it is different from English cricket; New Zealanders have always been happy to play cricket against anyone. "Kiwis" do not do things in the same way as the rest of the English-speaking world: they are more informal, less hierarchical, but no less effective. It was no surprise when New Zealand moved more swiftly and efficiently than anywhere else in the English-speaking world to quell Covid.

* * *

Cricket in New Zealand, as you would expect, has adapted cleverly. It has found a niche in the land of rugby by becoming a boutique summer sport, staged on small yet beautiful grounds, much like the intimate outgrounds that county cricket once used at the likes of Buxton, Harrogate or Horsham. No first-class ground in the world is more beautiful than Pukekura Park on the outskirts of New Plymouth, surrounded by native forest on three sides. No Test ground is more beautiful in its quiet rural way than Hagley Oval in Christchurch. The style of cricket that New Zealanders have displayed on them has become attractive too, to the point where everyone's second-favourite team was New Zealand, even before the World Cup final of 2019.

It has been a complete transformation since the 1990s when cricket was in crisis and close to financial and moral bankruptcy. *Wisden*'s review of the New Zealanders' tour of South Africa in 1994/95 captured the moment. It "ended with their squad in disarray," *Wisden* summarised. "The recriminations intensified when Matthew Hart, Dion Nash, Stephen Fleming and Chris Pringle were all suspended – the first three for smoking cannabis, Pringle for unspecified misbehaviour. Manager Michael Sandland and coach Geoff Howarth resigned in mid-January. Captain Ken Rutherford, who twice fell foul of ICC referee Peter Burge, was sacked after the home season degenerated into a series of traumas. Leading the critics in this series was Sir Richard Hadlee, who was commentating for New Zealand television and attacked the team's lack of discipline. The criticism was difficult to refute." Believe me as a former editor: this is as trenchantly damning as *Wisden* can be.

The whole country used to be not so much stuck in a time warp as wallowing in it. You drove into a country town for a late lunch or afternoon tea, and if you found anything so much as a milk bar open that late it had stopped serving hot food. Sunday opening – the opening of any shop other than a hotel or petrol station on a Sunday – did not begin in New Zealand until 1990, when Auckland's mildly Bohemian quarter of Parnell took the plunge into the 20th century. No wonder almost every young New Zealander used to emigrate or travel. The population was declining, because the country was boring.

Similarly, for all the individual brilliance of Hadlee and Martin Crowe, which had enabled the country to win Tests abroad as never before, the assets of New Zealand cricket by the mid-1990s were few. The domestic game was still dour, defensive, and dominated by medium-pacers wearing long sideburns and clocking up maidens; the main venues were rugby grounds, except for Wellington's Basin Reserve and Hamilton; the appeal of watching medium-pace on dodgy pitches in draughty stands was limited. The tour of South Africa in 1994/95 was a crisis-point like none before.

The consequence was that New Zealand became the first Test-playing country – and so far the only one – to reform its governance structure radically, and sensibly. A new constitution was placed before the old board, which was composed of committeemen from the constituent associations and therefore focused on their vested interests: what can New Zealand cricket do for my association so I can get re-elected? But so profound was the crisis by the mid-1990s that turkeys were compelled to vote for Christmas. A board of seven – later eight – independent directors took control: "great and good", not exclusively male, and experts in relevant fields, while a couple had played cricket to international level. Such a simple model of governance, yet impossible still for most cricket-playing countries to achieve. From this top, everything has flowed down, so that New Zealand teams consistently punch above their weight in global tournaments. An inch here or there and New Zealand would have won the 2019 World Cup; in 2021 they went to the top of the ICC Test rankings. By virtue of necessity, New Zealand Cricket learnt to make the most of resources.

* * *

"What do you think?"

"Awfully nice, dear."

"What about the colour – does it suit me?"

"It looks lovely on you, dear."

A husband, when asked for an opinion about his wife's new skirt or dress, has little choice. It is too late to ask how expensive it was; only the degree of enthusiasm can be adjusted. But I have to say that from my childhood I always hated dark green, until I saw the rainforest of New Zealand.

When my father married a second time, my stepmother had a flat in London. In its favour, it was situated roughly halfway between Lord's and The Oval. The drawback was that my stepmother had never been married before, and the time to adapt appeared to have passed.

On the fifth morning of the third Test between England and India in August 1971, my father and I took the Tube to The Oval. England, under Ray Illingworth, had collapsed in their second innings against the unique wrist-spin of Bhagwat Chandrasekhar, so India needed only 173 to win their first Test in England and their first series. Such a target nowadays would be knocked off, or missed, in 40 or 50 overs. India, at the end of day four, had reached 76 for two at a rate of less than two runs an over, so almost half a day's play was assured.

As a Yorkshire supporter, I wanted Illingworth – even though he had moved to Leicestershire – to lead England to victory. But as an English boy, I supported underdogs. I yearned for New Zealand's amateurs to score runs on their tours of 1965 and 1969; it was so romantic when Zaheer Abbas unfurled cover-drive after silky cover-drive when scoring 274 in the Edgbaston Test in 1971. Australia had to be beaten, but I wanted every other country to do well against England because they were amateurs whereas England were professionals (Illingworth the ultimate pro). I was more than half-thrilled when India inched home about teatime, after taking 101 overs to limp over the line. Illingworth's 36 overs had been wicketless, but he had conceded only 40 runs.

The flat had been trashed. We got back to find the kitchen floor covered in broken glasses, mugs, bottles – anything that could be swept off a shelf. The sitting-room had been recarpeted with books and papers. My little bedroom was unscathed, but every other room had been vandalised and smelt of gin or sherry. Stepmother had gone, if only temporarily, leaving behind the destruction she had inflicted on her own property.

The flat was decorated dark green.

* * *

As part of the New Zealand board's strategy, "boutique grounds" have blossomed. Even if the crowd consists of only a few thousand spectators, no more than at one of the old rugby stadiums in times past, these grounds look full on television. TV broadcasters are gratified: they have atmosphere to capture, crowd shots, scenes of excitement. When England played an ODI at the University Oval in Dunedin, the ground was packed with "scarfies": the city has the country's largest university and the students provided raucous encouragement, especially to the New Zealand fielders positioned in front of them. Was it a complete coincidence that Ross Taylor, having received particularly loud support when he fielded there, a few hours later played the finest one-day innings in a run-chase against England I had seen? His unbeaten 181 was the equal of Viv Richards's 189 when West Indies batted first in 1984 at Old Trafford. In his press conference, to which he had to be conveyed in a buggy because he had pulled so many muscles and suffered so much cramp, Taylor gave the crowd a favourable mention.

What makes a boutique cricket ground in New Zealand so delightful in real life, and to appear even more delectable on television, is the light. It is so clear, so clean, so unpolluted. Always in England the light has a hint of haze or pollution; at any cricket match in the subcontinent the sunshine filters through dust. In New Zealand it is as if you have taken off dirty spectacles and the optician has given them a thorough clean before you put them back on. Such is the clarity of the light that one might have entered heaven and the angels, to show one round, turn on the lights.

I once took the TranzAlpine train from Christchurch across the farming plains, over bridges and gorges, into the Southern Alps. At Arthur's Pass the train stopped: five diesel engines were added, so that having descended through native beech forest to Greymouth, they would be able to pull it back up the 1 in 33 gradient. The name of the station, and the settlement strung along the road, is taken from Arthur Dobson, who followed some Maori from the west coast when they made one of their occasional visits into these mountains.

South Island is similar to Scotland in its glens, with long vistas and craggy hillsides lined with firs. But if you walk along these valley floors, no rival clans swoop down from hiding among the trees; no memories of English troops who massacred the hopes of independence; and no midges either.

I wandered along the river valley at Arthur's Pass and up a path into the rainforest to find waterfalls gushing from the mountainside. We are accustomed to Britain being green, very green in South Wales, but what makes New Zealand unique, at least in the cricket-playing world, is the number of shades of green: the vastly wide spectrum of greenness, with every shade from the lightest to the darkest green, and everything in between.

It was wild flax which the Maori sought when they made their expeditions from the west coast. They could weave it into their finest ceremonial clothes as if it had been Irish flax. They found the plant growing beside these waterfalls; and this was the lightest green I saw, a radiant green, the flax dancing and waving in the sun like a lissom dancer in the Rio Carnival. Wordsworth kicked off the Romantic Movement by walking round the Lake District and rhapsodising: "The sounding cataract/Haunted me like a passion" but, in my eyes, it was primarily the sight of these waterfalls, secondly their sound.

On the southern shore of Lake Taupo in North Island the forest is not merely dense, the tree-trunks being much thicker than in the drier Australian bush. This rainforest, too, is so varied in its shades of green, from dark to luminous as if the sun lives behind the leaves. I felt like the Ancient Mariner when:

Ice mast high came floating by
As green as emerald.

Ferns spread their arms to implore the sun's benediction. A few of these trees have naturally died, yet moss preserves the appearance of life. The steam that puffs from the hillside was used by Maori for cooking food: they wrapped their pork and vegetables in leaves and steamed them, while they bathed and washed their clothes in thermal pools. In New Zealand the wind can be excessive, but here the forest absorbs it.

This is Aotearoa, the land of the Long White Cloud. So the sky is not supposed to be cloudless, yet the light is always radiant. You can see 30 miles across Taupo to its northern shore. If a boat from

Taupo comes this far south, it is a painted ship upon a painted ocean. Only ducks and swans disturb the silence, but not after they have breakfasted; horses graze amid the reeds. As Yeats said: "And I shall have some peace there, as peace comes dropping slow/ Dropping from the veils of the morning to where the cricket sings."

Waihi village is a Maori settlement of some 20 buildings at the end of a private road on the southern shore of Taupo. Behind it rises original native forest, because this is part of the Tongariro National Park, which a 19th-century Maori chief bequeathed to the Crown, preserving it from loggers by making it New Zealand's first national park. Hydroelectric cables climb the hillside, and the imported weed of old man's beard hangs from too many branches. Otherwise, non-indigenous life has not penetrated, leaving the green – in its innumerable shades – so serene.

In the mountains south of Lake Taupo I walked to two more lakes. One might have been Windermere 2,000 years ago, before Britain's original forest was reduced to less than 5% of the land mass. Flotillas of wildfowl floated. An island in the middle, once linked by a causeway, used to have a fortified village, where a tribal war was fought early in the 19th century. Access to the island is private, as it is to Waihi village; again I did not mind this exclusion because it preserves the lake for the long-term future. I saw no sign of human presence in the whole landscape, except two Maori meeting places, like Saxon halls without walls.

The second lake, on top of a mountain, sometimes has a whirlpool. Maori have their own theological explanation; the mundane one is that excess water drains out of the bottom, instead of splashing out over the top, to sometimes create a whirlpool. It took me two hours to walk round Lake Rotopounamu, which has a couple of beaches. On one a group of five people had just finished bathing. I waded in, and kept closing my mouth instinctively against the waves stirred by the wind, but the water was as fresh as could be, not salty, plenty of it having fallen the night before. Soon I had the lake to myself after the group had walked on, save for a couple of teal, like mallards, and a white butterfly. "All this, and heaven too," as one of the walkers had quoted.

Of these new boutique Test grounds, Mount Maunganui has the finest landmark for the cameras. The Mount itself, a mile from the ground, has fortifications built by Maori which are still visible amid the verdant vegetation of its lower slopes. It is of the same cultural piece as Hawaii. About 1200AD, for causes unknown, people hollowed out canoes, stocked them with dogs, pigs and yams, and set sail around the Pacific. Captain Cook found some of the same words being spoken from French Polynesia to Hawaii, although it did not save him from being killed when relations turned nasty.

The ground itself in Mount Maunganui is nothing special, as yet. It is situated next to the port and a salt factory, and during the day freight trains bring in wagon-loads of logs for export. It was an ordinary club ground until it grew in concert with the city of Tauranga and the Bay of Plenty region, and a grass mound was constructed around the perimeter and a long single-storeyed pavilion added. But on the screen, with one television camera trained on the Mount, and especially in the middle of a British winter, in the eye of the beholder this ground looks divine.

Mount Maunganui is going to grow, however, into NZC's headquarters and centre of excellence: this is the board's strategy. Auckland is by far the most populous city, but Eden Park can never be taken from rugby union; Wellington's Basin Reserve, being in the middle of a roundabout, is limited in its potential to grow. The climate in the Mount allows cricketers to practise outdoors almost all year round, and several New Zealand players live there, including Kane Williamson.

But give me Hagley Oval. Like Mount Maunganui, for most of the year it is just a cricket field with a single-storeyed pavilion, a mound and a groundsman's shed. For a big game, though, it can dress up like a young woman putting on a gown for her first ball of another kind.

While in New Zealand I do not feel as though I am at the ends of the earth and remote from civilisation – except when I think of my location on a globe, on the other side of the world from Europe. The first British settlers in Christchurch must have felt very remote from home at the end of their voyage on four sailing ships via the Cape of Good Hope. As in Australia and other parts of New Zealand, the settlers colonised what had been a feeding ground for the indigenous population. In Christchurch's case, approximately

800 Maori lived and subsisted in the freshwater meadows of what was renamed the Avon River.

As Dunedin was colonised by settlers from Scotland, Christchurch was by settlers from England – and what better way to make their new settlement more English than England than to create Hagley Park on the lines of London's Regent's Park, planted with British trees, and to play cricket there? Only six months after their arrival in 1851, these English settlers played a match, with equipment they had brought more than 12,000 miles, as the Suez Canal had still to be built. When an umpire called "Play!" for the first time in the new colony, how reassured the players must have felt: this colonisation was going to work, for them at any rate, they would have enough to eat, they would do more than survive. The first single scored in Christchurch may have been only 20 small steps for two batsmen, but one giant leap for the colony.

The city fathers accepted an invitation by the agent of the Nottinghamshire cricketer and entrepreneur George Parr to stage a match in Hagley Park in 1864: for English cricketers to come and play in Christchurch would have seemed like a validation of the colonial enterprise. To receive Parr's touring team, the city fathers built a fine two-storeyed wooden pavilion: it had a spacious changing-room, although the ceiling was lower than it would be for cricketers now, and a balcony upstairs from which they could watch the game unpestered by spectators. True, the standard of cricket in Christchurch was such that they put up a team of XXII to meet Parr's XI, and in their first innings Parr's underarm or lob bowler Richard Tinley took 13 wickets for only 18 runs, but they improved notably in their second innings, and the whole occasion was adjudged a success. Christchurch was on the map.

Look at the sketch of that 1864 match and the scene has hardly altered. It is a mere detail that Parr's match was played a few hundred yards away in another part of Hagley Park. The marquees are the same, and the feasting therein, although the wine is now locally sourced after the country's first vineyards were planted in the 1950s. Everything is in its place, just so. At the top of the mound a sign says: "Deckchairs only to be positioned behind this board": in other words low-slung chairs have to be used further down the mound so their occupants do not block the view of those behind. The wooden pavilion was relocated two years after Parr's match, to be used by the Canterbury Umpires' Association, and sits contentedly in the sun. It meant so much to the people of Christchurch when cricket opened at Hagley Oval after their earthquakes in 2010 and 2011 – the same sort of affirmation as the match against Parr's XI had been a century and a half earlier. I do not know anywhere in the world where a cricket match is better organised, not even at Lord's itself.

All around Hagley Oval, meanwhile, other cricket matches are in progress, perhaps half-a-dozen games being played by boys, men, veterans and ever more girls and women. Not even in Trinidad can one watch a Test and several club games simultaneously, because Queen's Park Oval is almost half a mile from the Savannah; the closest would have to be Eden Gardens in Calcutta when games are proceeding on the Maidan.

Anyone for punting on the Avon amid the moorhens? Shallower than its namesake in Bath, its banks more tidily trimmed, this Avon in Christchurch has been channelled to meander through Hagley Park and past Christ's College. It makes almost as handsome a background for the Far Eastern tourists to take their selfies as the college of the same name in Cambridge, where Milton and Darwin studied. One of the most eminent pupils of this Christ's College was John Wright, who had to observe a strict dress code at school, then wore a hair shirt when opening the innings for New Zealand and Derbyshire. After his retirement, I do not think I ever saw "Shake" with his shirt tucked in.

As in all New Zealand cricket, the security is the opposite of oppressive. Please don't walk on the pitch, one is politely requested two days before a Test, with no veiled threat and no rope around the square. When the game starts, the temporary perimeter fence of white plastic is not so secure that boys cannot wriggle under it to retrieve the ball which they have hit over it. Spectators are not merely allowed, but encouraged to inspect the square at the lunch interval, a custom that has long since died out elsewhere. The music on the PA system is tasteful, too. How could any spectator abuse a fielder at fine-leg or third man minutes after Louis Armstrong has sung "And I think to myself – what a wonderful world!" During England's 2018 Test, one spectator began an obscene chant and, after repeating the phrase twice, was muted. I saw no police wading in, so the England supporter must have censored himself, realising his chant was as inappropriate in these surroundings as rap in the Sistine Chapel.

Nowhere in the realm of international cricket do human beings and nature combine so harmoniously. And does such a setting have an impact on the players? For certain, at the end of the five-match one-day series between New Zealand and England in 2018, the television commentators said their stump-mics had not picked up a single sledge.

Do not, however, forget the wind. It can come as Friendly Zephyr, a blessed relief converting heat into warmth, but it can sweep all before it, or even drive you mad like the sirocco in southern France. Graeme Swann played a season in Christchurch as the pro for a league club, and tells the story of how one day all his team lay flat and face-down on the ground at the fall of every wicket, for respite. Some winds stem from Antarctica and lacerate the face like fine sandpaper. It is, I suppose, nature's payback.

A thousand years ago New Zealand was covered in unique forest inhabited by unique birds, most famously the flightless moa, of which there were estimated to have been between 100,000 and 500,000. When the Maori arrived, they cut down trees to build canoes and *marae* or meeting huts, and burnt many trees so their enemies could not hide and launch surprise attacks; they also found that some root crops grew more abundantly in charred earth, until that was exhausted and more trees had to be burned. Maori accounted for about 45% of the destruction of New Zealand rainforest, according to the Te Papa museum in Wellington, and European settlers for the other 55%. The latter wanted the wood, especially that of the kauri tree, for ships, houses and railway tracks. With such efficiency did they log and burn that little remains, except on the west coast of South Island where humans seldom go.

Farms which have planted tall hedges for windbreaks do not achieve the same overall effect. From Hagley Oval the spectator can see the hills beyond Christchurch stripped of every tree and, as he shivers, understand the cause. Once, I drove from Mount Maunganui to Taupo and in those couple of hours saw no indigenous trees or original landscape, just fir plantation after fir plantation where the land was not flat enough for farming. Where the land had been recently logged, one or two skeletons stood while a few other trunks lay like corpses. It could have been Stalingrad in 1945, except that men had destroyed nature rather than one other. It was reassuring to hear the NZ Prime Minister Jacinda Ardern announce that one billion trees were going to be planted, although nothing can replace the soil that has been blown away.

* * *

They had all day to kill in Wellington. The overnight train from Hamilton had arrived at about six in the morning. The boat train south to Lyttleltⁿ, the port for Christchurch, was not leaving until the evening. The following morning they would take the train south to Dunedin to play Otago. So all day to walk around Wellington, at one's own expense, since nobody got paid for playing in the Plunket Shield – and while it was the Christmas holidays, it would cost you money if you had to take time off work. First-class cricket in New Zealand in the 1950s was a different world.

In Hamilton I met David Hoskin, a genial old boy who played for Northern Districts for a decade as an opening bowler. The players in his day would ride to training – two evenings a week at Seddon Park – on their bikes, which is as good a way of warming up as any. Not until the 1960s did any of the Northern Districts players have a car, and it belonged to Bert Sutcliffe, the best cricketer New Zealand had produced to that point, the David Gower of his time and place, and a genial soul. Sutcliffe had to leave Otago when his sports goods business in Dunedin went bust – a common story for cricketers worldwide. When Rothmans stepped in and signed Sutcliffe as one of their handful of top sportsmen to represent the company, he moved to Hamilton and joined up with another rep in Don Clarke. Over 17st, Clarke held the points-scoring record for the All Blacks for 24 years, and earned a worldwide reputation as "the Boot". He also bowled for Northern Districts as Hoskin's opening partner.

Given two such celebrities, and the limitations of alternative entertainment in post-war New Zealand, crowds up to several thousand would attend Northern Districts' home games at Seddon Park, which used to have two grounds, unlike the one now. This revenue was sufficient to fund their away games, without frills. When they went to Christchurch and Dunedin, or Wellington and Auckland, they took a 12th man who had to double up as manager and look after the team kit big. Sutcliffe, being famous, had his own bat, but nobody else did, while their wicketkeeper Eric Petrie had his own gloves. Petrie was, according to Hoskin, "such a gentleman" that he played for the Gentlemen against the Players during New Zealand's 1958 tour of England.

For away games in the Plunket Shield, the ND players stayed in a boarding house, several to a room. There they would have their evening meal, which was on expenses, then buy Sutcliffe a pint of beer, which was not, and place it on top of the piano, and he would play by ear all evening while the rest of the team sang along. He would smoke some sponsored cigarettes, before they got him in the end.

The first discordant note was the sledging by the MCC team of 1960/61, a prototype of England A. Any touring team was a novelty, because Australian cricket still disdained New Zealand, and the crowd at Eden Park for the game between MCC and the Governor-General's XI attracted a record 23,000 on the second day. But neither the MCC captain Dennis Silk nor his vice-captain Willie Watson were disciplinarians. So when they were playing ND at Hamilton and Hoskin walked out to bat – and at No.11 he seldom hurt a fly – he found his ancestry being questioned by a couple of gnarled old pros.

A more harmonious sound was that of the ball fizzing through the air when Hoskin faced Alf Valentine on the West Indies tour of New Zealand in 1955/56: few finger-spinners get enough revolutions on the ball to do that. So, too, the cheers on the final day at Eden Park in Auckland, which Hoskin attended as a spectator, when New Zealand won their first Test after 26 years – in particular the roar when Everton Weekes smashed a long hop to midwicket. It was the only one of the four Tests in that series in which Weekes did not hit a century.

Mobility in international cricket was just beginning. New Zealand's wicketkeeper when they won their first Test was Sammy Guillen, who had played for West Indies on their inaugural tour of New Zealand in 1951/52 and had stayed on. In 1956 West Indies made no objection to Guillen playing for the opposition, even though he had not qualified by four full years of residence; and, perhaps less overawed than his teammates, Guillen top-scored in New Zealand's second innings at Auckland to give them enough time and runs to win. After the 1955/56 tour, Bruce Pairaudeau emigrated to New Zealand, became a sales rep in Hamilton, captained a local club and spent years talking about Weekes. Hoskin eventually became the president of New Zealand Cricket.

* * *

Thursday, 11.20am. A Dunedin hotel. Appointment to interview Kane Williamson for 20 minutes. How many have the privilege of saying they want to meet so-and-so, on a one-to-one basis, and usually have access granted within a day or two? Here is the chance to speak to one of the four candidates for the title of Best Batsman in the World, following the decline of AB de Villiers. Virat Kohli, Joe Root, Steve Smith and Williamson were born within a couple of years of each other, bat at No.3 or 4, and captain, or have captained, their respective countries, at least in Tests.

In England's previous game, the one-day international at the Westpac Stadium in Wellington to which I had walked, Williamson had scored an unbeaten century. But, when set to score 16 off the last over, he could only make ten so that England, not New Zealand, went 2-1 up in the five-game series. After shaking hands with the England players, and before walking off the field, Williamson had wiped his face two or three times. "Did you shed a tear?" I ask early in the interview. New Zealand's captain could have been affronted at having to reveal his emotions. "No," he says after a pause, and slowly adds: "Just frustration."

International cricketers have become adept at hiding behind stock vocabulary and conventional epithets. Even in a one-on-one interview, I have failed to break through the barrier. They have been briefed so well to say nothing controversial. Thus Williamson could have been predicted to say it was "not ideal" to have to score as many as 16 off the last over and he was "very disappointed" not to have got his team over the line but "all credit to the England bowlers." So normally I try to steer the interviewee towards what is uniquely individual: his, or her, early years and how they learnt the game.

This interview, over a coffee, went well. The NZ media manager did not exactly hover in the background, but he kept an eye out from the other side of the hotel lounge and told Kane when my allotted 20 minutes were up, but he kept going. By nature Williamson is not shy so much as reticent and the last person to blow his own trumpet. Yet he seemed interested in the comparison between his own upbringing and that of Steve Smith "across the pond". Smith had a garden in which to start programming his brain to batting as soon as he could hold a bat, a willing father to bowl at him, and a club ground over the back fence; Williamson also had a garden, and a willing father, but the primary school over his back fence did not have a cricket team – until his father and some friends raised the funds to install an artificial pitch, then found the time to coach a school team. The principal arranged with a local sports shop to give a voucher to every batsman who scored a century but, Williamson said, he never got one. What he did not say, characteristically, was that he scored so many centuries the shop would have gone bankrupt.

Having just come from Australia, where I had found that 55,000 indigenous cricketers had been registered by Cricket Australia, I asked Williamson about the apparent absence of indigenous players in New Zealand. He said his team had a player with Maori blood, and another had recently played for the Test side, but they were part-Maori as opposed to being brought up as Maori. We worked towards the conclusion that Test cricket did not suit their physicality, although T20 would do rather more. There was official encouragement, he said, and a Maori team, the opportunities were available, but there was a reluctance to take up cricket.

As Williamson spoke, I realised he would make a fine government minister after he has retired from playing – and that is not to suggest he was being in any way political in the sense of giving slippery or expedient answers. Listening to parliamentary debates in Wellington on the car radio, I came to admire New Zealand's politics as being more sincere and constructive than Britain's – none of the yahboo, points-scoring of the House of Commons.

The innumerable skills acquired by England's cricket captains have not been channelled into government in almost a hundred years, not since the Hon F.S. Jackson; but I hope New Zealand's maturer politics will be more accommodating.

Outside Dunedin, at the end of a peninsula, is Taiaroa Heads: nowhere on a mainland are you more likely to see the albatross in flight. Ungainly birds on the ground, they become majestic when they catch the thermals and need not flap their vast wings to soar or accelerate. When New Zealand qualified for the first World Test Championship final, I wondered if their flightpath had been comparable to that of the albatross: ungainly when playing dour defensive cricket in their rugby grounds until the 1980s, then take-off with Martin Crowe's batting and transformation from board level down, and soaring into the sky and becoming spectacular, with their ethical sportsmanship under Brendon McCullum and Kane Williamson.

* * *

Two of my three favourite places in New Zealand are Hagley Park and Hamilton Lake for a personal reason: they are where I did my two fastest 5km Park Runs. Immodesty forbids me from saying just how slow they were.

At the start of every tour one makes resolutions: to unpack at every hotel; to keep up to date with expenses; to either go to the gym or for a run every day; to have no more than two meals a day; to drink alcohol no more than 4/5/6/7 days a week.

Gradually these laudable intentions are derailed. Receipts are stuffed into the bottom of a bag or suitcase, unaudited; one lives out of the suitcase, not bothering to unpack; the flight next morning demands checking out of the hotel at 7.30am, before its gym has opened, and by the time one has reached the next hotel it does not have a gym, and it's dark outside, too late for a run. The gym or a run on the first day of a game, then? But by immemorial custom, the first morning is time to get to the ground early and play "baggsy-desks". All too soon, therefore, on an England tour one is gaining weight, especially if the hotel package includes a cooked breakfast. Buffets bring out the worst in people. I cannot remember ever eating mushrooms for breakfast at home, but there they lie in that hot dish, with a spoon only a few inches from your hand. The eggs should be sufficient, cooked one way or another, with a little bacon, and perhaps some fried bread, because one never has that at home either – but what about a few mushrooms? Follow that a few hours later with a cooked lunch at the ground and there is only way to go: outwards.

The English-speaking world saw the proliferation of Park Runs before Covid, or as the internet calls them: parkruns. In Anglo-Saxon society, outside the pub, few are the places where one can go up to strangers and talk, but it is allowed on Saturday mornings when you warm up or cool down with several hundred others who have run a course marked out by volunteers. Hamilton is an agricultural service city, intent on the functional, ideal if one's idea of a fun evening out is looking at tractor showrooms, but I am fond of its lake. At times on that Saturday morning it looked more like an inland sea, and after its circumambulation, a loop longer than a kilometre remained. There was also the constant risk of being overtaken by a man pushing a pram, or of cheering spectators shouting in the direction of the footsteps coming up behind: "Come on, grandma!"

Less than an hour's drive from Hamilton is the third of my favourite places – Raglan, on the west coast of North Island. The sand of its beach is grey, but that is a relief when the light dazzles. Harold Pinter was wrong when he said the two best things in life are cricket and sex, though I did not tell him when Vic Marks and I visited him one evening. There was little chance to diversify the conversation as the playwright was intent on talking about another Somerset all-rounder, Arthur Wellard. The truth is there are three great pleasures in life, the third being bodyboarding or boogieboarding as it is also known. Raglan is the perfect place in summer because the beach slopes into the Tasman Sea at a shallow angle, therefore the right wave can bear one 60 yards up the beach. I prefer it to surfing because of the immediate proximity to nature. One's face is four inches from the sea, if not in it after being tumbled off the board. Kane Williamson said his favourite pastime away from cricket was surfing and Raglan one of his favourite venues. A surfboarder is like a batsman frequently dismissed for a duck: his fall is very public, too humiliating for Narcissus to endure.

Grace is a security officer. She looks the part, Kiwi-style, polite, friendly, not confrontational. I met her at Eden Park towards the end of an Auckland Test, on one of those days on tour when England supporters are almost the only spectators in the ground. It might have been a Monday morning. In any event we both needed a coffee.

Security duties during a Test match in New Zealand being none too rigorous, Grace radioed to HQ to find out if a stall selling coffee was open; I had only found a couple of refreshment bars selling beer, burgers and pies. She was told about a stall, and came along too, telling me how she used to drink tea, and not smoke, but now she needed four mochaccinos a day to cope with the long hours of her job, and could not manage without a cigarette afterwards, hard though she tried to resist. One does not often meet self-effacement outside England, but Grace lived up to her name as she recounted the habits which she knew to be weaknesses.

I bought her a mochaccino, to which she added three spoonfuls of sugar. She said she was going to play cricket on Saturday, Samoan cricket, nothing like this Test match. It was the last day of their championship, held in south Auckland. Seventeen players a side. Bats enormously tall, shaped more like elongated baseball bats. Elongated stumps, too, presumably because back in Samoa the grass is very long. A ball made of baked cow-pat, traditionally. She liked the game because all the members of the team who had batted, or were waiting to bat, sat together and sang songs. Or, if they were fielding, one of them had a whistle and would blow it at the fall of a wicket and start a dance and all the fielders had to copy it. In cricket it is "not done" to be triumphalist at the fall of a batsman; in kilikiti, a send-off is a festival of song and dance.

Each of New Zealand's six major associations is allotted an area of the Pacific to nurture: Auckland promotes cricket in Samoa becasue south Auckland is where most Samoans in New Zealand live. The director of this project at the time was Adrian Dale, the former Glamorgan and England A all-rounder, who had first gone to

Auckland to play as a pro for Cornwall Park, Martin Crowe's club, and who ended up emigrating. But Samoan cricket, he found, was not an organic whole ready to be organised: "Different parts of Auckland and New Zealand have different competitions," Dale said. "Some players are ready to move closer to our official cricket but others want to stay as they are. It is a generational thing too: the younger players want a shorter game than the older ones."

When Christian missionaries moved into the Pacific in the 19th century, they found a culture that was highly physical because fighting had such a large role, and people tended to not only beat up but eat up their victims. Rugby made a suitable channel for their energies, and cricket was introduced successfully, too: not so much late-cuts and leg-spin as their own communal version of village against village, including customs and ceremonies unmentioned in the MCC Laws.

Samoans have been playing kilikiti since 1884. The British consul in Samoa at the time, William Churchwood, wrote in *My Consulate in Samoa: Four Years Sojourn in the Navigation Islands:* "For the first two years of my stay in Samoa, neither I nor any of the few British residents could ever persuade one single Samoan to join in our cricket." In 1884, the Samoans had a change of heart. "All at once," he wrote, "the village of Apia Samoa was seized with a most frantic desire to fathom the mysteries of the game, and to become proficient in its practice."

The reason was that Tongans had taken to cricket so avidly that a law had to be passed to prevent them playing more than once a week, and Samoans found themselves "being twitted on the subject of their ignorance of so grand an amusement" by a party of visiting Tongans. Deputations of local elders were sent to Churchwood and the crew of HMS *Diamond*, a British corvette moored off Apia. HMS *Diamond*'s crew, under the captaincy of another Dale, this one with the first name of Alfred, began to organise matches against the locals:

"The Samoans explained that as it was a British sport, we as British were likely to know more about it than the Tongans, and they thought that we could teach them in such a way that they might be able to beat these boasting

*men. We accordingly took them in hand, and soon
succeeded in instilling the initial idea into their heads.
For a time all went on very smoothly, but the quiet and
serious English style did not suit them long. One by
one, innovations of their own manufacture crept into
the game, until soon nothing remained of cricket, pur
et simple, but the practice of one man bowling a ball
to another man trying to hit it. Samoan cricket found
great favour all round, giving as it did in its improved
form the excuse, always welcome, and never rejected,
for feasting and parade, so dear to all Samoans. Soon
all the neighbouring towns were playing, and cricket at
last becoming quite an epidemic"* – not least because a
team could consist of 200 villagers.

T20 cricket has more appeal than a five-day Test to Pacific
Islanders, male and female, because of its greater physicality. Role
models would act as another incentive. The first Pacific Islander
to represent New Zealand at cricket was Murphy Su'a, and when I
saw him back in 1991/92 I thought he could have a decent career
as he could bowl left-arm pace and spin, and New Zealand did
not have much bowling after the Richard Hadlee era. Ross Taylor
was the next of Pacific Island heritage, but he was deposed as the
one-day captain and resigned as the Test captain, claiming to have
been pushed. The loss of face for a deposed leader in tribal society
cannot be easily imagined.

New Zealand's Test team, when England were last there, contained
as many Indian emigrants – from Punjab – as Maoris and Pacific
Islanders combined. In this way, the pros and cons of a satellite
broadcaster have become apparent. The pros are that cricket in New
Zealand is funded well enough to maintain its position as the No.1
summer sport; the cons are that the majority of the population,
the less affluent, do not subscribe to satellite television and never
see live cricket. These broadcasting arrangements stop the country's
cricket from going forwards and backwards.

* * *

During the Christchurch Test of 2018, Williamson gave me a present on behalf of New Zealand Cricket to mark my 450th Test. It was a Pounamu pendant, a precious stone from South Island, shaped like a fish hook. It represents "strength and determination, and brings peace, prosperity and good health. It also provides a safe journey over water." In addition to plane travel, I hope it includes boogieboarding.

ENGLAND IN NEW ZEALAND, 1929/30 — 2019/20

Overall

Played **107**   Won **48**   Lost **12**   Drawn **47**

In New Zealand

Played **51**   Won **18**   Lost **6**   Drawn **27**

In England

Played **56**   Won **30**   Lost **6**   Drawn **20**

England's record at each venue

Eden Park, Auckland

Played **17**   Won **4**   Lost **2**   Drawn **11**

Lancaster Park, Christchurch

Played **15**   Won **8**   Lost **1**   Drawn **6**

Basin Reserve, Wellington

Played **11**   Won **4**   Lost **1**   Drawn **6**

Carisbrook, Dunedin

Played **2**   Won **1**   Lost **0**   Drawn **1**

Seddon Park, Hamilton

Played **2**   Won **0**   Lost **1**   Drawn **1**

Bay Oval, Mount Maunganui

Played **1**   Won **0**   Lost **1**   Drawn **0**

Played **1**   Won **0**   Lost **0**   Drawn **1**

Played **1**   Won **1**   Lost **0**   Drawn **0**

Played **1**   Won **0**   Lost **0**   Drawn **1**

Series won	Captain
1929/30	Harold Gilligan
1950/51	Freddie Brown
1954/55	Len Hutton
1958/59	Peter May
1962/63	Ted Dexter
1970/71	Ray Illingworth
1974/75	Mike Denness
1991/92	Graham Gooch
1996/97	Mike Atherton
2007/08	Michael Vaughan

Highest scores

336*	Walter Hammond	Auckland	1932/33
227	Walter Hammond	Christchurch (Lancaster Park)	1932/33
226	Joe Root	Hamilton	2019/20
216	Keith Fletcher	Auckland	1974/75
200*	Graham Thorpe	Christchurch (Lancaster Park)	2001/02

Best bowling

7-47	Phil Tufnell	Christchurch (Lancaster Park)	1991/92
7-47	Ryan Sidebottom	Napier	2007/08
7-63	Matthew Hoggard	Christchurch (Lancaster Park)	2001/02
7-75	Fred Trueman	Christchurch (Lancaster Park)	1962/63
7-76	Frank Woolley	Wellington	1929/30

Chitral
Hunza
Swat
Nanga Parbat
Peshawar
Taxila
Islamabad
Harappa
Lahore
Faisalabad
Multan
Mohenjodaro
Larkana
Hyderabad
Karachi

PAKISTAN

CHAPTER FIVE

PAKISTAN

It is said that we retain a soft spot for our first beloved. I retain one for the country I first toured, Pakistan.

A dark-bearded 23-year-old Englishman came to Karachi in 1844, and was soon hailed as "the finest mind of his generation": Richard Burton arrived as a surveyor in what is now Pakistan, avid for adventure. I was 23 when I arrived there on my first England tour in 1977. Burton took a boat up the River Indus through Sind, or Scinde as he spelt it when he published the first account in English of this region. Another difference is that Burton was able to do enough local research to form the practical basis of his infamous translation of the *Kama Sutra*.

Karachi was more than 150 years old when Burton first saw it and, after the oysters that produced pearls had been exhausted, had become a fishing village of baked mud. The population of 2,000 was a mixture of Hindus, Muslims and African slaves, and as a whole "manly and well developed", while the women "seldom wear veils in the streets". Such was the potential of Karachi, or "Kurrachee", that Burton thought it was "the young Alexandria of our young Egypt". Beyond the settlement, however, "the plain around us is nothing but an expanse of sand, broken into rises and falls by the furious winds, and scarcely affording thorns, salsolae, and fire-plants, sufficient to feed a dozen goats and camels."

In order to travel around Pakistan, I arrived a fortnight before the start of England's tour, and before the snows cut off the mountain passes. Burton, multilingual, was making his survey of Sind as the only army officer who could speak Sindhi, and he was smitten when he beheld in Larkana a *nautch* or dancing girl. He called her "the Donna of Larkana", clad as she was in gold jewellery, brocade and satin. "Your eyes, weary with the beauties of her face, shift to her figure, where, if perfection ever was, there you discover it." She "floats forward so softly that trace of exertion is imperceptible: slowly waving her white arms, she unexpectedly stands close to you, then turning with a pirouette…" Reliable rumour has it that a Pakistan batsman, who had better not be named, and who was visiting a *nautch* girl of similar charms in Lahore, had to make a sudden escape and fell off a roof, thus ending his cricket career.

The Donna of Larkana was off limits; her younger sister, however, might not have been. After Burton's death, his wife unearthed a notebook of his unpublished poems, including one entitled "Past Loves". Burton in his youth had got around, she discovered, as much as his later Welsh namesake:

> The Nubians and the Abyssinians
> Sent me at least a score of minions.

Burton's total has risen already to 20. Yet his all-time favourite, so it would seem from this poem, was Nur Jan, the Donna's younger sister:

> But of them all the fair Nur Jan
> The Venus of Baluchistan
> Was most to my mind.

* * *

It was impossible to book a seat on a flight from Islamabad to Chitral: all you could do was buy a ticket, go to Islamabad airport at dawn and wait in the hope that conditions would clear to permit the one flight per day. I was fortunate: the weather forced a postponement of only one day, so next morning the PIA plane – a propeller-driven Fokker Friendship – weaved through the lower slopes of the Hindu Kush towards the Roof of the World.

This was where lads like Kim came to map the furthest extremities of British India and pushed on secretly into Afghanistan and Tibet, telling their beads to count each step and recording the number of miles on their prayer wheels. Shangri-La was secluded somewhere up in these mountains. Peter Fleming, most humorous of travel writers, had walked from China across Tibet through the Himalayan passes to Hunza. Rather dishevelled after his journey across quite a few deserts, he met on the approach to Kashgar an official from the British Consulate who said: "I don't know if you like beer?" The thirsty traveller wrote: "He soon did." Were I forced to live in another time and place, without cricket, I might choose the Consulate in Kashgar around 1900, officially keeping an eye on Russian spies and sending the odd telegram to London, but exploring Sinkiang in summer, enjoying the tennis court and local mulberries, in addition to the imported beer, and no duties at all in winter after snow had closed the passes!

It was not the altitude of 5,000ft which made me giddy after landing at Chitral's airstrip so much as the intoxicating view. Dark scree slopes served as background to snow-covered peaks and to the dazzling purity of a sky unsullied by cloud for months. The sparkling river was using little of its bed as the sun was no longer melting snow. The orangey-brown of the chenar or sycamore trees, as their leaves yielded to winter, was so lustrous I drank it in. Not quite the equal of the Donna of Larkana or Nur Jan, but I was in love.

The people were a joy too, these solid hill men in their Chitrali caps, more English than the English in their quiet reserve. Such was the mutual respect that after Colonel Durand, commanding a thousand rifles, had conquered the Gilgit Agency in the 1890s, he confirmed the local princes in their fiefdom in return for an acknowledgment of British sovereignty and some goats. Here, as everywhere else in Pakistan in those innocent days before proxy wars, one often heard this refrain from those who spoke a few words of English: "We are a simple people."

"You are mactully," I was told by a man during the Test match in Hyderabad – the one in Sind, not on the Deccan – on that 1977/78 tour. It had to be a male spectator: the only women who attended a cricket match in Pakistan then were the wives and daughters of politicians or generals in their VVIP stands. Elites in South Asia are seldom content with being VIP.

"I beg your pardon?"

"I think you are mactully," this man repeated, and again. Gradually it dawned: he thought I was the BBC's distinguished correspondent in New Delhi, Mark Tully. "Sorry," I said, and I was, to disappoint him.

"We are a simple people," he said.

So most Pakistanis were, in this era before drugs poured in from war-torn Afghanistan, to be transported through army and police checkpoints, with all the corruption entailed, to be shipped from Karachi to Europe. Pakistan's government, especially the military government which it was half the time, kept the people simple by not even offering many of them a primary secular education. Which only stored up trouble.

It has frequently been observed that people of the mountains are more straightforward than those of the plains, less sophisticated, less devious. I stayed at the Chitral Inn for less than two pounds a night. I bought a Chitrali cap: by rolling the folds down, you can pull the yak wool over your own eyes, and ears. It was still a shock to the system when the communal taxi left Chitral soon after dawn one morning: I could not cram my legs into the space allotted in the back to 11 other passengers, so had to stand on the tailboard and hang on to an icy bar without gloves, only a spare pair of socks on my hands. Frostbite was setting in as we reached the top of Lowari Pass at 10,000ft (this was before the Lowari Tunnel), where we were greeted by the sun and the track winding down to Dir. I had been looking forward to spending the night in Dir, thinking the name suggested somewhere pert and pretty, decked with flowers upon a hillside: Haarlem, especially Spanish Haarlem, had played a similar trick on my childish imagination. But it turned out a dismal dump, shacks selling tins and bottles of fizz beside the road, so I pressed on to Swat, at the opposite visual extreme, green and fertile, at least before the Taliban darkened the valley.

On a later England tour of Pakistan I flew past Nanga Parbat – straight along one side of it, a few hundred yards from the mountainside – before the pilot banked sharply and dropped into Gilgit. On another occasion, I returned to Gilgit and took the road up to Hunza: when Fleming descended from Kashgar, he had only a track hewn into the rock above the river, but Chinese engineers had built the Karakoram Highway. On one side of the river at the valley bottom lived Sunnis; on the other Ismailis, followers of the Aga Khan. It was quite a division as the winter drew on and the temperature was tolerable in the sun on one side of the ravine and freezing in the shade on the other. When I was there, the Sunni side of the valley was literally the sunny side.

After a night in Hunza I reached Gulmit. This village might have been the prototype for Shangri-La: some fertile fields and a woman who claimed to be 115 years old. This was on the basis that she remembered having seen Durand. She was said to be no longer compos mentis or able to receive visitors. But the castle in Hunza could have been the setting for *The Man Who Would Be King*, and a rope bridge could have been strung across any part of the ravine, instead of making the film in Morocco. On we drove to Passu Glacier where, after climbing scree slopes up to the glacier, I enjoyed the simplest yet most memorable meal. The guide from Hunza had brought some chicken, which must have ranged freely in the Karakoram, and fried some potatoes, and boiled some water to which he added a plant that flowered on these slopes in summer: a kind of tea, which I still have and keep for drinking once a year. We sat on a hill above a lake of snow melt and stared at Mt Rakaposhi in all its pure white majesty.

* * *

When Peshawar staged the third game of England's 1977/78 tour, against the North-West Frontier Province Governor's XI, we were treated to a trip to the frontier. We were told that we had to stay close to the bus – just the one for players and press – and never to wander away from the road, especially if any women were around, as Pashtuns are prickly when the honour of their womenfolk is perceived to be at risk. No chance of meeting my Nur Jan.

After carrying on up the Khyber to the border post at the top, we stopped on the way down and I felt the call of nature. Everyone climbed out of the bus for a photo while I walked up the rock-strewn mountainside to what resembled a heap of rubble: nowhere else for a bit of privacy in the absence of trees. Only it was someone's house.

"Come down!"

I thought the man on the road below waving his arms looked familiar. It was Derek Randall. A few others were shouting as well.

I scrambled down the hillside straightaway. I was relieved, yet unrelieved, to learn that a couple of tribesmen had been loading their Kalashnikovs.

* * *

Brought up in Western civilisation, I was led to believe in the Ascent of Man, and even watched the television series of that name. The Dark Ages had to be counted as a bit of a backward step after the Greeks and Romans, but otherwise Western civilisation had been – tally-ho – one long upward march of progress.

Different in Pakistan. Go for instance to Harappa, beside the river Indus in Punjab. New Harappa is a typical modern village: electricity would last for only a few of the 24 hours; no running water for most people, only a communal tap, so women were carrying jars on their heads; no hospital; no state school to teach basic literacy and numeracy, only a madrasa where an Islamic charity exploited the huge gap in the market. Men walked over the mounds in search of work, perhaps in the surrounding fields, to make a few ends meet, while women did the housework in mud-brick shacks.

Yet underneath these mounds of dusty earth lay one of the world's finest, most admirable, civilisations from four to five thousand years ago.

The Indus Valley Civilisation, which flowered in Harappa and Mohenjo-daro from 2500 BC, was not one of those societies where the ruler is a supreme autocrat, a god on earth who has loads of wives and servants buried with him when he dies, to carry on serving him in paradise. As in Egypt.

Far more of Mohenjo-daro, near Larkana in Sind, is preserved than Harappa. Generations have looked at Harappa's mounds and thought – yes, recycling! Let's use 4,000-year-old bricks for our new house rather than make new ones. It was the same when British engineers built the railway from Karachi to Lahore in the 19th century and found themselves short of material to make embankments above the Indus: what could be more convenient than those mounds of old bricks? So Mohenjo-daro was preserved while Harappa was plundered and ground down. Even in the time between my two visits the remaining walls and buildings of Old Harappa visibly shrank.

Mohenjo-daro was left, unknown and unexcavated, until the 1920s, whereupon the realisation dawned: here was probably the largest city in the Bronze Age world. About 100,000 square metres have been excavated, which is estimated to be only 10% of the city's extent, so it could have covered three million square metres; and for certain it had a population of over 50,000. It was not so much the size, however, as its civilisation which inspired my awe.

Indus Valley Civilisation was peaceful, humane, relatively democratic, artistic, domestic and fun-loving. Neither in Harappa nor Mohenjo-daro have weapons for fighting been found, nor anything more lethal than the spears and implements required to scare away or kill wild predators, like the lions and elephants that once roamed the Indus plain and forests. "Most spears of the Indus culture were made without pronounced central thickening to support the blade on impact," wrote Jonathan Kenoyer of the American Institute of Pakistan Studies in *Ancient Cities of the Indus Valley Civilization*. "Without a central rib, the blades would buckle on impact: this feature has led to the assumption that they were not specialised offensive weapons."

Mohenjo-daro has a citadel, or did when I visited in 2006. "Towering high above the plain, with gleaming red-brick gateways and light gray mud-brick walls, the city would have been a landmark, visible for many kilometers," as Kenoyer described it. But the citadel was not an enormous palace for an emperor, or a temple in honour of an omnipotent god. It consisted of the Great Bath, "without doubt the earliest public water tank in the ancient world"; and another large building which Sir Mortimer Wheeler identified as a granary, but was more likely a meeting-place for state or religious officials, and the Buddhist monastery which was added before this city inexplicably ceased to exist.

I walked along the streets: all had a well-made drain running along one side. Some of the mud-brick houses needed no more than a roof, a door and a few nice carpets and you could have moved back in. I went into what must have been a shop of some kind, or even a bank: a L-shaped wall about three feet high, like a counter, took up a quarter of the room, which the server would have entered from a different door from the one the public used. The difference in quality between the houses was relatively minor: those near the city centre had a well, and were bigger than the ones in "the suburbs" which did not have their own well, yet they were only marginally bigger, less than half as much again. The vast majority enjoyed a high standard of domestic housing, which suggests some notion of egalitarianism as part of their politics.

Surviving artefacts indicate an extensive trading network up and down the Indus and its tributaries, and east along the coast to north-west India and, in the opposite direction, Mesopotamia. Some of the pottery is so beautiful: a storage jar, painted red and black with peacocks and geometric designs, would take pride of place in one's dining-room, not kitchen or larder. Tools of bronze, and ceramics of terracotta clay; necklaces and all sorts of jewellery; bangles, seals and an Indus script invented around 2600 BC; figurines and gaming pieces, dice made of clay or stone, gaming boards of various designs. These people had delicacy – until their swift and sudden end.

It has been conjectured that they were too peaceable, and succumbed to invaders from the north, although no sign has been found of a violent end. Or that the Indus changed course and flowed too far away; or deforestation, owing to domestic heating and cooking, reduced the rainfall. Or did a pandemic strike? Similar cities on the north-west coast of India were submerged by the rising sea level. In any event, the standard of living in Indus Valley Civilisation – at least so far as domestic housing, sanitation and access to drinking water – seems to have been higher then than now.

A landmark legal judgment in the mid-1950s is partly to blame. The Supreme Court of Pakistan, by two votes to one, allowed the military dictatorship to take what it wanted from the annual budget: not so much for the navy and air force as for the army and Inter Service Intelligence (ISI). They could help themselves before passing on what was left to the civilian government. This was disastrous for the people of Pakistan. Once the army and ISI, then the politicians, have all taken their cut, very little has been left for health and education.

Starting in 1951, the Edhi Foundation has had to be Pakistan's NHS. The greatest humanitarian of the 20th century, according to *Time* magazine, Abdul Sattar Edhi, funded and organised the ambulances and hospitals which the state did not. Meanwhile, madrasas funded by Saudi princes and others abroad, occupied the void left by the absence of secular education.

This arrangement was fine for a cricket journalist: while 90% of society walked the streets, England cricketers and media were treated, like the elite, to efficient internal plane travel, imported cars and fine hotels. As in the case of every first love, I admired the brains and the beauty: the beauty of the mountains, the brains of the past.

The English team to Australia in 1863/64, including Edward Grace (back row, fourth from right)

The old Gabba in 1975/76

Rodney Hogg in full flow at Perth on the 1978/79 Ashes tour

Scyld, with Ian Chappell and Mike Atherton, interviewing Andrew Strauss in Australia in 2006

Scyld on a train in India in 1981/82 with David Gower being served tea in the seat behind

Ravi Shastri bowling for India v West Indies in 1983

The Hagley Oval in Christchurch, the world's most beautiful Test ground

Kumar Shri Duleepsinhji, inventor of the reverse sweep

A Chitrali woollen cap-maker in Pakistan

Imran Khan bowling against England in 1982

The first English team to tour the Caribbean, in 1895

Charles Ollivierre, the first black West Indian to play county cricket

West Indian superfan Gravy entertains the crowd at St John's, Antigua

David Houghton on his way to a century in Zimbabwe's maiden Test

Photo by Katie Borton

The author in action. NB the socks are white, but shinpads on top, because the ground is now such a long way down and batsmen smash it back so hard.

* * *

Imran Khan Niazi was the first Test cricketer to become a prime minister. He was also, in my estimation, the greatest of all Asian cricketers. There have been more splendid batsmen, but no finer fast bowler.

Having made his Test debut as an inswing and inaccurate bowler in 1971, aged 18, he went back to school again after that tour, to Worcester Royal Grammar. At Oxford he bowled his inswingers ever more rapidly, and batted ever more soundly, until county sides had to pick a first-choice team so as not to lose in the Parks (as seldom before and never since). In the Pakistan Test team, especially on their tours of Australia and West Indies in 1976/77, he learnt reverse-swing from Sarfraz Nawaz. At World Series Cricket, spurred on by the rivalry of the world's best fast bowlers, he became the equal of any before a back injury. As an imperious captain, he led Pakistan to the 1992 World Cup. It was all done with a charisma only surpassed, in my observation, by that of Viv Richards.

It was a shame Imran never played a Test against England in Pakistan: having joined WSC, he missed the series of 1977/78; he was injured in 1983/84, and too lordly to play in 1987/88 after the World Cup. I saw the tiger in his natural habitat, however, when I went to interview him for his profile as a *Wisden* Cricketer of the Year in 1983. He had led Pakistan to victory at Lord's in 1982 and, more likely than not, Pakistan would have won a Test series in England for the first time but for a home-town umpiring decision at Headingley which was as "blatant" – to use the euphemism before neutral umpires – as anything England ever experienced in Pakistan.

I interviewed Imran when Pakistan were playing Australia in Faisalabad in late 1982. "I should have been selected two years ago," was his immediate reaction, not belligerently, just matter-of-factly. I could neither concur nor disagree, not being then the editor of *Wisden*. Still, Imran remains the only *Wisden* Cricketer of the Year I have informed about his selection who did not radiate, or at least feign, pleasure and surprise – but instead made clear his opinion that he should have been picked earlier. Status, face, honour: so important in male hierarchies and eastern societies; not least for alpha males.

Far from "simple", as his fellow Pakistanis could once have reasonably been described, Imran was always complex. Before he was taken seriously as a politician, he was summed up well by William Dalrymple in *The Age of Kali*: "Imran is an intriguing compendium of contradictions: extrovert and cripplingly shy, openly arrogant yet disarmingly modest, austere and sensual, jet-set yet oddly primitive. He can switch from one persona to another with remarkable ease."

Imran was shrewd enough during my interview not to give away his trade secret: Pakistan had tipped the Lord's Test in their favour by delaying their taking of the second new ball, and by finishing off England's stubborn second innings with reverse swing – not only Imran's but that of the medium-pacer Mudassar Nazar – only this term had yet to be coined. While at WSC from 1977 to 1979, Imran had perfected this astonishing delivery, which he demonstrated during that Faisalabad Test. He went wide in the crease, leapt, launched the ball on a line at least a couple of feet outside off-stump, towards what is now the white line that demarcates wides in limited-overs cricket, then in the last two or three yards of flight made it boomerang into or onto a right-handed batsman's toes. Watching from exactly behind his arm in Faisalabad, I could only marvel at this inexplicable display of aerodynamics.

Imran, around this time, may have reverse-swung the ball further than anyone has ever done, before umpires became keener about the condition of the ball in the subsequent years of Waqar Younis and Wasim Akram. I cannot discover whether Bart King, the expert baseball pitcher on the Philadelphians' first-class tour of England in 1908, bowled not only conventional inswing but reversed it too; but I am certain he did not bowl at 90mph like Imran. But this trade secret Imran did not reveal, let alone the methods which he and his players used to make an old ball swing as never before. "Taking the new ball is such a cliché," was what he said, in a lordly tone. Imran had not taken the second ball at Lord's until the 117th over of England's second innings, which might have been unprecedentedly late for a Test in England, and then he had given it to his wrist-spinner Abdul Qadir. All way ahead of its time.

Imran was always detached, his own person, except when a beauteous woman hove into view; and always ready with a theory, though what he said one day was not invariably what he said or did the next; and, as a cricketer, he was above the battle that absorbed the common herd. It could now be seen as his first act of statesmanship when he persuaded the Pakistan board to hire two neutral umpires, England's John Hampshire and John Holder, to officiate in their home series against India in the winter of 1989. This new neutrality in the umpiring must have been one reason why the four-Test series ended, not in the normal home victory, but 0-0. Again Imran was ahead of his time, because the ICC did not appoint a neutral Test umpire until 1992/93.

Experienced Test captains acquire many of the skills required to be a government minister, even prime minister. Owing to his prestige as a World Cup winner, Imran when elected in 2018 was as likely as anyone to stand up to the Pakistan military and claim back a little of the national budget for civilian purposes.

One insight I gained but did not mention, for space, in the *Wisden* profile: Imran told me that when he was bowling and hit to the boundary, he saw red, literally. Blood came into his eyes. (The only time it has happened to me was when I was reverse-swept for the first time.) Imran claimed Pashtun ancestry – several generations earlier his Niazi clan had come down from the North-West Frontier to Lahore – and this may have been a trait he inherited.

I had been struck how the world squash championship title had been held for decades by the Khan family of Pashtuns. They had seen squash played by the Raj in Peshawar, taken up the sport, looked after the courts, and started beating the British at their own game. Pashtuns, perhaps because they see red, are famous for their capacity to pursue a vendetta until they get revenge: I wondered if what drove their squash champions in long rallies also spurred their fast bowlers in long spells with an old ball on pitches like concrete.

* * *

Rising above the rift between the Karachi faction and the Lahori faction, which then existed in the Pakistan side, must have been a useful part of Imran's training for the prime ministership. Too much could be made of it; on the other hand, no outsider could measure how deep the rift was in the dressing-room and on the field. Lahori players spoke Punjabi as their first language, Karachi players spoke Urdu, and Imran rose above the battle by speaking English. So had Pakistan's first captain, Abdul Hafeez Kardar. He also had the aura of being Oxford-educated, as well as a disposition which could be imperious, to the extent that Kardar was called Pakistan's Douglas Jardine.

Karachi and Lahore are as different as you would expect cities almost 800 miles apart to be. Once the population of Sindhis which Burton had observed had been multiplied many times over by the influx of Muslims from India in 1947, Karachi had been Muhajir (literally "emigrant"), trade, new money, hot, brash, volatile, sometimes violent. The most notable cricketers among them were the only family of four brothers who have played Test cricket: Wazeer, Hanif, Mushtaq and Sadiq Mohammad. A fifth brother, Raees, made it into a Pakistan Test squad. Javed Miandad, cricket's ultimate street fighter, was to personify the attributes which rupee-less refugees in Karachi had needed to survive and prosper.

Lahore is Punjabi, ex-Moghul, refined, old money, hierarchical, artistic. My love of Pakistan did not diminish when I ate at the Lahore Intercontinental's Moghul restaurant. It was not like one of those expensive ones in English-speaking countries where the best part about your dinner is the mint or chocolate at the end. Moghul dishes of mutton or goat that have been marinated for days, biryani and vegetable dishes steeped in gravies: such rich food that if you had it for lunch you would be comatose for the rest of the day, with or without alcohol (and nobody would check what exactly was in that teapot on your table).

If you had to walk off such a meal, you could turn left out of the Intercontinental and enter the Bagh-e-Jinnah, where cricket first took root in what became Pakistan. If it were still a Test ground, it would be a hot favourite for the title of most beautiful. It was modelled on the lines of the Oxford Parks by Sir George Abell, a Blue who hit the first double-century in the Ranji Trophy and became the private secretary of India's last two Viceroys. While the pavilions are similar, the Bagh-e-Jinnah is leafier than the Parks, surrounded on more sides by shade-giving trees.

Let us keep strolling through the Bagh or garden to the zoo, and on to the library, and the museum where Lockwood Kipling was the curator, while Kim, the creation of his son Rudyard, cavorted outside the museum on the great gun Zamzama. This museum lives up to its Urdu translation of Ajaib Ghar, or House of Wonders. Its treasures include rooms filled with the artefacts of Indus Valley Civilisation (Harappa and Mohenjo-daro have their own small museums); and of Taxila, where East and West met, co-existed, worshipped Buddhism and spoke Greek. Here was the exception to Rudyard's rule that "never the twain shall meet". Taxila claims to be the site of the world's first university, though it was dedicated to religious studies only, as a Buddhist foundation.

Again, when I visited Taxila, all you had to do to re-inhabit the site was put a roof on the rooms and spread a few carpets. The enormous size of the sink in the kitchen for doing washing-up, complete with plug-holes and drains, suggests several hundred students – and decent hygiene. Down the road was one of the castles which the Greeks left behind after Alexander's army had retreated, its stones fitting so neatly, its corners so shapely, like an armchair's curved foot. Eclecticism has seldom come better than this Greek-speaking, Buddhist, Gandhara civilisation.

Most sumptuous of all in Lahore's House of Wonders is the Moghul collection. When Persians and Afghans headed down from their mountains for an easier life in the plains of Punjab and engaged local craftsmen, what colours this culture produced! Not garish at all, but robes and dresses, Korans and other handmade books, of the most tasteful purple or gold. After an hour in this House of Wonders I felt as giddy as Burton at the sight of the Donna of Larkana.

The majority of Pakistan's first Test teams consisted of Hanif and his brother Wazir, from India via Karachi, and graduates from Lahore's Government and Islamia College. I met most of them at receptions in the course of England tours, and fine old soldiers they were. Kardar's team came to be supplemented by players – more often bowlers – brought up in club cricket on Lahore's maidans, most notably Minto Park. Often uncoached, but needing to find a way to take wickets on the grassless pitches, Lahoris were first as I understand it to devise both reverse swing and the doosra.

West Indian bowlers, such as Denis Atkinson of Barbados in the 1950s, had learnt how to swing an old ball by soaking one side with sweat, thus making it heavier than the other half, and therefore biased. By the 1960s Saleem Altaf, who opened the bowling for

Pakistan with conventional outswing, was finding that when he came back for a second spell the older ball swung the other way without the need for sweat. Numerous bowlers in several countries must have had a similar experience, without labelling it reverse swing, but I suspect Pakistan was the main breeding-ground – and on the maidans of Lahore, rather than Karachi where matting pitches prevailed. For the same reason, Lahori finger-spinners had to find another way to deceive batsmen, because their off-breaks turned little if at all on the unsympathetic soil. I heard that a cousin of Majid Khan was bowling a doosra ("the other one") at the Bagh-e-Jinnah in the 1960s, a generation before the Lahori who popularised it, Saqlain Mushtaq.

India is more conformist, and largely Hindu; Pakistan is can-do. Led by Kardar, and bursting with patriotic ardour to put their new country on the map, Pakistan's cricketers made a more immediate impact than those of any other new Test country, apart from the two founders Australia and England. Starting in 1952, they won a match in their first series against every country that had Test status.

* * *

There is, too, the sound of the first love to be cherished. It can resonate forever, long after the beloved has departed.

To my ear, the male voice, when not singing, is at its most handsome when reciting Arabic, hence the mesmerising effect of the Koran. But the male voice is at its most beautiful when reciting Urdu verse, which is close to Persian. Even after half-a-dozen tours of Pakistan, I do not understand more than a few words of Urdu, but it does not matter, the sound can still be sublime. To listen to the late Faiz Ahmad Faiz reciting his own verse is letting the warmth of a hot bath wash over you. Similar beauty can be achieved by the female singers of Faiz's poems or *ghazals*.

Faiz attended Government College in Lahore, became a captain in the British army during the Second World War, reaching the rank of lieutenant-colonel, and a Marxist. After Partition he became editor of the *Pakistan Times* inter alia, before being exiled. I cannot help thinking that if Faiz had been elected the head of government in Pakistan, the country would have fared better than it has under generals and other civilian leaders. I think of all the dusty villages which offer no public services, and never will so long as the feudal landlord is guaranteed his vote-bank, where Covid and corruption run amok, and the beginning of a social contract is still to be fashioned.

* * *

After the terrorist attack on the Sri Lankan team bus and the minibus of match officials, in Lahore in March 2009, Dubai, Abu Dhabi and Sharjah were the venues in the United Arab Emirates where Pakistan had to stage their home games. These Emirates are more sanitary and sanitised than the up-country venues where England played in 1977 – Faisalabad, Hyderabad (Sind), Bahawalpur, Sahiwal and Sialkot – and are therefore likely to be used again.

Starting at the Intercontinental in Rawalpindi, the journalists were downgraded to Ray's Hotel in Faisalabad, where the England team stayed in a government rest-house. Ray's a laugh, we said, but no it wasn't. It was right on the main street through the city, which had just changed its name from Lyallpur to commemorate the Saudi king. From 5am the horns of lorries, laden with cotton sheets and garments manufactured in the factories of "the Manchester of Pakistan", blasted bikes and bullocks out of their way. The communal toilet on each floor of Ray's was one of those, without a bowl, where one had to practise one's wicketkeeping. Breakfast, assuming the rumours of rats had not ruined the appetite, was either "eggs fry" or else "eggs fry", accompanied by bread as tasteless as only a sliced white loaf can be. Tea was the sweet syrup that is *masala chai* if one asked for it, or even if one did not. Occasionally the telephone line at the reception desk was clear enough to hear a faint voice from England.

On that 1977/78 tour several journalists decided to go from Bahawalpur – after England had played at the Dring Stadium, named after a British colonel who had been chief adviser to the Emir of Bahawalpur – to Lahore by overnight train. The dining-car had an open wood-burning oven on which to cook food. I cannot recall what I ate for dinner but I deposited most of it next morning on the track in Lahore.

Yet I still think fondly of Faisalabad. The accommodation, for a start, improved enormously after one of the Aga Khan's companies had built the Serena Hotel: news of the impasse between the England captain Mike Gatting and the Pakistan umpire Shakoor Rana, which led to the loss of a day's play in the 1987 Test, might never have reached the outside world if the media had still been reliant on the one temperamental telephone in Ray's.

Faisalabad was also one of the three venues where the England media made a clean sweep on the 1983/84 tour. England have only ever won two Tests in Pakistan: the inaugural one in 1961/62 and the one in the dark in Karachi in 2000. If in a pub quiz this question ever arises – who was the first English captain to achieve a 3-0 clean sweep in Pakistan? – I, if no one else, will fondly remember the answer.

We beat the Pakistan media at Aitchison College owing to a fine century from the Press Association correspondent Graham Otway, who was friendly enough with the England opener Chris Smith to borrow one of his bats. We won at the Karachi Gymkhana, where I made the best non-slip catch of my life, fielding at deep mid-off and diving half-forward and half-left to scoop up a skimming drive: my one and only fielding prize, though I had to spend it all on a tetanus injection. My main contribution though was to win the toss in all three matches. Journalists have to bat first: after the start of a tour, if not before, once the cooked lunches kick in, we do not have the fitness to field for 40 overs in the heat then chase down a target. And at Faisalabad, such was the courtesy of our hosts, we were each given a set of sheets and pillow-cases made of local cotton at the end of the series. A simple people, hospitable and generous, before Afghanistan was invaded and war spread its toxins through the country for decades.

* * *

Planes used to land and take off in Dubai more frequently than at any other airport in the world bar Chicago. Motorways, even of seven lanes, are brought to a standstill by the density of traffic. Air conditioning in the rows of tower blocks raises the ambient temperature by approximately 2°C and thereby makes itself indispensable. The Gulf, whether Arabian or Persian, is sterile. Its lifeless water heats up so much in the sun that at night it is hotter than the land which, being desert, has cooled: to be beside the Gulf at night is like being in a bedroom that has a hot steaming bath and no window. Dubai's cricket stadium is a fine one – so too the cricket grounds and nets at the ICC headquarters – but all around stand empty tower blocks, not finished since the recession hit in 2008, when Dubai had to be bailed out by the older, bigger and wiser brother that is Abu Dhabi. I find enormous buildings that are empty of humans disturbing – a portent of the end, not of the world, but humankind.

Ecclesiastical sources say that the Christian church was prominent in the Gulf before Islam. So there must have been settled communities, other than nomads, and according to one source the area which is now the UAE used to be "well-vegetated". So it is not only modern man who has destroyed his natural environment, but man ever since the agricultural revolution.

Yet in Dubai, I saw one immensely encouraging sight so far as the future is concerned. It was a public holiday, and one of the water parks was packed, mostly with young men, but one in four or five was a young woman. As it was a holiday, there were long queues for each of the rides or water slides; and I would guess some of these young men, mainly from South Asia, might never have seen a woman in a bikini before, let alone stood in a queue beside one. Yet social distancing, before its time, was voluntarily observed, and exemplarily. In spite of what some politicians have said about clashing civilisations, here were different cultures respectfully at play together.

Abu Dhabi is even more expensive than Dubai, but more tasteful. The Corniche could be southern France, around Marseille; the architecture of some buildings and bridges is ambitious, and works. Much less garish than the flaunting nouveau riche of Dubai.

Few sights actually take one's breath away, but one such lies in the western hinterland of Abu Dhabi, an hour or so's drive along motorways across the hard desert floor, past the oil fields to Liwa Oasis. Here Wilfred Thesiger, on his ships of the desert, came ashore after crossing the sands soon after the Second World War. I went to the wall which surrounded a hotel on the edge of Liwa, and looked over it. Beyond, in all its immensity, was the Empty Quarter: *ar-rimaal*, the sands, wave after wave of dunes stretching to the horizon, uninhabited and still not violated in any way by humans.

Sharjah is home to the manual workers, notably Afghans, Baluchis and Bangladeshis, who do the UAE's manual labour. Cricket means a lot to these men who live six to a room, only see their families once a year when they fly home, and have few other forms of entertainment on their rare days off. Sharjah's stadium is the most lived-in of the three Test grounds in the UAE, having staged more one-day internationals than anywhere else in the world – not least because none at Sharjah has ever been abandoned because of rain.

Unsavoury events occurred in the dressing-rooms at Sharjah, and on its field of play, when the one-day international format escalated in the 1990s: in a word, match-fixing. It is impossible to publish all the stories I have heard – lawyers would not allow it, however persuasive the circumstantial evidence – but we can determine the place, Sharjah, and date the time when it took off as common practice to the start of the 1990s. I interviewed Salim Malik at the end of Pakistan's tour of England in 1987 for his profile as a *Wisden* Cricketer of the Year. I went to his hotel room, sat in a chair, his suitcase and "coffin" were open, nothing to hide. He was not charming – match-fixers hide beneath charm – but shy at first, then open, straightforward, honest, nothing like what the Qayyum inquiry found him to have later become, or what India's Central Bureau of Investigation (CBI) reported.

When I met one of the authors of the CBI report in his department in New Delhi, he said their main witness, M.K. Gupta, being a bank clerk, had an excellent memory for names and the sums of money he had paid out, but not for dates. Their report went on:

> *"MK has stated that Salim Malik was introduced to him by Manoj Prabhakar at Delhi before a match between Wills Cup winners of Pakistan and Wills Cup winners of India. Prabhakar has accepted this in his statement.*
>
> *The match MK is referring to was played between Habib Bank of Pakistan and Wills-XI of India on October 13, 1991 at Feroze Shah Kotla. MK has stated that he paid a sum of Rs 8 lakh to Salim Malik to fix that match without the knowledge of Javed Miandad who was captaining the Pakistani side.*
>
> *MK has stated that he does not know who were the*

other players roped in by Malik. The match was won
by Wills-XI India after a tight finish. The scores were:
Habib Bank – 232 for 4 in 45 overs, Salim Malik 32
(run out); Wills XI – 236 for 8 in 44.3 overs.
    MK has also stated that Salim Malik had given him
the 'information' during Singer Cup, 1994 at Sri Lanka
that Pakistan would lose a particular match against
Australia in that series, which turned out to be correct."

The people who were actually punished for match-fixing, apart from the handful of players from India and Pakistan who were banned, and not for long in some cases, were those who could no longer wave their flags under the floodlights in Sharjah, and who could feel proud of their nationality, before being treated like dirt again the next day. Only after seven years without staging any international game, from 2003 to 2010, were Sharjah's stables deemed by the ICC to have been cleansed.

* * *

The first and last Test matches which I saw in Pakistan, both in Lahore at the Gaddafi Stadium, covered the spectrum of Pakistani cricket. The highlight – though not one that burned brightly – of the first Test in 1977 was the slowest Test century of all time: Mudassar Nazar pushed forwards on the baked mud pitch for nine hours and 17 minutes before reaching three figures. It should be added that England's over-rate was also slow, and the playing time restricted by the daylight hours of mid-winter, so the fact that Pakistan scored at more than three runs an over was disguised.

Much more intense activity was happening off the field: a crowd estimated at 50,000 turned up most days, not to watch Mud on mud, but to seize the chance to demonstrate. When Mudassar reached 99, a pitch invasion occurred, and the English media were keen to brand the crowd as "volatile", but how and where else to express an opinion under martial law? Zulfikar Ali Bhutto, the civilian president, had recently been deposed in a military coup by General Zia ul-Haq, who later had him hanged. Bhutto's daughter, Benazir, came to the Gaddafi Stadium and sat in the stands, not the VVIP area, in order to encourage her supporters and attract world attention for her cause.

England's last Test in Pakistan, to date, was in Lahore in December 2005. The visitors were forcing a draw by lunch on the last day, then abruptly lost their last eight wickets for 43 runs in little more than an hour to lose by an innings. Here was a classic case of how Pakistan's cricketers marched to a different drum-beat. England's four seamers had laboured assiduously for days with line and length, but to little avail as the pitch was heartlessly unresponsive to them, and Mohammad Yousuf so imperturbable: only Younis Khan, Shiv Chanderpaul and Hashim Amla have matched Yousuf in this ability to create an unburstable bubble of relaxed and never-ending concentration.

By contrast Pakistan's bowlers have always been ready to bide their time, to watch and wait, to bowl at less than full pace at unpromising times, then sense the opportunity and bowl flat out, inspired. Again, "volatile" was often the media's stock phrase, in contrast to the steady perseverance of John Bull. But this attitude was dictated by conditions, just as history is shaped by geography. Often in Pakistan there was no point busting a gut in a home Test, as the pitch would never deteriorate, and the day's play could be limited by bad light to five hours, so a draw was almost inevitable.

In this case it was Shoaib Akhtar who bowled faster than anything England could manage, although they had Steve Harmison and Andrew Flintoff, but it could have been Imran Khan, Waqar Younis or Wasim Akram at full throttle. (Shoaib differed in that he rolled his sleeves down, not up, when bowling flat out). At the other end was a wrist-spinner, the ideal complement to a fast bowler. Danish Kaneria was a less inspired version of Abdul Qadir, the wrist-spinner with a fast bowler's temperament who had taken nine wickets in one innings of the 1987 Test against England in Lahore. (This surpassed, in my eyes, the best spell by Shane Warne, but Qadir was up and down, Warne always at the batsman.)

It may not have been the most correct analogy, but I was reminded of one of the British Army's retreats from Kabul, when their soldiers had come through the passes and may have thought they were safe, before being wiped out in one fell swoop.

* * *

I do not understand why Pakistan has such a negative image. It is home to several wonders of the world, both natural and man-made, in the mountains and the plains, which would be centres of mass tourism if they were in India. Yet when I visited Mohenjo-daro, "the greatest city of the Bronze Age", the visitors' book listed one foreigner, a Norwegian, and two Pakistani visitors in the whole previous week.

When I spent my first complete winter in England since 1977, owing to the pandemic, I dug out of a cupboard my Chitrali cap. When I drink my annual mug of tea picked from the flowers growing beside Pasu Glacier, I think of those sturdy hill-men who live in the ravines north of Gilgit. Three or four accompanied the media on the England tour of late 2005, driving the bus, organising the baggage, and playing for our side in a media game: they were keen, wholehearted, as in everything they did, but I came to realise that the trajectory of the ball when it came to them in the field was not something for which they had been trained since childhood. There was nowhere to play cricket in their ravines.

These hill-men only ever had employment in summertime, harvesting the apricots and mulberries, the most delicious of all fruits, fit to be wine for Dionysus, yet so perishable that they disintegrate on the day of picking, so they cannot be transported for sale in the outside world. Otherwise, for work, the hill-men had walkers and mountaineers from overseas to equip and accompany on expeditions. This dried up after 9/11 and "the War on Terror" across the border in Afghanistan, and must have disappeared with Covid. I guess they have to eke out rupees in the plains to send home to their families.

A triangular tournament has recently sprung up on a plain near the Pamirs, where the skies and snows still dazzle, and where cricket teams from Chitral, Gilgit and Hunza compete in mid-summer in the Roof of the World tournament. I would love to participate, even if my bowling is 40 or 50mph slower than anybody else's. I would like to think that some batsmen would charge as if they were on their polo ponies, to create the chance of a stumping or two.

Yes, I want to be reunited one day. I am still in love.

ENGLAND IN PAKISTAN AND THE UAE
1961/62 — 2015/16

--- *Overall* ---

Played **86**	Won **26**	Lost **21**	Drawn **39**

--- *In Pakistan/UAE* ---

Played **30**	Won **2**	Lost **9**	Drawn **19**

--- *In England* ---

Played **56**	Won **24**	Lost **12**	Drawn **20**

England's record at each venue

--- *Gaddafi Stadium, Lahore* ---

Played **8**	Won **1**	Lost **2**	Drawn **5**

--- *National Stadium, Karachi* ---

Played **7**	Won **1**	Lost **1**	Drawn **5**

--- *Iqbal Stadium, Faisalabad* ---

Played **4**	Won **0**	Lost **0**	Drawn **4**

--- *Dubai International Cricket Stadium, Dubai* ---

Played **3**	Won **0**	Lost **3**	Drawn **0**

--- *Dhaka Stadium, Dhaka* ---

Played **2**	Won **0**	Lost **0**	Drawn **2**

--- *Niaz Stadium, Hyderabad* ---

Played **2**	Won **0**	Lost **0**	Drawn **2**

Sheikh Zayed Stadium, Abu Dhabi ───────
Played **2**   Won **0**   Lost **1**   Drawn **1**

───────── *Multan Cricket Stadium, Multan* ───────
Played **1**   Won **0**   Lost **1**   Drawn **0**

───────── *Sharjah Cricket Stadium, Sharjah* ───────
Played **1**   Won **0**   Lost **1**   Drawn **0**

Series won   **Captain**
1961/62   Ted Dexter
2000/01   Nasser Hussain

Highest scores

263	Alastair Cook	Abu Dhabi	2015/16
205	Ted Dexter	Karachi	1961/62
193	Marcus Trescothick	Multan	2005/06
173*	David Gower	Lahore	1983/84
165	Geoff Pullar	Dhaka	1961/62

Best bowling

7-66	Phil Edmonds	Karachi	1977/78
6-62	Monty Panesar	Abu Dhabi	2011/12
6-65	Nick Cook	Karachi	1983/84
5-18	Nick Cook	Karachi	1983/84
5-30	David Allen	Dhaka	1961/62

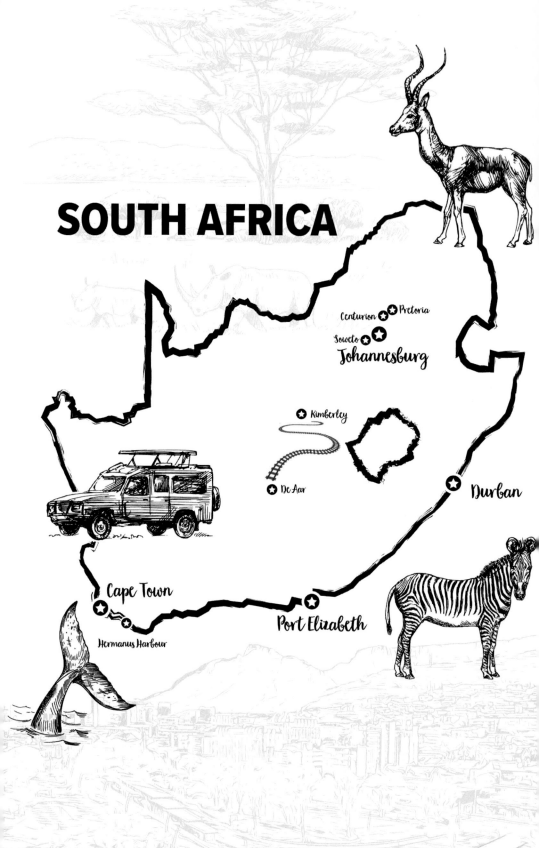

SOUTH AFRICA

Centurion ✪✪ Pretoria

Soweto ✪✪
Johannesburg

✪ Kimberley

✪ De Aar

✪ Durban

Cape Town
✪
Hermanus Harbour

✪ Port Elizabeth

CHAPTER SIX

SOUTH AFRICA

Nature, and human nature, turn the sunnier side of their faces towards the cricket correspondent. We meet people off the field who are pleased to have our custom, subsisting on expenses as we do. The hotel receptionist, after noting your request for a quiet room, smiles as she allots you one beside the dual carriageway; the chef might have spat in your food in the kitchen after you have sent it back, yet the waiter re-presents it politely. Press box colleagues are cheerful, as we should be when escaping grim routine. Only the gateman at Lord's, before MCC reconstructed itself, and the Indian bureaucrat, took positive delight in being awkward.

Nature too presents her sunniest face. Never do we wade to a ground through frozen mud and shiver in thermals, except in Dunedin. We escape the English winter by touring the Southern Hemisphere, or South Asia, or the West Indies outside the hurricane season, making shirt sleeves our dress code; although when I began, colleagues invariably wore dark trousers, blue shirt and tweed jacket.

Normally England have toured South Africa between November and February: hence the title of Alan Ross's book of the 1956/57 tour, *Cape Summer*. The first World T20 finals in 2007, however, were staged in South Africa in September. Thus I was treated not only to seeing whales in Hermanus harbour, the best vantage point on any mainland from which to watch them, but also to the gorgeousness of the Western Cape in spring. Having seen some of Australia's outback, I had never suspected that South Africa's bush could blossom, yet the Cape was radiant with red, blue, orange, white, yellow and even purple flowers, set against the background of verdant green.

On another England tour, I took the train from De Aar, a junction on the main line between Johannesburg and Cape Town, to Kimberley. It was late afternoon and the engine was plodding along at perhaps around 40mph to arrive in time for supper, when I saw across the plateau of deserted fields a light. After ten more minutes we still had not reached that light: it must have been 20 minutes before we reached it, a single light bulb at a country halt. Such immensity of space. Such silent immensity. Yet fertile and habitable.

Bowled over by this beauty, I began to understand the Afrikaner ideology: not agree with it, but understand. Dutch-speakers had disembarked from their ships in Cape Town and trekked with their carts, cattle and Bibles into the interior; and when they saw this grandeur and its gorgeous flora, they perceived that God had granted this land to them. Few were the natives – and where were their lawyers and legal documents to prove their ownership? These trekkers were the new children of Israel. This was their promised land.

History is written by the winners – except that this generalisation reckons without oral folklore handed down from one generation to the next, until it too is eventually written down. We now have an account of the colonisation of South Africa from the other side: *Land of My Ancestors* by Botlhale Tema, who became the first secretary-general of UNESCO in South Africa. By talking to the elders of her tribe, she pieced together how the trekkers had taken their land north west of Johannesburg near where Sun City is today. Although the author does not mention the word "cricket", she does use one of the game's metaphors: "... I also felt that I'd had my innings and deserved the rest". This suggests the sport had some small impact on the indigenous population outside the Eastern Cape.

To Afrikaners, ivory was "white gold"; and child slaves were "black gold". Missionaries told the trekkers, who wanted manual labour for their farms, that only orphans could be enslaved. So what better way to guarantee a child was an orphan? A quick commando raid on an African village. Find some unarmed parents. Bang, bang! Goodnight. And this, by Tema's account, went on well into the second half of the 19th century.

In 1913 the South African government passed the Native Lands Act. Indigenous people were permitted to own 7% of their own land. We can be fairly confident this was not the most fertile 7%. Black Africans, so as not to starve, had to leave their villages to work on white farms and in the mines. This coercion was so effective that in 1936 the government felt able to permit black Africans to own up to 13.6% of their own country.

"Colonisation is always inhumane," wrote a near neighbour, in what is now Namibia. The Governor of German South-West Africa around the turn of the 20th century was Colonel Theodor von Leutwein, and possessed of some objectivity. Too much objectivity in the opinion of the Kaiser, who sent the pioneer of concentration camps to take control of the German military there. But Leutwein left behind that damning assessment. Colonisation does bring out the worse in us, down to a neighbour's tree overshadowing OUR garden.

After such extreme polarisation, it is asking a lot of human nature for communities to come together in less than a hundred years.

* * *

Against this background came a PR company's field day. The first England Test team to visit South Africa after their readmission to international cricket arrived in 1995. They were to play the opening first-class match of their tour in Soweto against a South African Invitation XI captained by Hansie Cronje, a new, reconstructed role model, or so it was claimed, and including several non-whites. What better way to persuade the world that cricket was a frontrunner in social transformation in this "rainbow nation", as Bishop Desmond Tutu had tried to rebrand it?

Nelson Mandela flew in by helicopter, landing on the ground during a break in play. He and Tutu had lived nearby, in the only street to produce two Nobel peace prize-winners. Cricketers are normally bored by meeting dignitaries, but Mandela was the most famous person in the world; players were desperate to get a word, a touch, even a thin outside edge. "Meeting Mandela made me feel as strong as Samson," said England's fast bowler Devon Malcolm, who was privileged to be given extra time with South Africa's president.

So significant was this occasion, it remains the only cricket match which has had radio commentary – not all of it ball-by-ball – in all eleven of South Africa's official languages: Afrikaans, English, Ndebele, Northern Sotho, Sotho, Swazi, Tswana, Tsonga, Venda, Xhosa and Zulu. Only in the Kalahari could anybody in South Africa have complained about not being able to follow England's latest batting collapse.

The first democratic government in South Africa had come to power only in the previous year, so the country was almost as polarised as ever. The typical image was a utility truck driven by a white man, perhaps with a black foreman seated beside him, and black workers hired for the day standing or squatting in the back. The social divisions were rigid: whites went around in their cars, Indians in buses, Cape Coloureds in vans and lorries, while blacks walked.

During apartheid marriage between races had been illegal, and there was no sign of interracial mixing, by cricketers or anyone else. An even higher proportion of women than in most contemporary white societies, so I observed, had their hair dyed blonde – to make themselves even more distinct from the African majority? In almost every restaurant every guest was white and the staff were non-white, except for senior management and owner.

A single non-white had represented the country at cricket since readmission, Omar Henry, and then very briefly; no black African until Makhaya Ntini bowled his way into the national team. He was nicknamed "Boy". Even when Ntini had taken 200 or 300 wickets, over the stump mics on television you could hear him being encouraged and addressed as "Boy" by his teammates, notably the wicketkeeper Mark Boucher.

South Africa's team bus told the story of racial integration as the years passed after apartheid and Ntini: white players in the front and middle, the one black player at the back, and he was at the bottom of the batting order, always No.11, not given a chance to show what he could do to improve, only wanted for his manual labour of pace bowling. At one time it was Lonwabo Tsotsobe sitting at the back of the bus, alone. Not for one moment is it an excuse, but I was not too surprised when he was one of the seven South African cricketers banned in 2017 for match-fixing, in his case for eight years. Once No.1 in the ODI rankings for bowlers, never one of the lads.

The racial hatred in South Africa – far more potent than mistrust – remained tangible. White South Africans, whether Afrikaans or English speakers, were friendly to visitors from Britain, very friendly. If you were staying at a hotel or guesthouse and wanted to go out, the owner or manager would offer you a lift.

Sorry to trouble you, but please could you take me to the cricket ground?

"It's a pleasure!"

"Great, thanks. And tomorrow morning at 7am I've got a flight to Jo'burg. Please could you give me a lift to the airport?"

"It's a pleasure!"

"Oh well, in that case, do you mind driving me straight to Jo'burg? If we left at 6.30am we could get there in time for the England press conference at 11am."

(Through very gritted teeth) "It's a pleasure!"

Only later did you realise you were being co-opted. The warmth with which the manager or manageress greeted you was in complete contrast to the coldness with which they addressed their black staff. They would not look at the black porter or security guard, let alone in the eye, before making another effusively friendly comment to the white visitor. The object of the game was to bring the visitor on to your side, to make him an honorary member of the white tribe: safety in numbers.

Taxis were being taken over by black drivers. So we don't want good money ending up in their hands, do we? Not that it was ever said. One estimate by a black former banker, Sam Motsuenyane, was that one rand in 80 during apartheid circulated in black hands, whereupon he set up the African Bank.

Yet if you managed to talk with that African porter (because he might have come from Zambia or Zimbabwe for a job) or security guard, taxi driver or waiter – not talk at but with – you would be amazed. Of course, they would lose their job if they did not speak politely to the white guest, but scratch the surface and there was an astonishing depth of humanity. I would have been bitter as hell if I had reached the age of 40 or 50 and been denied every opportunity in life, yet somehow they rose above it.

Where are the world's most gifted linguists to be found? Not in the quad or common-room of an ancient university, but at the street corners of Cape Town, Durban, Johannesburg and Pretoria. Gaining a degree in a second language gave me every opportunity. Black South African taxi drivers speak a minimum of six or seven languages.

Whereas PR companies tend not to specialise in follow-ups or long-term outcomes, I went to the Soweto ground 25 years later. I even bowled a few overs, and during the fifth felt a little stab in my lungs. Most cricket correspondents are not exactly in peak condition during a tour, but still ... the altitude of nearly 5000 feet was having an impact. I was amazed South Africa had used the eight-ball over for almost 20 years after trialling it in their 1938/39 series against England: fast bowlers must have been exhausted after a one-over spell in Johannesburg. Another effect of the altitude was that the ball travelled further when I bowled, or rather straight after I had bowled! Towards the end of England's 2019/20 series, television commentators stated that in the thinner air of Johannesburg and Centurion the ball travelled approximately three metres, or 14ft, further than on the coast.

Soweto CC were playing the Barmy Army, who kindly allowed me to participate. The Army has risen enormously in my estimation since it first paraded in Australia in 1994/95, when children – and adults – were forced to listen to some fairly foul-mouthed excesses. Subsequently the Army have become admirable ambassadors. By playing this game in Soweto, they raised 15,000 rand – not far short of £1,000 – for the Soweto club, while another member of their group undertook to sponsor their Kookaburra match balls, which are imported expensively from Australia. (The locally-made Protea ball, not then used at higher levels, was much harder. Evidence: the dent in my hand after taking a catch in a media game).

While Soweto CC's clubhouse was intact, it did not appear to have been renovated since its launch in front of the world's cameras. In the home changing-room in 1995, Hansie Cronje must have eyed one of his bowlers, the Cape Coloured medium-pacer Henry Williams, and perhaps there and then decided to target him for his match- or spot-fixing manipulations.

The ground's outfield was nicely grassed for the Barmy Army game, but the pitch uneven. The game was being live-streamed by Cricket South Africa. I asked their digital expert which league Soweto played in.

"Achhh, no idea," he said.

And, by the guttural sound of it, he cared even less.

Soweto, it turned out, were in the top division of the Johannesburg league. Temba Bavuma played occasionally for the club, Kagiso Rabada infrequently. A fundamental change had occurred at the end of the 1990s. Before then, cricket coaches had been paid to go into the local schools and teach kids; now the kids had to make their own way to the club if they wanted cricket. So the sport staggered on in Soweto, for the few rather than the many, whereas the official vision 25 years earlier must have been for something more inclusive.

Yes, it had been a PR field day in 1995. Subsequently, not a single first-class game had been staged there. It became a regular feature of England tours: the team visited a cricket club in a disadvantaged area (Lenasia, where Indians only had lived, was another venue in Johannesburg, or Yorkshire CC in Kimberley): lots of handshakes and photos; some nice words; great PR for the South African Board, and a plug for their township programmes; then no contact ever again.

Soweto itself was flourishing – not so much economically, for the corruption of Jacob Zuma's presidency had made South Africa reel – as socially. Dark, intimidating streets in a country unravelling? No, roads were as tidy as could be, and buses ran in the centre of the main highway into and out of Johannesburg. Most houses were single-storeyed, a few no more than a couple of rooms, yet they were soundly built of brick and well-roofed against the Highveld's summer storms and winter chills; most dwellers took pride in a patch of garden. And we now know that state health workers had every street and settlement in South Africa under control with respect to Aids, and were therefore well placed when Covid came.

The municipal park was as delightful as anything you could see in an English town with its stream, benches, bushes, and absence of litter. In the quarter-century since 1995 the government had built millions of houses, equipped with running water, indoor toilets and electricity; and retro-virals were free for all, whether South African citizens or immigrant labourers, legal and illegal.

On the way back from Soweto, I admit I conceived a wish for legislation to regulate minibuses. They did not stop at red traffic lights, except at major intersections: as in Bangladesh, the drivers were paid by the journey, so they packed in as many as they could per day. In the shadow of the Orlando Stadium, built for the football World Cup of 2010, sprawled a squatter camp inhabited mainly by Zimbabweans, living in the same conditions as black South Africans under apartheid a generation before. Five million Zimbabweans were estimated to be working in South Africa, along with millions more who had crossed the border from the rest of Africa as far north as Ethiopia. No government, corrupt or incorrupt, could keep up.

* * *

South African cities have followed the trend set in the USA: white wealth has left the centres to poor blacks, and departed to affluent suburbs. On the outskirts of Johannesburg, the Sandton shopping mall is so huge it includes the hotels in which touring teams stay. The sleek Gautrain metro from Pretoria (via Centurion) stops short of central Johannesburg at Sandton, emphasising it is not intended for the masses. From their high-rises, bankers, financiers and directors have only to cross the road for lunch in the restaurant of a multinational chain. (The street stalls outside, where women cooked rich stews for taxi drivers, offered the best food I have had in South Africa.)

In the new surrounding suburbs, houses do not have a wall, as in England, or a fence, as in Australia or New Zealand; they have a wall then a fence on top, surmounted not by barbed wire but razor wire designed to slice off digits. Large notices inform you which instant response unit will shoot on sight if you intrude. Yet down the road in Soweto, no such wire, no such fear.

Of Johannesburg's three Test grounds, the original Old Wanderers ground was so central it was converted into the city's main railway station. (As in the rest of South Africa, pitches until 1930/31 were matting.) In 1905/06, England played three of their five Tests on this ground; between the second and third Tests was one day's break. This schedule reflected the belief that nobody at the time thought cricket matches between England and South Africa were of the same order as those between England and Australia. England's wicketkeeper, Arthur, or "Dick", Lilley, summed up the common position when he referred to "the first Test match ever played between South Africa and England at Lord's in July, 1907".

One of the six Tests at Ellis Park, the rugby ground used during the construction of the new Wanderers in Illovo, saw the unique sight of Hugh Tayfield being taken apart. Several bowlers conceded less than two runs an over during the dour 1950s, but South Africa's off-spinner did it without ever being clobbered, except once, in 1953/54, by New Zealand left-hander Bert Sutcliffe. Sutcliffe's reaction to being hit on the head by a ball that took off at Ellis Park – although New Zealanders could hardly complain about the risks of batting on rugby grounds – was to run down the pitch after returning from hospital and belt Tayfield for seven sixes. Three years later Tayfield was bowling 137 balls in a row against England, mainly to Trevor Bailey, without conceding a run.

The new Wanderers, or the Bullring, became one of the most hostile grounds for touring teams. The tunnel with a plastic roof was installed to protect them from physical if not verbal abuse. South Africa's bowlers were hostile, too, whether Allan Donald and Shaun Pollock, or Dale Steyn and Makhaya Ntini and Morne Morkel. At almost 5,000 feet the ball flew through to the keeper. No ground in the world had a higher percentage of "caught behind" dismissals in Test cricket than the new Wanderers at 37%. According to the data garnered by TV cameras, the new ball swings for a longer period at altitude, which also helps to find an edge, whereas the old ball reverse swings later in an innings than on the coast, and less.

* * *

Slag heaps were flattened when it became economically viable to sift through them, so the reminders that Johannesburg was built on gold are less visible on its skyline than they were. But the mentality of settlements built on exploitation, whether of the earth or other humans, takes time to move on. Mining camps in Johannesburg in the late 19th century merit a mention in Roy Porter's history of medicine, *The Greatest Benefit to Mankind*: "Europeans exported tuberculosis to the 'Dark Continent', especially once native labourers were jammed into mining compounds and the slums of Johannesburg. In the gold, diamond and copper producing regions of Africa, the operations of mining companies like De Beers and Union Minière de Haut-Katanga brought family disruption and prostitution. Capitalism worsened the incidence of infection and deficiency diseases for those induced or forced to abandon tribal ways and traditional economies."

For the fortunate, this gold rush funded tall buildings in the city centre, the first skyscrapers outside the USA. Such was the gold, glitz and glamour that the manager of the England touring team of 1938/39, Jack Holmes, reckoned they were offered three different entertainments every evening of their stay in Johannesburg, which included two Tests. The opposite of lockdown.

Gold also funded the private schools of Johannesburg, based on the English model, with Houses and plenty of sport. Founded in 1898, St John's hired Alfred Atfield, who had represented Gloucestershire and Wiltshire. Atfield was one of the first of numerous cricketers to find that spending the summer in England and winter in South Africa made for a pleasant lifestyle (in 1901, while on the MCC groundstaff, Atfield managed to score a century for Cross Arrows and get married on the same day.) Another feature of these professionals, who followed the sun from hemisphere to hemisphere, seems to be that they lived to a greater age than their contemporaries who wintered in England.

An exception was George Lohmann, he who has the lowest Test bowling average, 10.75, of those who have taken 100 wickets: he contracted tuberculosis, even before he took 35 wickets at 5.80 in England's three-match "Test series" in South Africa in 1895/96, and died in South Africa aged 36. Lohmann, in my reading, was a T20 bowler before his time: that is, he had everything in his medium-paced repertoire to have been a success now. He was "a perfect master at varying his pace without betraying the variation to the batsman", said C.B. Fry.

Atfield, according to the annals of St John's College, was "remunerated by Sir Abe Bailey", the diamond tycoon who had South Africa inducted into the Imperial Cricket Council in 1909, alongside England and Australia. Atfield then moved to the new Johannesburg College, or King Edward VII School as it was re-named in 1910. "Cricket began with the arrival of AJ Atfield, a former Gloucester player who established cricket at King Edwards," states the history of the school which produced such world-class sportsmen as Gary Player, Bryan Habana and Graeme Smith. The school has had a discernible trend of producing wicketkeepers. It cannot be a coincidence that the school's pro in the early 1920s was Jack Board, the former Gloucestershire and England keeper. The line has extended from Edward van der Merwe, who kept wicket for South Africa in a couple of Tests either side of 1930, and Louis Duffus who, after keeping for Transvaal, became South Africa's first cricket writer of note, to Quinton de Kock, Dane Vilas, Nic Pothas and Ray Jennings, arguably South Africa's finest keeper to pace bowling.

Hence, I conclude, the similarity of styles. Are any other Test-playing countries so close as England and South Africa in style and, for long periods, results? Play straight, with plenty of leading elbow; plenty of disciplined pace bowling, supplemented by tidy finger-spin; and never let your side down in the field. After all, the same coaches coached in both countries. Australia and New Zealand were too far away for English professionals to winter there, the cost of travel prohibitive. Only India's maharajahs before the Second World War offered employment on anything like the same scale as South Africa, and that was for the likes of Jack Hobbs, Wilfred Rhodes and Herbert Sutcliffe: trophy professionals.

The results were also remarkably close between England and South Africa, as between no other two countries over a prolonged period. Before 1930 South African sides, brought up on matting, could not adapt to English conditions. From then until 2015 England won nine Test series, South Africa seven, and four were drawn. In actual Tests, the score was 28-21 to England.

This balance was tipped by South Africa's loss of many of their best players to English cricket under the Kolpak system. On the condition that they gave up international cricket – temporarily in a few cases – South Africans could earn a living in pounds, not ever weaker rands, without being classified as overseas players. Most Kolpaks followed the tradition set by Barry Richards and Mike Procter in being excellent value, raising the standard of Championship cricket, especially with their pace bowling – but at the same time lowering South African standards. From 2015, England won the next three Test series rather too easily.

The re-profiling of the Test teams of the two countries since they ceased to be all-white has been interesting, too. South Africa, as a generalisation, have black fast bowlers, a spinner of South Asian origin, and batsmen and wicketkeepers of European origin. The difference is that England no longer have black fast bowlers. Devon Malcolm quickly faded after his tour of South Africa. Nelson Mandela made him feel like Samson; the England management did not.

* * *

Centurion's press box has everything to be desired: right behind the arm, at the right height – not too low, so the view is blocked by the umpire, not too high as at Edgbaston – and open to the elements, yet roofed against rain and midday sun. One can see, hear and feel the body language of the players and reactions of the crowd. But I used to stay in Centurion itself, rather than Sandton, only because a week living in a shopping mall for the Johannesburg Test was sufficient, not out of love for this new suburb of Pretoria.

Of all the ways to earn a livelihood, standing in the middle of the road at traffic lights is not the best way to promote longevity, yet it is a common way of making a living in Centurion. Whatever colour the lights may be, you stand facing the traffic. If they are green, you have one lane of cars whizzing past you on your right, the other on your left, both within touching distance. On a dark day, in the absence of a luminous safety jacket, you pin your faith in a sheet of white paper or cardboard strapped to your chest. When the lights turn red, you have less than a minute to sell one of your newspapers, or scrubbing brushes, or bunches of flowers, or to wipe a car window, or simply beg, and thereby make your living.

South Africa offers a safety net for its young, and pensions for its old. For its middle-aged population, beyond retro-virals, the state offers nothing. Personally, the hero of South Africa's freedom struggle was Steve Biko, more so than Nelson Mandela who transformed the politics but left the economy undisturbed. In Sandton's main square stands a large statue of Mandela, though rather too rounded and fleshy for someone who has spent 18 years working in a quarry on Robben Island. Around his statue, prostitutes – "Hello sweetie!" – who have come in from Alexandra township of an evening try to find work. Neighbouring Botswana nationalised its diamond mines, and prospered.

Everywhere has extremes of rich and poor, but nowhere in my experience is the distinction quite so stark or rigid as in the suburb of Centurion. I walked past a church or "kerk" which listed five pastors on its noticeboard, all of European origin if the names were anything to go by. Sunday attendances in these parts must be pretty high, judging by the only bookshop I could find in Centurion: books lined the whole of the wall opposite the entrance, but the shelves contained only one title, the Bible, in several languages. On a hot weekday afternoon the gates to this church were closed, emphatically. Entrance was physically impossible. Behind the high fences topped with razor wire, a car park was neatly laid out for the faithful's four-wheel drives on Sunday, all white lines immaculately painted. On the other side of the razor wire, two young able-bodied black African men worked their way down the street, one on each side, rummaging through rubbish bins.

* * *

Port Elizabeth is an old dear, living on her widow's pension, one rapidly eroded by inflation. She has to darn her skirts and socks, and struggles on. She has her memories of being young and fancy-free, however, and clings to the hope that her future will perk up before she dies.

For PE could yet be one of the world's great cities, not only a centre of industry – as economists visualised when making it part of the Nelson Mandela Bay metropolis – but the whole of Africa's summer capital, ahead of Durban, which becomes drabber and dingier, ahead of Cape Town where icy sea makes wetsuits indispensable. Half of PE's seafront is taken up with the port, railway lines and flyovers, but that still leaves several miles along the coast to Summerstrand where the Indian Ocean surfs ashore.

Here everyone can swim in summer, without wetsuits, or sharks as in Durban. This could be one of the grand corniches of the world, up there with Nice or nicer, because no billionaires are flaunting their yachts to excite envy; or Alexandria, which has far more history but has faded even further from grandeur; or the Malecón in Havana. If Cuba's capital can be resurrected after decades of being boycotted, so can PE.

South Africa's first international cricket match was staged in that halfway point along the coast between the industrial and beach-resort areas, and up a ravine in St George's Park. Dotted with sub-tropical vegetation, this ravine is reminiscent of a Windward Island, one with a government so indifferent to tourism that it does not pay to have the litter cleared. Nevertheless, sea breezes on top of this hill are delicious, although the humidity can become intense, as the city's merchants knew when they built their late 19th-century mansions. One was a Mr Dorkin, who chose a site beside St George's Park to build a handsome home that is now a prep school. It is his wife Elizabeth who lives on, as the city is named after her, not an English queen.

Team photographs have not altered for aeons: here we are, a keen and athletic touring party who know our stuff, and you locals had better watch out! The photograph of the first English touring team to South Africa, in 1888/89, differs: you are to be impressed by their social status. Everyone is dressed in frock coat and top hat; some also sport a walking stick or cane. They have played a spot of cricket at Eton or opened the bowling for Harrow, and possess a title, like the Hon Charles Coventry; or Aubrey Smith, who secured a knighthood after emigrating to Hollywood; or even the manager Major Warton. Inset, so as not to lower the tone by their humbler clothing, are three professionals who did the hard work (and drinking): Johnny Briggs of Lancashire, George Ulyett of Yorkshire, and Frank Hearne of Kent. Hearne stayed on after the tour for his health, activated cricket in Cape Town as a sports outfitter and coach, and later represented South Africa.

After retiring from the General Staff in South Africa, Warton had returned to England to raise his team. The other arrangements were made by William Milton, who had played rugby for England and was private secretary to Cecil Rhodes, and he obtained sponsorship from Sir Donald Currie, who owned the Castle shipping line. Currie also paid for a trophy for the local team that put up the best show against these tourists; hence Kimberley won the first Currie Cup, before it was reserved for domestic competition. Fielding several club players as they did, Warton's team went short of runs initially on bare, baked grounds and pitches where the ball came on more quickly and bounced higher than at home – until they persuaded their hosts to play on matting.

Thus it was that two elevens arrived at St George's Park on the morning of 12 March 1889. Hitherto the tourists had been playing teams of XV or XVIII or even XXII local players; this was the first eleven-a-side match. Posters in PE had advertised the game ("A limited number of Carriages will be admitted at 10s 6d each") as being Major Warton's team "Against South African XI" – not a Test match at all, not for the English players at any rate. Yet for the South Africans the game was something unprecedented, and Mrs Dunell, their captain's wife, embroidered their green caps with two words: South Africa.

The English team won, in only two of the three scheduled days, by eight wickets. The *Port Elizabeth Advertiser* conveys no great sense of occasion, just mundane run-of-play, but for a while it was a competitive game, rather similar in shape to Sri Lanka's inaugural Test against England almost a century later, before the visitors won comfortably.

The teams entrained for Cape Town for a second fixture between Warton's chaps and this South African XI, but the pros were far too good at Newlands. Bobby Abel scored one of his 74 first-class hundreds and, without needing a fielder, the left-arm spinner Johnny Briggs took 15 wickets for 28 runs, the best figures of their kind in Test cricket, if they can be classified as such.

During apartheid non-white Africans were allowed to watch South Africa play cricket if penned in their own enclosure; occasionally one of their better bowlers might be permitted in the nets. Otherwise, before 1948, black Africans were out of sight and mind for touring teams, who came from Australia and England only. After the Second World War, and the rigorous implementation of apartheid under Daniel Malan from 1948, black Africans began to make themselves heard, firstly by cheering South Africa's opponents, secondly by singing songs which the players and authorities did not understand; besides, it was a bit awkward to tear-gas church bands. St George's Park became a focal point for these protests because cricket had been played in the Eastern Cape, in Fort Hare and schools founded by Christian missionaries, since the 19th century, when Britain's colonial ambition was still to turn native elites into English gentlemen.

I am grateful to have heard St George's Park in full song. During the Tests of 1995/96 and 1999/00 the church bands belted out "Shosholoza" and "Stand By Me", impervious to the state of play, and almost raised the roof of the old wooden stand. The music at the Recreation Ground in Antigua used to be animating, provided you did not have to think or write, but my most joyful musical experience at any cricket match was in PE.

On the hill where the merchants made their homes the numerous late Victorian houses are equipped with delightful terraces or verandas, shutters and iron railings. They are as handsome as any of their contemporaries in inner Melbourne or around Sydney Harbour. Here, among the few cafés and restaurants, might lie the seed of a middle-class harmony and multiracial future. But, for this to happen, where is South Africa's answer to Silicon Valley – the glassy new buildings of the IT hub which the Continent needs, next to these potentially trendy houses for the graduate workforce? The work ethic of South Africans of every race seems exemplary; where is the intellectual capital to make the most of this physical effort? The immediate future, at least, remains blighted by apartheid's legacy: whites got jobs simply on the basis of being white, irrespective of qualifications, while non-whites were deterred, or prevented, from ever exercising their initiative.

Instead, PE's inner suburbs contain long straight streets leading down to the port, lined with concrete-and-glass buildings of the 1960s, and deserted except for car showrooms on the ground floor. Eerie, in this world of rapidly expanding populations, is the emptying city centre. A couple of outer suburbs around Summerstrand are affluent; too many others are made up of bungalows on derelict land, with an old vehicle on blocks in what might once have been a garden.

So PE is not so much the Friendly City, or the Windy City, which have been her sobriquets, so much as the threadbare one. Still, the widow is going to put on her old coat and go out for a brisk walk along the sea front, thinking of what might yet be, and will enjoy tea – or a tipple maybe – on her return home.

* * *

Durban was the place where my father came closest to being mugged. It was 1940 and he was on a troop ship from Liverpool to

Malta via the Cape of Good Hope, as the Mediterranean was rather busy. When she stopped in Durban, he was walking through the port back to the ship one evening when he realised he was being followed – by how many men, of which race, he never said. After reaching Malta, which was bombed every day for months on end, he took sleeping pills every night for the rest of his life.

During my touring I have spent a happy, unhassled hour in the central bus station in downtown Kingston, Jamaica, so I am not quickly alarmed. But I too, like my father, felt more threatened in Durban than anywhere except Port-of-Spain. Pickpockets and muggers probably have a partiality for ports. Following the same trend as the rust-belt of the USA, and Johannesburg, white wealth has left the city centre for North Durban, where the beaches are clean and the shopping malls packed with national and international chains. This is where the cricket teams now stay, driving down the carriageway to Kingsmead, if they play in Durban at all.

"Durbs" was where Johannesburgers went for summer holidays in the sea-front hotels and high-rise apartments, walking and drinking on the beaches, swimming and surfing and going to Kingsmead for the Boxing Day Test. Not any more. It is a walk of only a few hundred yards from the hotel where England used to stay to Kingsmead, but across waste ground where the air is pregnant with dereliction and danger as well as humidity.

My father did not tell me, and maybe as a soldier in the ranks he had no opportunity to savour it, but central Durban in 1940 was anything but drab. If a photograph taken a year earlier is evidence, it was Party Central. The photo shows England cricketers in their best suits sweeping like Hollywood actors into one of the theatres or cinemas along the sea front, society girls hanging off their arms. The England touring team of 1938/39 was captained by Wally Hammond, who led from the front, day and night, and surely ranks still among England's highest scorers, not only of runs. Bill Edrich was one of his favourites; and next to their hotel was the Athlone Gardens nightclub. Hours of play pre-war were less than six per day, so plenty of time remained for the carefree cricketer to change into his dinner jacket and hit the town. Cities on the verge of war, if not actively engaged in it, have added zest in living life to the full.

The most famous timeless Test lasted 12 days from start to inconclusive finish, including two Sundays and a day washed out, which left plenty of time for dalliance. Edrich had scored no more than 88 runs in his Test career, and went to bed early, so we are told, until the sirens of Athlone Gardens could be resisted no longer – and he went to score 219 (runs). After the war, Hammond remarried and settled in Durban.

The finest initiative in South African cricket had occurred in Durban earlier on that tour, during the third Test, not the fifth. Lord Nuffield, wealthy after founding Morris Motors, attended the match and offered £10,000 for a worthy project: hence the Nuffield Schools Week. Australia has its National Under-19 state championship as its most important building block; South Africa, Sri Lanka and Zimbabwe depend on their elite schools. Some South African schools can produce a better all-time Test team on paper than some English counties. I remember A.B. de Villiers, in his second Test, aged 20, and saddled with wicketkeeping, batting out for a draw against England as they were peaking for the 2005 Ashes. His unbeaten half-century steered South Africa to safety with two wickets in hand. It was the innings of a head boy, given the responsibility to do a man's job, and doing it with the utmost maturity.

The trouble, by 2020, was that the games during Nuffield Week featured all three formats. Fifty-over games, I think, are varied enough to train up the best teenagers to become Test, ODI or T20 players.

Durban still dons party clothes for an evening out at Kingsmead. The World T20 finals in 2007 were the spark, when Yuvraj Singh hit Stuart Broad for six sixes in an over. Under floodlights the ground makes an attractive setting, as warm as India for an IPL game, its air cleansed by sea breezes, and the crowd as mixed as could be, for Natal's Indian population has Hashim Amla and Keshav Maharaj for role-models.

* * *

Newlands in Cape Town has traditionally staged the New Year Test. Before South Africa's readmission, England would often play over

162

Christmas in Johannesburg then make the 900-mile train journey through the Great Karoo to Cape Town for New Year. The two sets of cricketers would live, drink and sleep in each other's pockets, stretching their legs at dawn or dusk at the junction of De Aar. Beating England was never the raison d'être of the South African cricketer as it was for the Australian. The relationship was, if not fraternal, cousinly.

Players arriving at Cape Town today come through the airport, to be driven past the townships of Langa and Khayelitsha, which are inhabited mainly by Xhosas who have bussed from the Eastern Cape to find a job. In 2016 I went to Langa after Temba Bavuma had scored the first and, to date, only Test century by a black African for South Africa; Hamilton Masakadza had been the first for Zimbabwe 15 years earlier. It was practice evening, and Langa's players were so friendly – as well as delighted at the success of one of their own – they let me bowl in their nets after I had seen the modest bungalow where Bavuma had grown up, before he won a cricket scholarship to pukka schools.

It is almost an inflexible rule that the future top-class batsman has to grow up in a house which has a garden or driveway where he can bat from the age of two or three and condition his reflexes, specifically the synapses linking the brain to muscles. As the years passed, and Bavuma batted very correctly, and compiled neat 30s and 40s but did not add to his maiden century – nor did any other black African for South Africa – I found myself wondering whether there was more to this conditioning than the physical and physiological. To score a Test century is to lord the crease, to dominate your opponents, to believe you rank among the best, to have watertight self-assurance. But how can someone dominate an international bowling attack after he has been brought up not to be assertive in any walk of life? During a Test against Sri Lanka during lockdown, I even saw Bavuma – well-set for a century – "walking", giving himself out caught behind, after he had missed the ball by some distance according to television replays.

Langa's nets in 2016 were not so good as they had been when part of a flagship programme; the club's hockey was thriving more than the cricket. English professionals used to coach in and play for township clubs, before T20 tournaments filled their off-season. Langa had slipped into the third division of Cape Town's league.

Cape Coloured cricket, on the other hand, has become ever more vibrant: so many role models on television, like Jean-Paul Duminy, Vernon Philander and Ashwell Prince, and so many livelihoods to be made in domestic cricket when filling the non-white quotas. (The community originally consisted of slaves imported by the Dutch East India Company from Malaya, although Basil D'Oliveira told me his ancestors came from Madeira.)

When I attended a club game between two Cape Coloured clubs, I thought the closest analogy was West Indian club cricket of a generation before. Players turned up in big throaty old cars; most bowling was quick; so too most innings, as the ball was to be hit as far and high as possible, a display of machismo that was admired by female spectators. Did batsmen from this community also need what South Africa's elite schools had supplied? Duminy made a spectacular start to his Test career, in Australia, scoring an unbeaten 50 in a match-winning stand on his debut in Perth, followed by 166 off his own bat in another victory in his second Test at Melbourne, only to fade gradually like a Cape spring flower.

* * *

At the end of my last tour as the *Telegraph*'s cricket correspondent, the England captain Joe Root kindly presented me with a copy of a painting of Newlands signed by his team, in pencil, in accordance with their custom. It depicted the Cape Town Test on the 2019/20 tour, which England won, and the famous view from the ground towards Table Mountain. (I have climbed it, then the cable car stayed shut all day, owing to strong winds, so I had to descend as well: the stream towards the bottom tasted delicious.) It was the first Test England had won at Cape Town since 1956/57, and Root jested I must have covered that one as well. There could not have been a happier note on which to end my touring, or a happier career.

During that Cape Town Test, the second of four in that series, I have to admit I was struggling: not sleeping properly since arriving in Centurion on Boxing Day after an overnight flight; finding my hotel booking there had been cancelled and no room at the inn; losing my credit card in a cashpoint scam and part of a front tooth. I could only make emergency calls on my phone, and had to visit the dentist twice. It had been the most momentous year in English cricket, what with the Ashes and the World Cup victory, and tours of the West Indies and New Zealand as well as South Africa, and by the morning of the Newlands Test I was exhausted: not the way to start a game which lasts five days, each consisting of eight or nine hours at the ground before the process of writing up begins. I was walking round the garden of the Vineyard Hotel at 2am, not enjoying the silhouette of Table Mountain. I was hearing Mussorgsky's *Night on a Bare Mountain* and the bell tolling.

The morning after the Newlands Test, a 20-over media game was going to be staged on the same ground. I dragged myself out of bed, and got smashed for two consecutive sixes by someone who turned out to have been a teammate of Joe Root's at Sheffield Collegiate and who slog-swept with exactly the same bobbing of the head to sniff the ball the moment before contact. I was nearing rock bottom. However, I took the two catches which came my way: no need for footwork, thank goodness, but both hit fairly hard – and that was the bottom line. If you hold your catches you can retain some self-esteem. England's head coach Chris Silverwood had come to Newlands – the morning after a Test which England won with half-an-hour to spare – to watch two of his sons playing; and after I had lent him my trainers he joined in, as a batsman, then batted afterwards on the boundary against his three-year-old. My love of the game was reinvigorated.

On my last evening in Cape Town I attended an open-air concert in the botanical gardens of Kirstenbosch with a long-standing colleague, Simon Wilde of *The Sunday Times*. It was bright afternoon and, such was the clarity of the light, one of those times and places when the Cape looks impossibly lovely; again you knew how those original trekkers must have felt. Kirstenbosch is flanked by the most desirable suburbs of Bishopscourt and Claremont, with Constantia and Table Mountain beyond; below the gardens, the townships of Cape Flats spread beyond the airport and along the coast.

A local band played, the music's beauty not quite equal to this setting, so we agreed, but this was not what mattered. What struck us both was the ten thousand people sitting on the grass banks, trying to detect a rhythm to which they could dance. They were more integrated than crowds at 20-over games in South Africa where black, brown and white sit next to each other in separate groups; here they all mixed in. Ten thousand made a representative sample, but of course they represented middle-class Cape Town, those who could afford the entry fee, and the proportion of middle-class people was not going to increase in the foreseeable future after Zuma's cronies had plundered the economy.

Here, nevertheless, was colour-blindness on a scale I had never before seen in South Africa, and as the sun set behind Table Mountain, the country's future appeared as though it could be bright. On Mussorgsky's Bare Mountain the bell had rung at the advent of dawn, and here was a multiracial beginning.

When Covid appeared, the silver lining was that it gave South African cricket time for reflection (they did not play another Test for 11 months), when the contracted players went into a training camp of a different kind. The time was used, in part, for soul-searching, which I suspect had never been done before. The assumption had always been that any non-white cricketer had to fit in with the traditional South African, i.e. the white way, of doing things. Now, at last, players like Lungi Ngidi were heard and attitudes altered under Mark Boucher's coaching.

When South Africa played their first Test series abroad during lockdown, in Pakistan, I detected – albeit only on television – that cool civility between the races had been replaced by warmth and genuine delight in each other's success. Instead of white players lining up alongside each other for a presentation, and the non-white players tacked on, there was a new colour-blindness. The South African team lost the series, but they had gained something which they had never had before.

South Africa's women's team may have gone even further down the track. The permutation, of white batters and non-white bowlers, became similar to that in their men's team, but with almost all their bowlers non-white: like everywhere else in the world, batting is more a matter of nurture, bowling a matter of nature. In any event, the South Africa women's team was skilled enough, and united enough, to win their first T20 series in India in March 2021.

The next time I see a bus carrying a South African cricket team, I expect new seating arrangements and everyone to be integrated. If South African cricket can access all the potential players in the country, no matter the value of the rand, their future is going to be rainbow-bright.

ENGLAND IN SOUTH AFRICA
1888/89 — 2019/20

Overall

Played **153**   Won **64**   Lost **34**   Drawn **55**

In South Africa

Played **85**   Won**34**   Lost **20**   Drawn **31**

In England

Played **68**   Won **30**   Lost **14**   Drawn **24**

England's record at each venue

Newlands, Cape Town

Played **21**   Won **10**   Lost **5**   Drawn **6**

Old Wanderers, Johannesburg

Played **17**   Won **6**   Lost **7**   Drawn **4**

Kingsmead, Durban

Played **16**   Won **6**   Lost **1**   Drawn **9**

St George's Park, Port Elizabeth

Played **10**   Won **6**   Lost **1**   Drawn **3**

The Wanderers, Johannesburg

Played **10**   Won **4**   Lost **3**   Drawn **3**

SuperSport Park, Centurion

Played **6**   Won **1**   Lost **2**   Drawn **3**

Played **3**   Won **1**   Lost **1**   Drawn **1**

--------- *Ellis Park, Johannesburg* ---------

Played **2**   Won **0**   Lost **0**   Drawn **2**

Series won   Captain

Series won	Captain
1888/89	Aubrey Smith
1895/96	Lord Hawke
1898/99	Lord Hawke
1913/14	Johnny Douglas
1922/23	Frank Mann
1938/39	Walter Hammond
1948/49	George Mann
1964/65	Mike Smith
2004/05	Michael Vaughan
2015/16	Alastair Cook
2019/20	Joe Root

Highest scores

258	Ben Stokes	Cape Town	2015/16
243	Eddie Paynter	Durban	1938/39
219	Bill Edrich	Durban	1938/39
195	Cyril Washbrook	Johannesburg (Ellis Park)	1948/49
187	Jack Hobbs	Cape Town	1909/10

Best bowling

9-28	George Lohmann	Johannesburg (Old Wanderers)	1895/96
9-103	Sydney Barnes	Johannesburg (Old Wanderers)	1913/14
8-7	George Lohmann	Port Elizabeth	1895/96
8-11	Johnny Briggs	Cape Town	1888/89
8-56	Sydney Barnes	Johannesburg (Old Wanderers)	1913/14

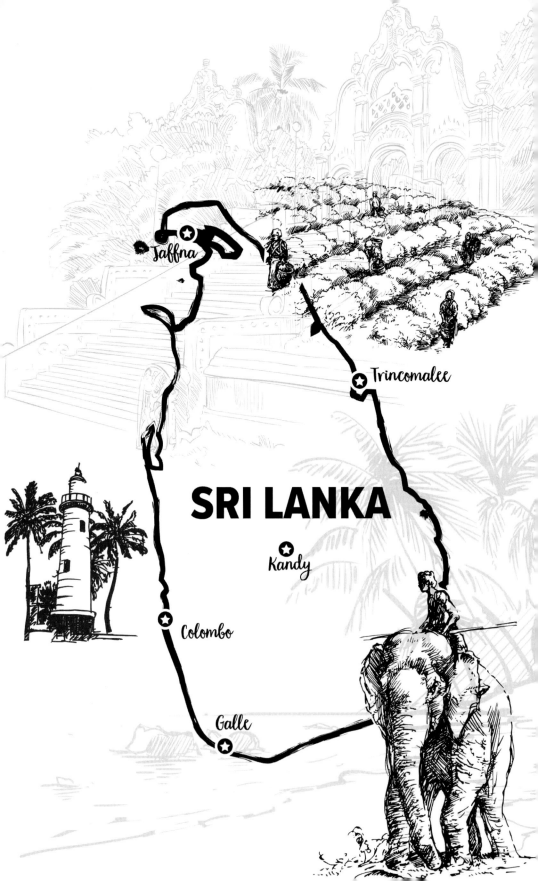

CHAPTER SEVEN

SRI LANKA

Green fields. Woods and forest. Tiled roofs of russet – and russet is my favourite colour. Lakes, ponds, villages. From the air, at 5,000 feet, Sri Lanka could be Sussex. Houses are socially distanced, each with its patch of ground, not crammed side by side as in most of South Asia – while in the alleyways they play cricket even more than in Sussex. The people may be shorter but the names are longer. Sri Lanka can outstrip Shoreham-on-Sea or Bognor Regis any day, as even the smallest settlement could be called Wijagunawardenehagarama.

Sri Lanka is larger than Wales and smaller than England, which makes it curious that the island was never a single polity until British colonisation. The Portuguese made their presence felt in ports; the Dutch searched for cinnamon; and the British wanted, above everything else, to keep out the French. In the central mountains around Kandy, meanwhile, the Sinhalese kings held out, their authority based on being the guardians of a relic of Buddha. It was like Wales before Edward I conquered: the mountains forbade a single ruler.

Closer inspection before landing identifies the fields as being designed for rice, and many trees are palms not oaks and elms; and the houses are not priced at £850,000 or £1.4m, for that is not a swimming pool in the garden but a pond left by the monsoon. After landing, the moment you leave your air-conditioned plane, you add another layer of epidermis: a film of sweat. Starting at Colombo airport, wash basins in Sri Lanka seldom have more than one tap because such is the ambient temperature there is no need for hot. This island on the equator is similar, superficially, to the West Indies.

Underneath this luxuriantly green surface, the similarities to England run deeper – though darkness lurks too – for this is the most Anglophile of all the Test-playing countries. If one connection is cricket, so too rugby, which is played with astonishing zeal, thanks to the rainfall softening the grounds. Rugby Union, of course, not League. The Christian missionaries of the 19th century would have preferred martyrdom, even burning at the stake, to being paid for playing for Featherstone or Hull Kingston Rovers.

Schools and colleges still bear the imprint of these Victorian missionaries. It seems as though anyone who is anyone has attended St Thomas or St Sebastian's or St Mary's, or Trinity or Holy Trinity, or Holy Family Convent or Ave Maria Convent or, in the absence of any other deities or saints, then Royal College. After these cricket and rugby matches, parents down whisky as heartily as the Raj did. Tonic water lives on in Sri Lanka, at least until sunset when it is drowned in gin.

"The London Grill" and the "London Coffee House" have been expunged from India as Hindu nationalism grows, and they may never have existed in Pakistan or Bangladesh; but in Sri Lanka, strident as Sinhalese Buddhism has sometimes been, the upper echelons have yet to reject the colonial past. Ceylon was not India, whose earth and people were compelled to yield their resources to Britain, and where some resentment was bound to remain. Like nowhere else I have found in the Commonwealth, one can still dine in Colombo as if one were in Oxford Street in the 1930s: the whitest of tablecloths in the London Grill, the napkins ironed, a waiter in dinner jacket taking your order for Beef Wellington: medium rare, sir? Very good. And after a proper pause – is that Somerset Maugham by the way at the next table? – he will set fire to the crêpes at your table with dashes of brandy and panache.

A Test match in Sri Lanka moves to much the same leisurely rhythm for the first half of its existence. It feels like weeks, but it can only be days, that I have spent at the Sinhalese Sports Club watching Sri Lanka, after winning the toss and not unsurprisingly electing to bat, score 570 for eight declared. Centuries by Kumar Sangakkara or Mahela Jayawardene were fine enough, indeed very fine, but a more obstinate customer, Thilan Samaraweera, pushed defiantly forwards on the slow pitch and averaged 77 at the ground. Samarawearisome, I came to think. But, like a breeze springing up, a refreshing change of tempo occurs on the last two days of a Test in Sri Lanka. After sweltering heat has made the pitch dust and disintegrate, the ball spits and the game does not peter out as a draw after all.

This may be fanciful, or self-deluding, but I sense among Sri Lankans a deeper respect for law than in most of Asia; and for Westminster-style democracy, even when Parliament degenerates into a boys' dormitory as at home. On a weekday morning, anywhere on the island, crisply uniformed schoolchildren – the boys wearing that most useless of inventions, especially in the tropics, the tie – line the roads; rural police stations are open buildings, not Soviet-style blocks; public libraries may be dilapidated yet they survive. The onslaught of American-style consumerism was delayed for a whole generation by the civil war. When one crosses the first half of a dual carriageway in Sri Lanka, one is not forced to look both ways, which has been known in South Asia.

* * *

The Galle Face Hotel in Colombo was cricket's first watering hole. London used to have a department store which boasted that, provided you stayed outside it long enough, you would meet everyone you knew. Similarly, the Galle Face was where from the late 19th century onwards you could meet most of the world's best cricketers. The first touring teams stayed there, whether English cricketers on the voyage to Australia, or the other way round.

In addition to cricketers, all manner of dignitaries have found their land legs amid the white marble columns, and savoured the sea breeze in their rooms or wicker armchairs: Emperor Hirohito and Sir Donald Bradman, for instance; both, in their way, were commanders of ruthless attacks. Obviously Somerset Maugham passed through, and Evelyn Waugh, while D.H. Lawrence – en route to Australia to write *Kangaroo* – still scowls behind his beard in the Terrace Bar, perhaps troubled by the thought he is betraying his roots by wallowing in such luxury? David Lloyd George and Alec Guinness were also guests, their partners not identified. All must have enjoyed gin slings and Collins cocktails on the terrace, while the sun slipped into the Indian Ocean like a well-oiled guest between the hotel sheets. Most of us muddle along, and scrape by, but such grand settings can delude us into thinking that we add up to more.

The Honourable Ivo Bligh, who captained the first England team to regain the Ashes, stayed at the Galle Face Hotel in 1882, not once but twice on the voyage out: his ship had been holed at night in the middle of the Indian Ocean by a poorly lit tramp steamer and barely made it back to Colombo for repair. Of delicate constitution, Ivo retired from cricket after this tour, though not quite 24, when his players had achieved the highest honours; only when he became

Lord Darnley and the owner of Cobham Hall in Kent did he find another purpose in life. Exactly 50 years later a captain of even more aristocratic bearing, Douglas Jardine, invited his two fast bowlers from the Nottinghamshire coalfield to dinner and plied them with plans for regaining the Ashes, marking out fielding positions with candles and cruets. Dinner does not have to be consumed quickly in Colombo, ambient temperatures being so warm.

From the 1960s, when cricket teams began travelling by plane, the Galle Face lost its pre-eminence to the MCG Hilton in Melbourne and the Taj Mahal Hotel in Bombay. (Before the 1960s a national team visiting Bombay would be put up at the Cricket Club of India at the Brabourne Stadium.) Once teams flew, Colombo was no longer on the beaten track until Sri Lanka were promoted to Test status in 1981. Besides, in the age of air conditioning, a sea breeze is not a prerequisite for sleep on a tropical night; new hotels, built inland, are not penalised for failing to have a prime location. Also, the Galle Face might not have been large enough to accommodate touring teams once they included coaches, physios, analysts and digital experts in almost the same quantity as players.

Yet, it is still the place for late afternoon tea and sundowners, if not dinner. I avoid a buffet dinner – the lugubrious meat has been cooked so many hours before – while tourists in shirts and sandals do not observe the dress code of "the good old days" when an essential ingredient of the England cricketer's trunk, whether amateur or professional, was a dinner jacket. Still, hedonism is seldom so quietly enjoyable as it is of an evening here.

* * *

Sri Lanka's first full-time national coach was Don Smith, of Sussex, who played three Tests for England in 1957. He told me in an interview that Sri Lankan cricketers were astonished in 1976/77 when they played against MCC, who paid a visit during their winning tour of India and were captained by Tony Greig, also of Sussex.

For the first time in their careers the Sri Lankan players found themselves verbally abused during their matches against MCC, as England were then called. The masters and coaches at their schools in Colombo had not introduced them to this world. "Sludging," they said to Smith. "What is this sludging?" Sri Lanka's age of innocence, in more ways than one, was about to end.

* * *

I never attended Eton v Harrow matches at Lord's in the 1920s – not until I saw Royal College v St Thomas in Colombo. Here the époque was still very "belle", and the "vita" still "dolce", so much so that Galsworthy's Forsytes would have been at home.

This annual cricket fixture is a three-day game, but whatever happens in the middle comes second to socialising. I attended one of these rituals at Tamil Union CC or, as it was renamed, the P. Sara Stadium in Colombo. The attendance was around 13,000. Old Boys had flown in from Canada, Britain and Australia to attend. The whisky was flowing faster than the River Clyde in full spate.

"Have another chota peg," an Old Boy shouts so loudly he almost drowns out the school band.

"Chin, chin, old boy!"

Newspaper coverage was staggering. On the day before this game the back pages of the daily papers had been covered with photographs and profiles of every player in both teams. Schoolboy cricket in Sri Lanka, like Premier League football in England, is the default back-page lead. Even Eton v Harrow at the height of the Edwardian era did not command such attention. Far more English than the English.

In the first recorded match between Royal College and St Thomas in 1879, masters were included on both sides, to drill values and discipline into their young teammates. So well trained were the boys that from 1880 they were permitted to play by themselves, untutored. It now claims to be the longest-running annual cricket fixture in the world after Eton v Harrow. On the first day of one Test match between Sri Lanka and England, the back pages were devoted to reports of the second day of Royal v Thomians, while a preview of the Test was confined to a column inside. What do you expect if a mere Test clashes with so mighty a match?

Back in the 1950s, so I was told by Ranjit Fernando, who kept wicket for Sri Lanka in the first World Cup in 1975, Ceylon were playing India and the hosts were not doing well on the final afternoon: they needed a partnership if they were to draw the match.

"Oxford or Cambridge, please save us!" a spectator shouted. Not your normal cry at Edgbaston or Old Trafford. At one end was John Arenhold, a South African, representing the country where he worked, and an Oxford Blue; at the other end was Gamini Goonesena, a wrist-spinning all-rounder. A couple of Sri Lankans, Oxbridge Blues, had represented Middlesex before the Second World War, but Goonesena was the best cricketer from the island to represent an English county, and New South Wales too, before Sri Lanka acquired Test status. He not only made the highest score for Cambridge in a Varsity Match, 211, but did the double of 1,000 runs and 100 wickets in 1955 and 1957.

Oxbridge graduates who came to be the headmasters of schools and colleges in Colombo not only instilled cricket and rugby into their pupils, but BBC pronunciation for generations to come. The fruitiest English accent you will hear nowadays outside Buckingham Palace is that of a Sri Lankan cricket commentator.

And so long as Sri Lankan cricket consisted of club matches between middle-class members of the European, Sinhalese, Tamil and Burgher communities in Colombo, in addition to prestigious school fixtures, it seems to have been fundamentally honest. When West Indies made their inaugural tour of India in 1948/49, they were verbally promised a share of the profits. Every day for months on end, without any time lost to rain, they played in front of packed stadiums; and, lo and behold, their share of the profits from this leg of their tour amounted to £10. In Ceylon, after playing for a fortnight on the same contractual basis, they were presented with a cheque for £500: so Jeff Stollmeyer, the West Indian opening batsman, narrated in his book *Everything Under The Sun*.

This upper-crust nature of Sri Lankan cricket was broken when a less than pukka boy was such a promising batsman that he was permitted to join Sinhalese Sports Club, the upper-crustiest of all the clubs in Colombo, once Europeans had left town. Shortly after joining SSC he was insulted to his face about his social origins by one snotty member. Highly motivated from that moment, Arjuna Ranatunga went on to represent Sri Lanka in their inaugural Test and to captain them to the 1996 World Cup. Only West Indies, twice, India, Australia and Pakistan had won the World Cup before. Ranatunga selected the best players, irrespective of their social background, and thereby set Sri Lanka's successful pattern: batsmen from the elite schools, bowlers from anywhere.

* * *

"I'm going to hit a six tomorrow," England's captain announced on the eve of the 1996 World Cup quarter-final against Sri Lanka. It was not the sort of pugnacious thing that an England captain said in those days, because it was not the sort of pugnacious thing that an England captain did in one-day cricket.

We were staying at the Serena Hotel in Faisalabad, when Mike Atherton passed a group of us in the reception area and made his announcement. The hotel was a far cry from the crumbling concrete dump where I had first stayed in the city, when it had only just changed its name from Lyallpur. England's players, however, were exhausted: their five-Test tour of South Africa had culminated in seven one-day internationals – seven – in less than a fortnight. Such a schedule ensured they were drained on arrival at the sixth World Cup, and their timing entirely out of sync with conditions in Pakistan and India. They reached the quarter-finals by winning nothing more than their games against the amateurs of the Netherlands and the United Arab Emirates.

The next day bore a similarity to the Crimean War. Then, 40 years had passed since the British Army had last been tested at Waterloo; and England's one-day cricket was similarly antiquated. Bat rather like a Test match to keep wickets in hand for a fling towards the end, then plenty of seam bowling to tie opponents down. In this quarter-final against Sri Lanka, England were 59 for two after 15 overs; nobody hit a six until Phil DeFreitas was promoted to No.5 and injected some impetus. England reached 235 for eight in their 50 overs, whereupon it hit them that one-day cricket had left them far behind.

Sri Lanka had topped their group, but this could be explained away: Australia and West Indies had refused to go to Colombo for their group matches owing to a terrorist threat, conceding the points, and so what if Sri Lanka made mincemeat of Zimbabwe and Kenya? The only sign that something special was afoot was their fielding which, under the Australian coaching of Dav Whatmore, was far better than it had ever been before; and their qualifying round win against India in Delhi, when Sri Lanka's opening pair were revealed as a novelty because they smashed the first ball, not to mention all those that followed. These openers were all-rounders, not specialists: Sanath Jayasuriya was one opener, as well as a left-arm spinner, the other Romesh Kaluwitharana, also their wicketkeeper. As a result of this doubling up, Sri Lanka needed only four bowlers, and packed their side with batsmen down to and including No.7. They allowed the opening pair to hit as they pleased, and hoovered up if anything went wrong.

In this quarter-final, Jayasuriya hit England for 82 from 44 balls. Nothing so old-fashioned as playing himself in; no fear of getting out cheaply; no allowing the bowler to settle into his spell. Thus far in the history of cricket, attacking was what bowlers did; now it was the openers, hitherto the most defensive of batsmen, who attacked. Some of the England players might have recalled Jayasuriya in the one-off Test at Lord's in 1991, when Sri Lanka's batsmen, set to bat out the last day, all lasted for an hour or two, as if it were another 50-over club game on which they were raised. While most scored around 20 in that time, Jayasuriya blazed 66 off 70 balls. Now he battered England until they did not know what had hit them. A 20th-century side was playing a team from the 21st.

When Jayasuriya was dismissed, Sri Lanka were 113 for two in the 13th over. Such a scoring rate is standard now – in T20. Back in 1996 this was Bob Beamon-plus: way beyond the limits of what the human imagination had thought possible. In the end, the margins of five wickets and 9.2 overs might have looked modestly close, but this was deceptive. The Light Brigade had been wiped out.

"Sri Lanka are going to win it," said Asif Iqbal, the former Pakistan captain who presided over the stadium at Sharjah and was a commentator: he told me that when our paths had crossed before the quarter-finals, when Sri Lanka were 66-1 with official bookmakers. Inexplicably, in the semi-final at Calcutta, India sent Sri Lanka in on a pitch which was certain to disintegrate in the game's second half – and did. So that was another obstacle hurdled by one means or another. India's captain was Mohammad Azharuddin, who was subsequently banned from cricket for life after he had been interrogated by India's Central Bureau of Investigation, before being pardoned later.

No question who was in command of the World Cup final in Lahore, after Australia had batted first and made a bright start. Sri Lanka's four spinners bowled for the rest of their innings. Four spinners, bowling at the death? Such things were undreamt of in England's philosophy. Ranatunga supplied solidity in the middle order, the steadiest of hands on the tiller, and a disdain for established orders, such as the one that had snubbed him. I was at the Gaddafi Stadium in Lahore that evening, but the celebrations in Sri Lanka were almost audible.

* * *

Lord's, like any other cricket ground, had grown accustomed to spectators running on the field whenever they felt like it, but that was normally at the end of a game, so they could applaud their heroes and be seen on television. When several dozen Tamil protesters ran on during Sri Lanka's inaugural Test in England this was a political demonstration such as Lord's had never seen before.

It was August 1984, and already the civil war had started, and the never-ending sequence of atrocity followed by reprisal. Two Sinhalese policemen were killed in Jaffna; the police responded by burning Jaffna's public library, where unique Tamil manuscripts and books were housed. A spark to light a conflagration.

In that Sri Lankan side at Lord's was a Tamil pace bowler, Vinothen John, a burly fellow who took four wickets in England's first innings, bowling mostly from the Pavilion End with good pace. Apart from John, only half-a-dozen or so Tamils – defined as those whose first language is Tamil – have represented Sri Lanka in Test cricket. It is disproportionately few, given they are one-seventh of the population.

* * *

In the almost ideal world that was Cricket BC (or Cricket Before Covid), or so it now seems, the most agreeable way to go to a ground was a walk of about a kilometre. Any less and the exercise is insufficient; any more and the backpack with a notebook, laptop and plugs, starts to feel weighty.

In England my favourite commute is from a hotel in Great Portland Street across Regent's Park, past the lake's swans and pedalos, to Lord's; or from the centre of Nottingham across the river to Trent Bridge. Other Test grounds involve car parks, often a distance away; or else trains, taxis and queuing. For some reason Birmingham New Street has barriers strategically placed so that only a couple of taxis per minute can exit. On foot, one can be sure of arriving either in time or on time.

In Galle, the walk from the Fort to the ground is no more than a few hundred yards. So near to the Equator, this is sufficient to warm up, and to nip back to the hotel at lunch time (or rather to avoid the media lunches which in Sri Lanka are all too copious). Two consecutive Tests at any ground is a little too samey, but then no journalists were allowed inside the Galle Stadium in January 2021: only a lone English spectator on the wall of the Fort.

In Galle itself, across the causeway which connects the Fort and on which the cricket ground stands, Sri Lanka's far-right party went on the rampage in search of minorities during the civil war. But in the Fort religions come closer to peaceful coexistence than anywhere I know.

Cinnamon was the big attraction for the *Vereenigde Oostindische Compagnie* (VOC), or Dutch East India Company, arguably the first multinational. A rather straggly tree, cinnamon grew in sparse soil on the south coast of Serendip, and the Dutch discovery brought about the word serendipity. When walking through the alleyways of the Fort, I bought some in a spice shop and it was nothing remotely like the sawdusty powder that coats an American apple pie. I chewed a strip of bark from a cinnamon tree: just a hint of cinnamon, rather than the overwhelming sawdust, with an overtone of sweetness like honey. A piece of bark is almost edible on its own; in coffee or tea it is a highly acceptable substitute for sugar. Try real cinnamon: a bite is as good as its bark.

Galle harbour, in a detailed sketch in the *Illustrated London News* of 1872, is filled with the tall masts of sailing ships at anchor, and fishermen's boats so narrow they are less than two feet wide, balanced by a fixed rigger on one side. It is argued that Galle was Tarshish of the Old Testament, from where King Solomon shipped his ivory, apes and peacocks. But as ships grew bigger, Galle's sharp coral sank them, so the Raj moved up the west coast to make

Colombo its main port en route to Australia. Once that was opened in 1875, Galle Fort was abandoned until UNESCO made it a world heritage site.

The Portuguese set up the first trading post, to be expanded when it was captured by the VOC, whereupon both the prison and the long white warehouse were packed with prisoners. It is nice to hear that Britain introduced trial by jury in 1811, if only for white men; while in Colombo a representative of each of the Sinhalese, Tamil and Burgher communities was nominated by the island's Governor to the Legislative Council from 1833. By then the Dutch had built the sewerage system "in which the high tide acted as a flush and the ebb tide removed the debris," according to Christopher Ondaatje in *Woolf in Ceylon*; and Dutch-designed drains still cope with monsoons by using the slight gradients.

No tall new concrete buildings are allowed to alter the skyline and disrupt the demographic balance by overwhelming the locals. Houses are so handsome, some with porches looking onto the straight streets: through unshuttered windows you see furniture of hard wood copied from European styles by local carpenters. Most restaurant menus are not advertised in the street with a national flag beside each language. It is in these streets the faiths live side by side. No synagogue, if Solomon ever endowed one, but here is a Buddhist temple and it is stocked with Hindu deities, as these two religions in Sri Lanka are intertwined like vines. Similarly, in the main square, an ancient banyan – gorgeous at night when lit from below – holds Hindu and Buddhist statues in its branches. Here is a Dutch Reformed Church, here an Anglican, here a Methodist, here a Roman Catholic, all painted white as white can be. Yet half the Fort's population is Muslim. They came from Batavia, or Malaya, or the south coast of Arabia, to trade in jewellery. Their mosque dates from the 1880s, and the call to prayer is never strident. In Southeast Asia many a mosque, funded by a Saudi prince, blasts out an amplified call to prayer, and long, recorded sermons raise the community's temperature.

Monkeys, eating hibiscus flowers on russet roofs, concentrate on their food as if they own the place. The Fort's circumference is little over a mile, on a road inside the ramparts and without a single pothole. I tried a couple of laps not long after dawn while the streets were still shaded. It was a rainy morning, but so what? Warm rain is delicious in Sri Lanka. Rudyard Kipling was wrong. In Galle Fort, East and West still meet.

* * *

At the other extreme of commuting comes Kandy – not the old ground of Asgiriya in the centre of town which belongs to Trinity School (it was the only school in the world to have a Test ground), but the new ground at Pallekele, out of town.

It's all right if you are one of the England or Sri Lankan cricketers or management staff, because police motorbikes roar ahead to blast a path down the middle of the narrow road, scattering stalls and carts selling piles of avocados and pineapples. The army also want to pile in with some of their vehicles, along with a fire engine and an ambulance. This convoy is followed in hot pursuit by cars and tuk-tuks which cannot resist this rare opportunity to drive along this road at more than 15kph.

For lesser mortals the drive from Kandy to Pallekele is unconscionably slower. The journey might only be ten kilometres, but one has to estimate that it will take the worst part of an hour. As in the rest of South Asia, the Highway Code can be summarised in two words: biggest first. So, once the cricket convoy has shot past, the pride of place goes to lorries which ignore the double yellow line in the middle of the road and merrily swerve into your lane, roaring, fuming, and accelerating until you see nothing but LANKA ASHOK LEYLAND bearing down on your taxi. If I could remember my dreams, most would consist of subcontinental lorries and buses about to crush me. LANKA ASHOK lorries are assembled locally, but some have been imported from India, displaying the maker's name TATA. It seems the apposite word, as the moment rapidly approaches when one has to say goodbye.

As on the coastal plains, rugby is surprisingly popular in Kandy, which has a ground in its centre beside the old prison; so tuk-tuk drivers on the Pallekele Road know how to swerve like outside centres, especially where there are no pavements so they can swerve both ways at pace. Newer tuk-tuks have a lock on them, so they cannot pirouette on a 20-rupee note and turn over, but the older sort can resemble Darcey Bussell in her prime. None of them has a glass window except for the windscreen; they are open to the air on either side, unless it is raining and the canopy is drawn down. Even then you cannot keep out whatever the Sinhalese term is for "carbon emissions", assuming there is one.

If you select this mode of transport, and your tuk-tuk driver is at all worldly-wise, he will seize on the fact that you have come from England to watch the cricket, and he will soon devise a plan that could pay off his mortgage. A day trip to the Tea Country, sir? Or else take you back to Colombo after the Test, which would take seven or eight hours in his tuk-tuk? If you do say yes, and are too tall to sit up straight in a tuk-tuk, you will bang your head on the bar that holds up the canopy at least a hundred times.

In addition to cars, lorries, buses, carts, cycles, motorbikes, tuk-tuks and the odd elephant – this, after all, is a trunk road – are the dogs which decide to cross the road to Pallekele. If most drivers were not Buddhist, these dogs would not get a yard across the road before being flattened; but the respect for life – the possibility the dog might be a relative – allows them to cross miraculously, like firewalkers stamping over a fire. Pedestrians, being more rational creatures, do not try to cross the road, except if they can find a zebra crossing, pack down like rugby forwards and charge in numbers. The absence of pavements works two ways, both to the driver's advantage: pedestrians have nowhere safe to go, while he always has an escape route.

As Kandy is the Sinhalese cultural centre, numerous are the Buddhist monasteries, and Buddhist Cultural Centres, and Buddhist bookshops, and monks robed in orange. Doctrinal differences aside, few of these monks bear any similarity to the Dalai Lama (I once stood a yard in front of him and, as he walked past, his eyes looked straight into me like nobody else has done). Some monks in Sri Lanka could walk straight into their local rugby team. No tuk-tuk driver is going to mess with them: stocky, close-cropped and armed with stick or stave.

As the start of play draws near, what could be better than inching uphill while being overtaken by tuk-tuks on the inside and lorries on the outside? But, if you think yourself unfortunate, look at the signs outside several establishments on the Pallekele Road that proclaim "Wedding Suite available". Their plate-glass windows are blurred with dust, their red curtains less than five yards from the road, and shaking. The music on many a wedding night will be dominated by bus drivers demonstrating their horn's latest tunes. I suppose these establishments can at least guarantee that the earth will move for the happy couple.

Eventually your vehicle swerves to the right into a green expanse of valley and you have arrived at Pallekele. Older, dustier, more migrainous, yet surprised and delighted, not only at the navigational skill of all concerned, but at human nature too. In all that snarling bedlam of traffic, on a road which Dante would have seized upon as a path to Hell, you have not seen a single angry face or heard an impatient word.

* * *

Kandy has the air of an Indian hill station, except that the air is hotter. The views may be as sumptuous as in the Nilgiris if you are staying at the top of a hill and look over the Mahaweli River, which is dammed, so that trees along its banks are reflected in limpid muddy water, but well before 8am the mist will have been burnt off. Do not be startled by what sounds like a gun but is a firecracker thrown at a wild boar, intruding to dig up gardens.

The focus of Kandy is the Temple of the Tooth. The focus of the Temple is the Buddha's tooth. One might deduce from his doctrines that the Buddha was ascetic and lean, but not according to statues, which portray him as being at the opposite end of the scales. And this larger-than-life image does fit with the size of his tooth, which is 3in long, according to Leonard Woolf. He saw it several times in 1911 when working in Kandy for the Ceylon civil service, before marrying Virginia.

Near the Temple is the Queen's Hotel, yet to be renovated because mass tourism has not reached Kandy apart from cricket followers; it is the cultural tourist who visits. A walk round Kandy's lake, no more than 1.7 miles, can be attempted because there is a pavement, unlike on the road to Pallekele, and it is largely shaded. Some trees dip a branch into the waters to sip the lake, as delicately as female members of the Kandy Club took their tea around the time of the First World War – or more so if they came hot from the tennis courts.

One could be walking round Lake Como at the height of summer, for there stands the Hotel Suisse, except for the monks who are carrying an umbrella, whether parasol or parapluie.

Although most of Sri Lanka's cricketers have come from Colombo, Kandy has given birth to the country's finest batsman and bowler. Kumar Sangakkara benefited from the extra bounce that cricket pitches have in the hills, especially at Asgiriya, where he played for Trinity School. He had to learn how to play off the back foot, unlike his contemporaries in Colombo who could play forward to almost anything. Thus, so he told me in an interview, he was equipped when he went down to Colombo to become a lawyer, and joined Nondescripts CC as a way of passing his weekends. Unlike any other Sri Lankan, he averaged 60 in Asia and almost 50 outside. Only Sachin Tendulkar, of those batsmen I have seen, seemed to programme his brain as well as the mature Sangakkara, who studied the conditions and bowlers he had to face, and rehearsed in the nets every stroke he was going to play in the next innings. One exception? He did not rehearse against the simple full toss and was sometimes dismissed by the worst ball he faced.

Sangakkara also gave what must be the finest speech by any international cricketer. The MCC Spirit of Cricket annual lecture has been delivered by a range of individuals from poachers to gamekeepers. Nothing, in the world of sport, could have been more moving than Sangakkara describing the anti-Tamil riots of his childhood in Kandy, when his family hid Tamil friends in his house from the Sinhalese mob. He ended his speech by proclaiming he was a Buddhist and a Christian and a Hindu and a Muslim, a Sinhala and a Tamil and a Burgher and a Malay: he was a Sri Lankan.

Sangakkara was not my all-time favourite Sri Lankan batsman, however, nor his companion in huge partnerships, Mahela Jayawardene. It was Roy Dias, for whom the promotion to Test status came a little too late, as he was already 29. He nevertheless batted like a combination of Michael Slater and Sunil Gavaskar in that he drove as firmly as an Australian but also had the wristy strokes square of the wicket of an Indian. Dias scored a dazzling 80 against England at Pune in the 1987 World Cup – with a straightish bat he hit a six that soared over midwicket – and left me wanting more. Sri Lankan batting at its best, I would say, is not the most beautiful but the handsomest: those missionaries instructed their charges to use their leading elbow à la MCC and, to this orthodoxy, a little Asian wristiness has been added, but not half so much as in India. The first Sri Lankan to be named a *Wisden* Cricketer of the Year, Sidath Wettimuny, who scored 190 against England at Lord's in 1984, told me in the interview for his profile that he and his two brothers, who also represented Sri Lanka, were brought up on a coaching book by C.B. Fry.

If Sangakkara authored the noblest words by an international cricketer – Samuel Beckett represented Trinity College, Dublin at cricket, not Ireland itself – then Muttiah Muralitharan was the author of the finest deeds. His father was a humanitarian, who visited the old Kandy prison and gave out food parcels to prisoners. The prison was none too humane when Woolf had to attend executions before the First World War, and overcrowding became abominable before the construction of a new jail at Pallekele.

When Muralitharan was on course to becoming the highest wicket-taker in Test history, all 800 of them, I visited the factory which his father owned, making the Lucky brand of biscuits, on the outskirts of Kandy. If the machinery and conveyor belts were rudimentary, the workers – mostly women – appeared content in their work. They were transported to and from their homes by company bus, a generous provision in parts of the world where so much time is spent waiting for public transport, and wasted.

The boy, grinning mischievously yet inwardly insecure, was the father of the man. He was sent as a boarder to St Anthony's College in Kandy – Roman Catholic whereas Trinity is Anglican. I met his housemaster, who remembered Muttiah in the dormitory for his grinning and spinning, for even at school he was a wicket-taker, using his wrist with its unique physiognomy: a trait running in his family. Murali had to perform in the annual fixture against Trinity, in front of crowds up to 10,000: both school grounds have large stands to accommodate old boys as well as present pupils. In one Test, Sri Lanka's spin attack consisted of three former St Anthony's boys: Ruwan Kalpage, Piyal Wijetunge and Muralitharan. Not even 19th century Eton or Harrow could match that.

Muralitharan came from the Tamil community of the Tea Country, or Indian Tamils, whom the British had imported as bonded labourers to work the tea plantations in the 19th century. They usually had to borrow money for their passage from their south Indian village across Palk Strait, and often the terms were such that they never paid off their debts. And they were stateless, citizens neither of India nor Sri Lanka, some until as late as 2003. Depoliticised too: for safety's sake, surrounded by Sinhalese, they – including Murali – stayed out of the civil war involving the Jaffna or Sri Lankan Tamils, who had inhabited the island's north for more than a thousand years.

When the tsunami struck on Boxing Day 2004, Murali was driving from Colombo to a charity event at the Foundation of Goodness on the west coast, until he saw a policeman running towards him to tell everyone to turn inland. On 28 December, having liaised with the UN's World Food Programme, he loaded up one of his father's lorries and along with two others set off for the northern area governed by the Tamil Tigers. Part of the food he was donating were Lucky biscuits, and lucky the people who received his humanitarian aid. I can see him grinning at the wheel, disarming border guards, using his fame entirely for the benefit of others from all communities, while governments around the world made promises of aid for tsunami victims which has yet to materialise.

Murali loaded up his lorry again and drove to the east coast, around Trincomalee, and the south coast. He learnt how more than 30,000 died; and how the best way to survive the immense waves was to climb a palm tree, because palms knew how to bend with the wind and could do the same with the sea. He heard about a six-month-old baby that had been placed on a mattress in a bedroom: nobody had been able to reach the baby until the wave had devastated the house then receded. There, like Noah's Ark after the Flood, was the baby still in the middle of the mattress, alive.

* * *

Sri Lanka have won the 20-over World Cup, and the 50-over World Cup, and were a successful Test team between 2005 and 2016. They did so because they had some outstanding individuals, who were largely the product of the island's elite schools (Sanath Jayasuriya and Chaminda Vaas were the two main exceptions). It was not on the strength of their domestic structure that they flourished.

The government has always held a grip on the national cricket board. After the selectors had chosen a national squad, their list would often have to be submitted to the Minister of Sport for his approval. But when a window briefly opened, and Wettimuny became the interim leader of the board, he brought in Jayawardene and Sangakkara to advise, and they recommended a domestic first-class structure of five or six teams – much like Australia, which also has a population of just over 20 million and six first-class teams.

But Sri Lanka stuck to its existing structure and even expanded their number of first-class teams to 24. It makes no cricketing sense to take every club in the Colombo area – Moors, Nondescripts, SSC, Chilaw Marians – and suddenly make them play, not 50-over club matches as before, but three-day first-class matches without a huge investment in new infrastructure. Only in one way does it make sense: every club when it becomes a first class team has a vote, and that vote can be bought by presents to its officials, and thereby those in power stay in power.

Yet one problem still remains: Sri Lanka is Colombo-centric. Suppose you do organise the island into six first-class teams, how do you go about it when almost every player lives and plays in Colombo or its outskirts? Kandy has grown to the point where it could have a first-class team of its own, with a few locally-born players, notably the excitable wicketkeeper Niroshan Dickwella, from Sangakkara's school if not exactly the same mould. But how can you send a player, born and bred in Colombo, to represent a region he has never been to before? In the Lanka Premier League in December 2020, one team was named Jaffna, but the players did not come from there, and the matches were staged in Colombo. Pakistan at the outset had a similar problem in having only two major cities, Karachi and Lahore, but subsequently Multan and Rawalpindi and others grew to become cricket centres.

* * *

Taking the train from Kandy to Colombo is a pleasure for every sense save the nasal. At the start of Platform 2 in Kandy, the urinals of "the Rest Room for Gents" might not have been properly cleared out since the station was built in the 1860s. Unlike most stations, however, this one has a bookcase, below a sign in Sinhalese. As the express to the capital was delayed (the similarities with Sussex never end), the *Social History of Early Ceylon* by H. Ellawala whiled away my time – and contradicted Woolf's statement that "there is no caste system in Buddhism." After the new religion had arrived from India in the 4th century AD, the number of castes was effectively reduced from four to two (no more Brahmins). In the cities of Sri Lanka, money has replaced caste as the key social factor.

In Far North Queensland I once took a skytrain over a canopy of rainforest. The Kandy train goes *through* rainforest. The Raj built a botanical garden outside Kandy to cultivate different kinds of coffee and tea; but for a whole hour after leaving Kandy the train rattles along – any pace bowler would be proud to gain so much sideways movement – in tropical luxuriance. Streams pour through culverts under the single wide-gauge track, and carry on sparkling down the mountainside. Vines and grasses are red and yellow. Could we but see them, leopards perch on branches and look down, yawning. It is sufficiently beautiful to make you giddy if looking outside your window has not already done so. Several signs, standing above a pretty sheer drop into the valley below, proclaim: 25kph WEAK RAILS AND SLEEPERS. Matt Prior, having seen one, concentrated on his book. It is a risk worth taking, however, to inhabit for an hour this primitive world in which nature has not been made subservient to man.

* * *

Colombo eventually resumed its status as cricket's chief watering-hole, in the shape of the Cinnamon Grand. This hotel is not so grand as the most palatial hotels of Dubai and Abu Dhabi, or even some of the new hotels in Colombo that have sprung up along the waterfront since the civil war, where Chinese and Indian investors have moved in. Yet the doormen of the Cinnamon, in their white gloves and bow ties, who admit one to the delicious cool – it is the opposite of coming home in winter to a warm fire – are dressed more smartly than I have ever been.

The Cinnamon is not one of those hotels from which locals are, in effect, excluded. Right beside is a shopping centre with a food court where at almost any time of day a cricket match is being played on television, live or repeated. If one had had the misfortune to forget the finer points of the third one-day international between Bangladesh and Zimbabwe five years ago, one can catch up over a Mongolian hot pot or nasi goreng.

The Cinnamon is all the more congenial for being spacious, with a couple of tennis courts in the grounds, two gyms and more than half-a-dozen restaurants, a couple nestling around the large swimming pool. It is not a soulless, sanitised, seven-star prison. And I am all for everyone having a job, but not if it is wiping the dust off every glass bauble of a chandelier before winching it back up to the ceiling.

When two England coaches of recent times, Trevor Bayliss and his deputy Paul Farbrace, were in charge of Sri Lanka, they used to live in this hotel; and when they returned to Colombo with England, far from sick of the Cinnamon, they resumed their armchairs in the coffee shop. They watched the cricket world go by as benignly as a pair of affable aunts in their favourite tea room in Southsea or Margate. Isn't that the new Australian umpire on the international panel? The South Africans, who have arrived for a tri-series, don't they have the No.1 in the batting and bowling rankings – A.B. de Villiers, now he has come out of retirement again, and Kagiso Rabada with his seriously smooth run-up? Have you seen that English school team who are going down to Galle – apparently they have a very promising young batter at Hampshire's academy.

> In the coffee shop cricketers come and go
> Talking of AB and Kagiso.

Live music is played much of the day, whether a pianist in the morning or a quartet of an evening. A Parisian pâtisserie would not sneer at the tortes and tarts and truffles, cooling in the coffee shop's glass displays. If the women do not seem quite so seductive as in the foyer of Mumbai's Taj, where receptionists float like yachts, then some are slim and sari'd – and a hair salon adjoins the coffee shop, so that daughters emerge at their finest to rejoin mothers or fiancés. Between the tables and sofas a waiter moves deftly with a fly swat, square-cutting like the finest of Sri Lankan batsmen, leaving no fly unmiddled. Best of all, the sons of Sri Lankan society do not exude the same sense of entitlement as those of India, where all too often the attitude of the first-born son is that of one who has never been denied.

Every department of the Cinnamon has its own cricket team when the hotel organises its annual competition. Only six-a-side, and ten-over games, but still; the last time I heard, the competition had been appropriately won by the Health Club. And as lattes are sipped in the coffee shop, coiffures assessed and gossip exchanged, one catches sight of a pair of male eyes. It is not the resigned, bloodshot stare of one who has spent a lifetime consuming drugs or betel nut. This is an expression which is alive, but haunted. He is fit and strong, too, this middle-aged Sri Lankan who may be talking – at times earnestly – to his wife. Nothing ostentatious in his word or manner, nothing overtly wrong, except for that expression in his eyes; and it is only after returning to one's book or conversation, and looking again later at this man, that a rupee drops: that he could have been one of the many thousands conscripted for the civil war, who saw action in the Jaffna Peninsula or the Vanni or Mannar, who may have been involved – under orders – in the genocide at the end, and who will never forget the horror.

Those were the days. A couple of terrorists then checked into the Cinnamon Grand in 2019 and committed carnage next day at breakfast-time.

* * *

Sri Lankan girls' schools, like one beside the lake in Kandy, may have a cricket net on an all-weather concrete surface. Otherwise, from the perspective of an England cricket tour, the sport in Sri Lanka appears very male – more so than India, as much as in Bangladesh or Pakistan. Off the field there might be a woman in the board's media department, or one working for the television broadcaster, but on average I have seen fewer than one female official per tour. Women do not appear until the end of a match-day or a game, when the men are leaving, and they have to sweep the stands and collect the rubbish, or change the sheets in the hotel. At least the country now has Chamari Atapattu as an exciting role model.

The trouble is that, after the civil war, Sri Lanka has buried its past too hastily. Maybe the island is not simply the shape of a tear drop. Maybe the island is a tear which has yet to be wiped away.

Merely in the sphere of cricket, there was never a commission of inquiry into match-fixing, such as India had in the probe by its Central Bureau of Investigation and Pakistan had in the form of the Qayyum inquiry. The allegations made in the CBI report about Sri Lankan players were never followed up. The darkness was never exposed to daylight. Four Sri Lankan international cricketers, most notably Jayasuirya, have been banned by the ICC, more than any other Test-playing country. Their Anti-Corruption Unit has warned that Sri Lanka is the one country where people can get killed if caught up in match-fixing.

I still do not see how there was a way to end the civil war except militarily so long as the Tamil Tigers leader Velupillai Prabhakaran was still alive: he was, inter alia, implacable. But the evidence is persuasive that genocide took place as the war was in the act of being won. Afterwards the truth commission appointed by the government was nothing like the one in South Africa that helped to heal some of the wounds inflicted by apartheid. In 1999 the UN ranked Sri Lanka second in the world table for the highest numbers of enforced disappearances. Two decades later, and a decade after the war, Sri Lanka withdrew from the UN Human Rights Council.

> *"The Sri Lankan Government has launched a renewed crackdown on dissent that is severely curtailing civil society freedom and obstructing efforts to deliver justice for conflict-era crimes under international law,"* said Amnesty International in February 2021. *"The report, 'Old Ghosts in New Garb: Sri Lanka's return to fear', exposes how the Sri Lankan government has targeted human rights organisations, media, lawyers, political opponents, and law enforcement officers in a concerted bid to suppress opposing voices and hamper the transitional justice process for crimes committed during the country's 30-year armed conflict."*

We have to be careful here. "The whole apparatus of peace is sometimes colonial and racist in that it implies the transference of enlightened knowledge to those who lack the capability or morality to attain such knowledge themselves." So the editors of *Post-War Reconstruction in Sri Lanka* warned, quoting Oliver Richmond. OK, but here goes.

Trincomalee on Sri Lanka's east coast was hit not only by the civil war – at its maximum extent the Tamil Tigers stronghold reached to the north side of the town – but also by the tsunami. Even as late as 2018, when I travelled there from Colombo, it had not been exactly rebuilt and few jobs were available apart from subsistence fishing. No postcards of the place – with all its natural advantages and historical associations – were on sale. I was reminded of the north coast of Jamaica and several beaches in Australia: Trinco is up with them for natural setting; and if it is people who make places, the courteous, innocent, unexploiting nature of its population makes Trinco even more of a delight.

Lads were playing with bat and ball on scrubland outside the main bus station, opposite the Kali Temple: an ideal place for a cricket stadium right in the centre of town. The train station is a kilometre away, although it takes ten hours to reach it on the overnight train from Colombo: if the rolling stock were upgraded, and the concrete sleepers had the odd shock-absorber, England supporters would choose this mode of transport. Across a neck of land, little more than a kilometre away, is what Nelson called "the finest natural harbour in the world", all ready for the affluent to arrive by yacht or cruise ship. It is more sheltered than Sydney Harbour, so the waterskier, jetskier or parasailor could not ask for anything smoother.

Galle's ground can never seat more than 5,000 people, or have floodlights, because UNESCO would not allow it. Trincomalee could accommodate thousands of overseas visitors along its beaches. Innocence may be lost, but more and better incomes earned. Material reconstruction – the building of an international cricket stadium in Trincomalee – would, or might, lead to economic prosperity and reintegration. Not integration, but reintegration: Sinhalese and Tamils used to live side by side until colonisation came along to divide and rule.

ENGLAND IN SRI LANKA
1981/82 — 2020/21

—————————————— Overall ——————————————
Played **36**   Won **17**   Lost **8**   Drawn **11**

—————————————— In Sri Lanka ——————————————
Played **18**   Won **9**   Lost **5**   Drawn **4**

—————————————— In England ——————————————
Played **18**   Won **8**   Lost **3**   Drawn **7**

England's record at each venue

—————————————— Galle International Stadium ——————————————
Played **7**   Won **3**   Lost **2**   Drawn **2**

—————————————— Sinhalese Sports Club, Colombo ——————————————
Played **5**   Won **2**   Lost **2**   Drawn **1**

—————————————— Asgiriya Stadium, Kandy ——————————————
Played **3**   Won **1**   Lost **1**   Drawn **1**

—————————————— P. Sara Oval. Colombo ——————————————
Played **2**   Won **2**   Lost **0**   Drawn **0**

—————————————— Pallekele International Cricket Stadium ——————————————
Played **1**   Won **1**   Lost **0**   Drawn **0**

Series won	Captain
1981/82	Keith Fletcher†
2001/01	Nasser Hussain
2018/19	Joe Root
2020/21	Joe Root

†One-match series

Highest scores

228	Joe Root	Galle	2020/21
186	Joe Root	Galle	2020/21
151	Kevin Pietersen	Colombo (P. Sara)	2011/12
146*	Keaton Jennings	Galle	2018/19
128	Robin Smith	Colombo (SSC)	1992/93

Best bowling

6-33	John Emburey	Colombo (P. Sara)	1981/82
6-40	James Anderson	Galle	2020/21
6-82	Graeme Swann	Galle	2011/12
6-106	Graeme Swann	Colombo (P. Sara)	2011/12
5-28	Derek Underwood	Colombo (P. Sara)	1981/82

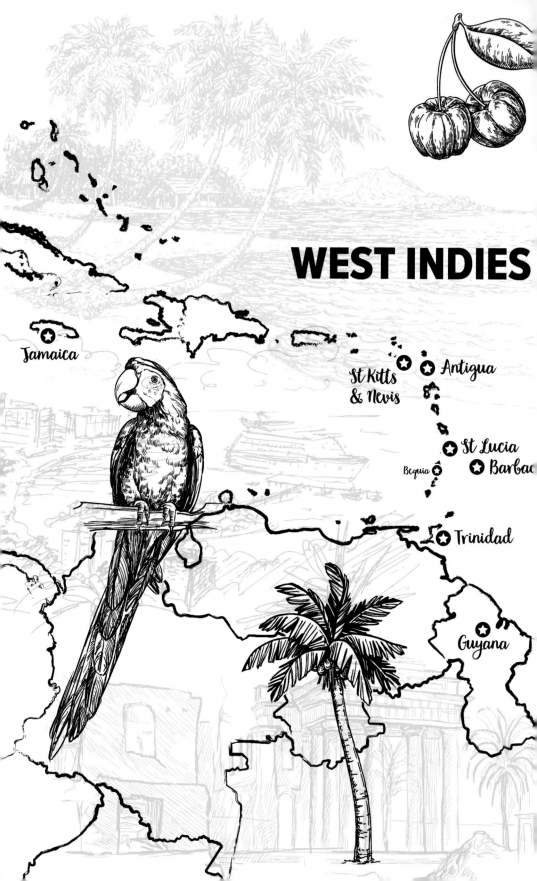

WEST INDIES

Jamaica

St Kitts & Nevis

Antigua

St Lucia

Bequia

Barba[c]

Trinidad

Guyana

CHAPTER EIGHT

WEST INDIES

Michael Holding was fielding at fine leg as I recall – more than 40 years have passed yet the memory remains vivid – and he had about 20 yards to run to his right to pick up the ball. The shot that had been played might have been a hook, or more likely an involuntary fend-off, by one of England's left-handed batsmen, perhaps David Gower, in this Kingston Test in early 1981. But it could have been a hook, because this was one belter of a pitch if you could bat, one of those old-time West Indian pitches. Walk out there before the start and you could see, not the actual details of your face as in a mirror, but an outline of your head reflected in the surface. Sabina Park's groundsman had gone up and down his pitch, twisting the roller from side to side, ripping out the blades of grass until the surface was bare, then polishing and buffing up the sheen until the pitch almost dazzled – unlike England's batting in this series.

What happened next was the most astonishing athleticism I have seen on a cricket field, and the most extraordinary sound I have heard at a cricket ground. Holding, running to his right, did not bend down, he simply extended his right arm telescopically, swooping and scooping the ball up. Then he jumped in the air, as so many Jamaican athletes do, including Holding in his schooldays doing track and field. But he not only leapt in the air, he swivelled or pirouetted to face almost the opposite direction, with his momentum still taking him to his right, and while in mid-air threw the ball back to the wicketkeeper on the full. Sabina Park's boundaries never have been long but still, try running one way, picking the ball up and while in mid-air throwing it 50 yards in almost the opposite direction from which you have come. Most of us would end up on the ground in a ruptured heap. Holding, head high, sauntered back to his place.

The crowd meanwhile emitted a sound I have never otherwise heard. The press box was at the opposite end for that Test, in the George Headley Stand, and therefore open not enclosed, and when Holding leapt and pirouetted, I heard the crowd groan in something like ecstasy. And Jamaicans, of all people, know athleticism when they see it, for this is the island of Don Quarrie and Merlene Ottey, Arthur Wint and Herb McKenley, and, more recently, Usain Bolt, Asafa Powell and Yohan Blake, in addition to the great cricketers: Headley himself, Collie Smith, cut down before his prime, Lawrence "Yagga" Rowe, and the greatest T20 batsman Chris Gayle.

This groan – it went deeper than admiration or patriotic pride – was Sabina Park's initial, spontaneous reaction. As Holding sauntered back, it turned into an eruption of applause, and not only human voices cheering and shouting, but musical instruments like steel drums, and all sorts of banging on wooden benches, and maybe the odd conch-shell joining in, as the crowd gave praise to *their* Mikey. It could have been a coronation, of one of the people by the people, except that Holding had been crowned in 1976 after taking 14 wickets on the flattest of Oval pitches.

England's players were also affected by the sight of West Indian cricketers. Through the 1980s England played West Indies in 24 Tests. The score was 17-0 – and not to England. When Micky Stewart became England's first full-time coach in the mid-Eighties he immediately noticed how overawed the players were. "In all my time in sport I'd never experienced top players, really top players, speaking in such awe of their opponents. Out in the Caribbean I think the England players, even the experienced ones, had got to the point where they were going into games accepting that they were going to come second. It was terrible." Terrible perhaps, but understandable, even rational. West Indies v England in the 1980s, in terms of physicality, was men against boys.

England were not alone in regarding West Indies as masters of the cricket universe. West Indies' score against all Test countries in the 1980s was 43-8. An Australian colleague would, as part of his job, meet touring teams at the airport on their arrival in Australia. He observed English players exiting from customs and immigration in ones and two, pushing their trolleys perhaps, eyes down, their bodies saying: "I've played county cricket in England, and I'd like to play some Tests out here, and it would be nice to win a game." The West Indians would emerge together in their maroon blazers, strolling nonchalantly, heads high, and were 2-0 up against Australia before a ball was bowled.

I mean, having first seen West Indies live in the 1969 Test at Headingley – how did Roy Fredericks point his maroon cap upwards at an angle like a miner's lamp? – and having seen not only Rohan Kanhai and Bernard Julien score centuries in their 652 for eight at Lord's in 1973, but Sir Garfield Sobers stroking his last Test hundred, 150 not out, and then having covered all their Tests against England through the 1980s and beyond, I could not understand how anybody could view West Indians as being in any way inferior to white people. Not only physically, for the best cricket book to this point, having been published in 1963, was indubitably C.L.R. James's *Beyond a Boundary*. The only mural I have painted, on the wall of my first flat, was a reproduction of the sketch on the back of his paperback edition, of palm trees, an open book and a set of stumps.

Michael Holding had given me an interview on the West Indies tour of England in 1980. When he retired to the commentary box, he immediately stood out as one of the very few former players who did not automatically look down on those of us who have not played Test cricket. Integrity, too: I have spent long hours talking to him about match-fixing, even if the libel lawyers have seldom been satisfied with sufficient proof. Have you noticed how television commentators do not mention match-fixing? They have to protect the value of their product, but could there be more to it?

Ethically, too. Of all Test-playing nations, without proof but also without question, West Indies have sledged the least.

Education is the only answer, or re-education. In so far as cricket is concerned, the Bodyline series of 1932/33 is ingrained in English folklore as the time when Don Bradman could not stand up to Harold Larwood and Bill Voce. Yet we completely disregard the subsequent MCC, i.e. England, tour of the West Indies.

England rested their main bowlers in 1934/35 after two hard winters. They did not rest their main batsmen. Five of their top six – Wally Hammond, Patsy Hendren, Maurice Leyland, Les Ames and the captain Bob Wyatt – scored more than 600 first-class centuries between them. Only Hendren had passed his prime. Yet the highest average of any England batsman in that series was 28, while George Headley averaged 97 for West Indies.

England's batsmen, their top batsmen, could not cope with the West Indian fast bowling. Constantine was warned for short-pitched bowling. Martindale broke Wyatt's jaw. None of the hosts' three pace bowlers – Martindale, Constantine and Les Hylton – averaged so much as 20. This piece of history has, in effect, been suppressed.

* * *

SS *Medway* was piloted into the Careenage in Bridgetown and moored on 28 January 1895. Arriving in the West Indies is exhilarating at any time. The Caribbean can span the spectrum of blueness from aquamarine to navy in the space of a gaze; palms are rich green, casuarinas sway like dancing girls, and if the sand on some beaches is not golden yellow but the light brown of caster sugar, it looks all the more appetising. Arriving by night is magical because of the sounds, if not sights: nature's band of tree frogs, creaking in time like an old water wheel, backed by lower-pitched cicadas, is almost as tuneful as Mozart's *Eine Kleine Nachtmusik.*

Thirteen young bucks from England had sailed on the *Medway* to Bridgetown for the first cricket tour of the West Indies. What better way to escape the English winter than to combine two of life's greatest pleasures, visiting the West Indies and playing cricket? Most of the players were members of MCC, moustached, young and fancy-free, so a third of life's pleasures was not inconceivable. On going ashore at the Careenage, they would have been almost intoxicated before the speeches and rum punch. Named in India after its five (or 'panj') ingredients, the punch might have had an impact on R.S. Lucas's party because, instead of a gentle net next day to find their land-legs, they agreed to play their first game, against Barbados, at what is now Kensington Oval. They were dismissed for 48.

Barbados is the same shape as Sri Lanka: a pearl orientated north-south, or a tear drop falling to earth. Not the same size, though: Barbados is much smaller, only 14 miles at its widest, so almost everywhere you can see the sparkling Caribbean to the west or Atlantic to the east. These luminous glimpses are like laughter in a conversation, brightening up your day.

"Barbados is not paradise unalloyed," wrote the late Jan Morris, doyen then doyenne of travel writers, but "well away from the clubs and big hotels, you may well feel yourself in some lingering old Arcadia … The people of Barbados have the oldest, homeliest, quaintest,

200

most rustic and evocative of accents, with a rich West Country burr and a thin sliver of Irish on top of it, like cream. It [Barbados] seems to be inhabited only by kind and courteous people."

Morris wrote this in the 1950s, after attending a service at St John's church on the east coast, but so much of it still applies because the social fabric has not unravelled as much as in most societies. It is a country that still has yellow school buses and red pillar boxes. The bell still tolls each quarter of an hour in the tower above the barracks at the Garrison, while other public clocks in the region have not stirred for decades. Racehorses in the Garrison stables are still bathed in the surf at dawn. It was here that the inaugural first-class cricket match in the West Indies was staged, when Barbados hosted Demerara, later to be British Guyana, in 1865; and not only George Washington's former house but most of the infrastructure surrounding the Garrison has not altered.

Outside Bridgetown you see the old Bajan way of life when a driver on a country road halts to talk to a friend at a bus stop; even when he slows down simply to toot his horn in recognition of someone ("it's all in the beep," said a colleague when we were driving to Crane beach). You see it in the unattended roadside stalls of fruit and vegetables, where you are expected to leave the right money for the gardener who has grown them. Such glimpses into human nature in Barbados buoy one as much as a sight of the sea.

Institutions have slowed down the fabric's unravelling. On attaining the age of 100, a Barbadian citizen is visited by the Governor-General, or the President as it is now: the citizen does not have the hassle of travelling, but receives the head of state at home. Thus the centenarian Coral Agard had her hair done two days before her 100th birthday, according to the *Daily Nation*, and received Dame Sandra Mason, who talked and toasted Coral's health. Coral has four great-great-granddaughters. For a living she used to "head cane" i.e. carry loads of sugar cane on her head to waiting lorries. She loves vegetables, as well as a "touch" of brandy with milk once a week.

Even in St Lawrence Gap, which might be termed the Butlin's of Barbados, you can see the old values – not so much the Anglican Church itself, which tries to turn its back on the nocturnal excesses, but in the tiny harbour. Half-a-dozen fishing boats are anchored with their outboard motors attached, overnight, not stowed away for risk of theft.

Everywhere people say "You're welcome" or "Have a nice day!" Partly this is the tourist industry speaking to North Americans: it does not matter what you say, the reply will always be one or the other. If you say: "This morning I've got to visit my best friend who's got such bad elephantiasis that his head is four times bigger than normal, then I've got my dad's funeral this afternoon," the reply will still be: "Have a nice day!" But I also ascribe this cheerfulness to the Bajan way of life and temperament.

Barbados is trying to industrialise, as a regional hub, instead of importing everything from Florida – and good for its government that it does not just bewail the economies of scale. So factories are appearing inland along the freeway. Yet the three Cs remain: conservatism, Christianity (the phone directory is packed with page after page of churches and names of clergy, male and female), and cricket; together with the unspoken fourth, class. Just as C.L.R. James described the intricate social niceties of cricket clubs in Port of Spain when he was deciding which to join – black working-class, black lower-middle-class, or black and brown middle-class? – the same considerations have applied in Barbadian cricket.

The socially acceptable place to play was the Barbados Cricket Association league which, well into the 1950s, contained the first XIs of the three most prestigious schools, in addition to the top men's clubs such as Pickwick, Wanderers, Spartan and Empire. Workers in the countryside had no chance of a formal game until the Barbados Cricket League was established in 1937 by the leader of the trade union movement, Mitchie Hewitt. Yet, I would say, democracy has ultimately won the day. Cricket has become less of a middle-class preserve in the West Indies than any other Test-playing nation (except perhaps Afghanistan). An echo comes down the years at mid-afternoon in a match at Kensington Oval when the announcement is made: "Here comes the water cart". Nothing so fancy as "drinks".

I went to St John's on the east coast where Jan Morris had attended the service. It is not the original church from the 17th century because that was destroyed by hurricane, and a successor by fire, but the stone building is still handsome and the setting no less so, on a hill above the Atlantic. Had I to live at some period in the past, I would be tempted to be a Rector of St John's, living next door in the Georgian rectory with its panelled dining-room. Nothing much to do except a weekly sermon – and journeys into Bridgetown, for net practice and games, on the little train that trundled across the island until the 1930s. A notice outside the church states that landowners (whites, that is) ruled the parish council until 1959: not until then could non-white Barbadians participate in local government in their country.

So it was Barbados that staged the inaugural first-class cricket match in the West Indies, and the inaugural home Test in 1929/30, as well as being where the first touring team from England came ashore. In 1966, to celebrate Independence, Barbados challenged the Rest of the World, and lost, but partly because Garfield Sobers was unfit to bowl. This island has been the hot-spot of West Indian cricket, as the West Riding has been to England, Sydney to Australia, and Mumbai to India. Other islands and territories have had their surges when they have been better at cricket, but the flame will never die in Barbados. The government, I am glad to say, makes sure of that: all children at primary school receive two hours of cricket training per week from one of the seven national coaches employed by them to cover the island. From the age of 11 the Barbados Cricket Association takes over, although many fall through the net. If I was a millionaire, I would sponsor an annual T20 competition between the villages outside Bridgetown, with a little prize money, and a communal meal of curry goat, rice and peas. But, above all, a fee for the groundsman.

* * *

Morris may have called the island paradise not unalloyed, yet on some visits to Crane beach on the south coast I have found no alloy. The gateway to paradise is a rough single-track road covered by an awning of colourful trees, exactly which I am too preoccupied to notice. Will the tide be out, what will the waves be like, will seaweed have floated over from the Sargasso Sea, will the shack that hires out bodyboards be open?

There was a slight obstacle to paradise, but maybe that is normal. In this case, stepping stones led from the track down to Crane beach, and if the wind was blowing hard or the tide was splashing waves over the stones, walking across them could be precarious: and no chance to look along the beach to see if Ray-Ray was there. On my last visit, a path had been constructed on top of the stepping stones, so visitors could reach the beach without mishap.

After jumping onto the sand I have to restrain myself from running to one or other of the shacks which hire out the bodyboards: not cool. I slap on sun cream while talking to Ray-Ray and his brother Andrew about the cricket. They say they both played softball and tape-ball cricket when young on the street in St Michael's or any flat ground; both have torsos which would not need pre-season training, but neither has ever played a formal 11-a-side match. Unspoken is the fact that neither has ever had a thousand Bajan dollars to buy boots and pads, a bat or ball, all imported.

I rush off, as I guess one does when the pearly gates open, and it is only for the first few seconds that you notice the water is slightly cooler than body temperature, in other words ideal for a hot afternoon. But what makes Crane beach perfect is the right frequency of wave. Every seventh wave can be jumped on, but even a couple in between are serviceable, sufficient to reach the damp sand, if not the wonder-wave that sweeps you right up the beach into heaven.

Take your mind off the sea, by thinking about work for a minute, and you will likely be tumbled. Yet even this can be refreshing at Crane, as I have yet to land on a stone or break a collarbone. The higher the wave, of course, the more thrilling the risk. You want a wave bearing down above head height, and if you do not catch it exactly right you end up in a spluttering, humbled heap.

Only a tingling on your back reminds you that time is passing: a break for more sun cream and one of Ray-Ray's drinks. He takes a coconut from a palm at the head of the beach, machetes the top off, drains a bit of the milk, then adds pineapple or mango juice, rum and plenty of ice. Then beach cricket with an old bat and a tennis ball, with Andrew or Ray-Ray and any other locals, fizzing the ball around with their bullet arms ("pace off" is all I can offer), and you recall the words of the late Malcolm Marshall, surely the finest of fast bowlers, who grew up in St Michael's: "There were many of my contemporaries who I considered every bit as good as me but, for one reason or another, simply failed to carry on the promise of their childhood and youth … the harsh realities of making a living got in the way."

Andrew says he is a cousin of Sir Everton Weekes. Only a cousin, and "removed", but still! I had first met Sir Everton when he was doing radio commentary on Tests and I ghosted a couple of columns he did for *The Sunday Telegraph*. He had struck me then as one of the great men of cricket, inspiring awe and affection without trying. He's in the phone book, his cousins said. What, Sir Everton Weekes in the phone book? So he was, without the Sir, simply E. Weekes.

I met him again at Kensington Oval during a Test. Even in his nineties Sir Everton was still luminous, as if fashioned from Bajan sun and sea. Rarely in my experience does a piece "write itself" but this interview did, as a reflection of the inspirational nature of its subject. It is the only article I have written before breakfast, as I rose at dawn the next morning and within an hour had done my best to capture the last of the three Ws – that Barbadian triumvirate who had done so much not only for West Indian cricket but, imperceptibly and immeasurably, for race relations in Britain:

> *Not many people have been a top cricketer, a top commentator, and a top human being. Sir Everton Weekes was the first of this kind. Some might argue that at the age of 93 – next month he turns 94 – he is also the last.*
>
> *Weekes scored 15 centuries in his 48 Tests and averaged 58. He is, still, the only man to have scored five centuries in five consecutive Test innings – and in his next he was going strong on 90 when he was adjudged to have been run out for 90 against India, in Madras as was. Those were the days before neutral umpires and tv cameras.*
>
> *He was a top commentator too. Has there been a better pairing at the microphone than the late Tony Cozier doing ball-by-ball commentary and Sir Everton, summarising at the end of an over – a better combination of informed observation and relaxed yet insightful criticism? During the first Test between West Indies and England at Kensington Oval last week,*

which Sir Everton watched from the Worrell, Weekes and Walcott Stand, the Prime Minister of St Vincent, Ralph Gonsalves, told him he was his favourite commentator.

A top human being too. His philosophy has always been "live and let live" – those four words to which the world's wisest philosophies can be boiled down. Weekes inspired such friendships that during the Australian tour of the West Indies in 1954/55, a significant moment in the history of race relations in cricket occurred. When one of the white West Indian players threw a party, the Australians refused to accept the invitation if the black West Indian players were not invited as well. England had toured the Caribbean the year before, but I am afraid they had not drawn the same line in the sand.

And now Sir Everton is serenity. The last of the three Ws has his marbles intact, and if he is a little frail – might not be able to square-cut and pull with quite the same withering power – he has the richest of smiles, the warmest of hearts. Not for him any self-aggrandisement: mention his triple-century against Cambridge University at Fenner's in 1950, which helped to spark the Calypso summer, and he immediately recalls the runs scored by David Sheppard – "he was made a Bishop" – and Peter May, the future England captain; and, free of bitterness, he speaks as warmly of current cricketers as he does of those in his playing career.

"For starters I would say the word 'hate' has been removed from my vocabulary," said Sir Everton on the final day of the first Test when asked how he keeps going. And that is an achievement itself for a person born in 1925 in Barbados, a white plantocracy where even the notion of social justice did not exist, especially for a boy rich in nomenclature – as Everton DeCourcy Weekes – but otherwise poor.

His batting was conditioned by his upbringing all right: he hit the ball along the ground and recorded only two sixes in his Test career – and one of them was

*all run – because he had to learn the game in the small
yard of his home in central Bridgetown, some 300 yards
from Kensington Oval.*

*"There was no fence. If you hit the ball through
somebody's window, that was the end of that ball" –
balls he and his friends made for themselves, knitted
together from cork, paper and cloth. "The actual
six was in Trinidad against Australia, over mid-on
against Bill Johnston. We were both born on the 26th
of February." Weekes had to join the army to gain the
chance to play organised cricket, express himself and
have his gifts recognised.*

*"I used to swim every day up to two years ago, at
Miami Beach (near Oistins on the south-west coast of
Barbados), but I've got high blood pressure and I've been
advised not to go into the sea water because it can be
very rough at times. I've missed it. I've missed it. But the
doctor thinks drowning is not a very pleasant way to go."*

*Sir Everton represented Barbados at bridge "for about
ten years" as well as cricket. Indeed he put the bridge
into Bridgetown. "I play once maybe twice a week now.
Most of the bridge is played at night and I no longer
drive at night. The traffic is not very pretty in Barbados."
And again the chuckle in the understatement.*

*"Ever since I retired from Test cricket I've been playing
bridge seriously. Actually I've played bridge against
England, I've played bridge against Australia, and
I've played bridge against India." Needless to say, he
does not point out that he also scored a lot of Test runs
against these countries. In the 1950 series it was his
partnership of 283 with Frank Worrell in the third Test
at Trent Bridge, when the series stood at 1-1, which
basically alerted the cricket world that non-whites too
could bat, sometimes in more entertaining style; if his
one poor series was in Australia in 1951/52 when the
West Indian board made the basic error of arranging
only one first-class game – in a new country, with*

*pitches of very different bounce – before the first Test,
he made up for it in 1954/55; and in both of his series
against India he averaged more than 100.*

*"I do a lot of reading – most of the stuff is Biblical."
But he also has a copy of the new book about John Arlott
and Jim Swanton which he is going to read, because he
was friends with the late cricket correspondent of* The
Daily Telegraph *– "we got on pretty well" – and used to
play for E.W. Swanton's XI in several countries. "I spend
a lot of time watching the television," he added. "Your
knowledge can be expanded quite a lot if you have time
to watch BBC for instance.*

*"What I like about cricket now is that the players
are being paid properly." In his day, to make a living
from cricket, Sir Everton had to play in the Lancashire
League, for ten years, before a thigh operation went
wrong and stopped him playing. He not only opened the
batting for Bacup – with a future Lancashire captain
Bob Bennett – but the bowling too: he gave up his leg-
breaks and bowled outswingers. "In fact I got 75 wickets
there in my first season at Bacup."*

*Does he watch T20? "Of course, of course. I like
quite a few of them [the T20 players]. The top one in
my opinion, and the one I like most, is the opening
batsman, left-handed, from Jamaica – Chris Gayle. He
was in my view a very good cricketer, and it suited his
style. He also made two triple-hundreds in Test cricket –
he must be a very great player in my view."*

*With Shannon Gabriel and Kemar Roach, the West
Indian fast bowlers who rather alarmed England, he
has sympathy. "The pitches don't seem to give them
much help, compared to fast bowlers in years gone
by." The secret of West Indian cricket when they were
world champions, according to Weekes, was that
"groundsmen would get up early to roll in the dew." And
not just professional groundsmen at the Test grounds
but those who did it for love at club grounds around
the Caribbean: those pitches that shone in the sun,*

that brought the best and bravest out of batsmen, those pitches that do not exist any more except possibly St Lucia, the third Test venue, which is now said to have the only pacey pitch in the West Indies.

"For me to watch cricket here [at Kensington Oval] in the late '30s, I would go out and help roll the pitch in the mornings with the groundstaff so that I would be in the ground when the game starts. If I went back out, I'd not have much money to get back in, so I'd remain out there to help and roll the pitch. In the meantime I was able to watch all the games and some very good players."

George Headley was his hero above all. When Weekes played for Barbados in Jamaica in 1947, Headley made 200. What did he learn from the one who used to be known as "the Black Bradman"? "That occupation of the crease is extremely important. It didn't matter how you looked, style did not come into play, the main thing was to spend plenty of time in the middle. He was a very fine example of that. He was not the type of person that would not help you – he was a very fine gentleman and we became very good friends."

Then he speaks glowingly of today's players. What about the captain, Jason Holder? "He is a good cricketer, and a nice young man too. Most of them are very nice people – the young West Indian players."

Sir Frank Worrell and Sir Clyde Walcott are buried at Cave Hill, above the cricket ground belonging to the University of the West Indies, overlooking the north of Bridgetown and the Caribbean, sparkling in all its shades of blue – and space has been set aside. "I'm the only person on earth who knows, to an inch, where he is going to be buried," jests Sir Everton.

Not yet, please, not yet.

* * *

"Shot boy!"

Nowhere in the cricket world is the press box louder than in the West Indies – not before the start of play, when the England media have arrived early and bagged seats and phoned offices about the day's requirements, but once the local media have arrived and the day's play has warmed up.

"Shot boy!" Not "Good shot, old boy" but "Shot boy!"

From this shout it can be deduced that West Indies are batting. The word "boy" is not used in the old South African sense – of a house-boy, liable to be labelled "lazy" – but in the filial sense. The West Indian journalist or radio broadcaster who has shouted "Shot boy!" feels paternal pride towards the batsman who has swiped England's medium-pacer for six.

"Give Mattis a break!"

On my first tour of the Caribbean in early 1981, England played a West Indies Board President's XI in a four-day game in Pointe-à-Pierre in the oil fields of central Trinidad, to the smell of petroleum. The West Indies Test team needed a new batsman at No.4, between Viv Richards and Clive Lloyd, so this match was a talent parade. The uncapped Jeffrey Dujon scored a dazzling hundred, swiping the off-spin of Geoff Miller way over midwicket with what came to be known as a slog-sweep, and Dujon's time was soon to come as the Test wicketkeeper-batsman; but for this series the selectors went for Everton Mattis, a poor Jamaican boy with Rastafarian roots. The trouble was that he scored only a few runs in the first three Tests – the one in Guyana was cancelled because Robin Jackman was called into the squad, having played recently in South Africa – so by the fifth and last match, in his native Jamaica, Mattis was not fitting the bill. Nobody was shouting "Shot boy!"

"Give Mattis a break! That's all I'm saying to you, Reds! Give Mattis a break!"

A Jamaican journalist had button-holed the radio commentator Reds Perreira in the press box at Sabina Park. Reds was born in Guyana – up the Pomeroon river in the time before electricity – so inter-territorial rivalry was coming into this dispute. Never mind that Reds was as impartial as could be. Baz Freckleton was a sport journalist who had previewed a world heavyweight contest in Jamaica: "The citizens of Kingston must not become too worried when they hear a large thump tomorrow, because it will be George Foreman hitting the canvas at the National Stadium." Yes, it has happened to us all: Foreman defeated Joe Frazier in two rounds.

"Give Mattis a break! He's a boy from Trenchtown! That's all I'm saying to you Reds, give Mattis a break!"

Perhaps the most famous phrase in cricket commentary on radio or television (Brian Johnston and Jonathan Agnew could barely utter a word during the leg-over incident) was what Fazeer Mohammed shouted on radio at the end of the 2017 Test against Pakistan in Dominica.

"Why did he do that???!!!"

Shannon Gabriel went to swipe a spinner for six, instead of blocking out for the draw that was only seven balls away. Nothing could better illustrate how profound the West Indian interest in cricket still is, even if the Test grounds are empty, than the depth of Fazeer's passion.

Barbados has the press box which becomes the loudest. When Jason Holder scored the double-century that defeated England in the first Test of the 2019 series, many were the shouts of "Shot boy!" Until local sentiment was summed up by one journalist crying out:

"God so loves Barbados that He created Jason Holder!"

* * *

Something else binds the West Indies, besides cricket and a few organisations.

In a short story by the Barbadian writer Karl Sealey, "My Fathers Before Me", published in 1960 in a collection by Faber & Faber, a man called Dick is due to emigrate to Britain the next day. He is literate, quick-witted and looking for an opportunity to use these abilities that he could not find in Barbados. His grandmother warns him he is "going to a land where you ent got a bird in the cotton tree, where nobody'll care a straw whether you sink or swim, and where black ent altogether liked."

After more reflection, this grandmother says to her daughter Bessie: "I's just been telling Dick, Bessie, how no good ent ever come to our family leaving our land and going into nobody else country." The grandmother's husband went to fight in the Boer War;

before he went, he used to sing about "the pound and a crown for every Boer they down." When he came back, after shoeing horses in that South African war, he had "a foot less".

Bessie's son also emigrated to find employment. Before going to Panama, he swaggered around singing songs about the money he would make by digging the canal. Except he, and other Barbadians, did not come back but "died like rotten sheep in the Panama mud."

Dick thinks it is going to be third generation lucky. The women of his extended family plead with him to learn from the family's past and not go to Britain, but he rejoins: "My grandfather and dad didn't go [abroad] because they were foolish, but because they were brave. They didn't go because they wanted to be rid of their wives and children. They didn't go because they wanted an easy life. They didn't go for a spree. They went because their souls cried out for better opportunities and better breaks. And just like them, I'm going for the same thing." Herein lies the dilemma of Afro-Caribbean existence, summed up by the Nobel Laureate from St Lucia, Derek Walcott: "There is too much nothing here."

It is one of the world's most beautiful regions – yet it seems to me almost impossible to make a decent, legal, living in order to stay there and enjoy it. Working in the tourist industry, as barman or waitress or chambermaid, is no ladder to greater prospects. Illegal ways to make money are far more plentiful when the drugs of South America are smuggled via the Caribbean into North America. Even the money, or most of it, which is spent by tourists in the West Indies, emigrates – into the bank accounts of multinationals, not invested in the West Indian economy and society. To modify Bob Marley's "Redemption Song" with a synonym: "How long shall they kill our profits/While we stand aside and look?"

Emigration has long been the one legal alternative, usually to North America or Britain. So for all the drawbacks inherent in leaving home, half of West Indians live abroad. In Boney M's song "Rivers of Babylon", an even greater pathos is captured. It has been a double diaspora for people who came from Africa – or were "stolen from Africa" as Marley sang – and, having settled in the West Indies, feel forced to leave again, to earn a living, in a second exile. As Harry Belafonte sang:

But I'm sad to say I'm on my way
Won't be back for many a day
My heart is down, my head is turning around
I had to leave a little girl in Kingston Town.

* * *

Cricket used to offer a pathway, to making a decent living abroad, without demanding permanent exile. From the 1920s the leagues of Lancashire, then beyond, offered opportunities to Afro-Caribbeans which they could never have found outside the professions. From 1968, when first-class counties were allowed to register overseas players with no qualification period, the jobs increased to the point where at least a hundred West Indian professionals would have been playing for British clubs and counties every season – until the British Home Office cut this connection to the point where only cricketers of international experience were granted visas and work permits.

I have traced, so far as I can, the first of this kind; but then any excuse for going to the beautiful island of Bequia will do. He was Charles Ollivierre, one of five non-white members of the first West Indian team to tour England in 1900, who topped their batting averages. The games were not awarded first-class status, but Ollivierre scored 159 against Leicestershire in an opening stand of 238 with Plum Warner, later Sir Pelham, and stayed on to qualify by two years' residence for Derbyshire. The Hill-Wood family effectively owned Derbyshire CCC and Arsenal FC and while in the course of time their investment in the latter may have been ever so slightly greater, they contracted Ollivierre to play as an amateur. He did not play as a professional, because Derbyshire's professionals, so rumour had it, did not want a black man in their dressing-room. The only three non-whites to have played county cricket by then were all from the subcontinent, most notably Ranjitsinhji of Sussex and England, and sufficiently affluent to be genuine amateurs. While Ollivierre was qualifying, Derbyshire finished 13th out of the 15 counties in the Championship in 1900, and last in 1901.

Ollivierre used to be registered as having been born in Kingstown, the port and capital of St Vincent. When I asked around there in 1981, I was told the Ollivierre family came from Bequia – the island that lies behind the sightscreen at one end at Arnos Vale – and subsequently his birthplace has been altered. I needed no other reason to take the ferry across the few miles of Caribbean Sea. I met the last active harpooner in Bequia, which was allowed by the United Nations to catch three whales per year by traditional methods from a rowing boat. This member of the Ollivierre family was in his sixties, if not seventies, decidedly dodgy on his pins, but in the excitement of the moment the adrenalin must have made him rise to the occasion, like a latterday Ahab, harpoon in hand.

In his first full season of 1902 Derbyshire improved to tenth position, and Ollivierre rose to several occasions. His first-class debut for Derbyshire, at Crystal Palace in 1901, must have provided reassurance for the Hill-Woods as well as the player himself. London County – W.G. Grace's team after he had fallen out with Gloucestershire – dismissed Derbyshire for 64, but in their second innings Ollivierre was promoted to open, against South Africa's finest pace-bowling all-rounder arguably until Jacques Kallis, Jack Sinclair. Ollivierre top-scored with 54 in Derbyshire's second modest total.

I doubt whether Ollivierre could have created this pathway – from Bequia to county cricket more than a century ago – if he had not moved to Trinidad. For them, on the Savannah in Port-of-Spain, in a two-day game now ranked as first-class, Ollivierre batted against the first English touring team, R.S. Lucas' XI. More significantly perhaps, he opened the bowling in the visitors' second innings. Trinidad were always short of bowlers: that is why they allowed non-whites to represent the island, so they could beat their major rivals, Barbados and British Guiana, who were all white, and touring teams. Trinidad had one of the best non-white pace bowlers of his generation in Joseph Woods, who bowled through R.S. Lucas' XI's first innings to take six for 39 (in his first-class career Woods took 107 wickets at only 11 runs each). When the visitors followed on, in Woods's absence, Ollivierre took two wickets and Lebrun Constantine, father of Learie, took three

– though he was normally a wicketkeeper; such was Trinidad's need for bowlers.

Ollivierre was never consistent for Derbyshire. He had a wristy, risky style: contemporaries said he had a little something of Ranjitsinhji about him. It is all too likely as well that his eyesight, which forced him to retire at the end of 1907, was already troubling him, and in those days it was an unavoidable handicap: the first England player to wear spectacles is believed to have been Richard Young in 1907. Hence the story about Ollivierre playing at Queen's Park in Chesterfield for the first time is not so funny as it would otherwise seem. Derbyshire, according to one of their former players, Fred Root, in his autobiography *A Cricket Pro's Lot*, had won three matches on their southern tour and Ollivierre had done "remarkably well" and "had celebrated accordingly on the return trip. He had never seen the spire before, and having snatched what early morning sleep was possible, he arrived very late on the ground" where Derbyshire had to field.

"Charles took up his accustomed position in the slips, not feeling too good. First one catch went down, then a second, followed by a third, and still a fourth. This was most unusual, for Ollivierre possessed to a high degree the coloured man's well-known agility and quickness of eye in the field. He kicked the ball back disgustedly to Arnold Warren after his fourth lapse and, hands on hips, surveyed the view. Suddenly he dashed off to the pavilion without either asking the captain's permission or giving any explanation for his extraordinarily hurried exit. An investigation found the West Indian dousing his head in a wash-bowl of ice-cold water. He eventually returned to the field, but again it was obvious there was something wrong. After gazing at the spire with much the same 'peeking' action as a captured pigeon, he made a bee-line for the skipper and said, 'It's no use, captain, you must find a substitute for a bit; I am ill, I am awfully ill. No wonder I drop catches. Why, even the church steeple seems to be falling on me!'" Root concludes: "He took a lot of convincing that the famous spire seemed to be falling on everyone else, too."

Before his eyesight failed him, Ollivierre engineered the most astonishing comeback in the entire history of the three-day Championship. Chesterfield has always been free-scoring; even so, after Percy Perrin had hit 68 fours in his unbeaten 343, and Essex had totalled 597, the Derbyshire players cannot have given themselves much of a chance. Yet "Mr C.A. Ollivierre" scored 229, so they were only 49 behind on first innings; and Essex collapsed in their second, as even the best have done against Derbyshire's pace bowlers. Derbyshire knocked off the 146 they needed in only 30 overs, Ollivierre finishing unbeaten on 92. Thus they ended the season tenth, above Surrey, which was respectable. Had he not played that disastrous final season in 1907, Ollivierre's first-class batting average would not have been 23 but 25, respectable for its time, especially for a struggling northern county. Before the 1970s, the highest average among Derbyshire's leading all-time run-scorers was 31.

Ollivierre died in 1949, a long way from his native home, in Pontefract. Between the wars he coached in the Netherlands during the summer, and I received a couple of letters from a Dutch cricketer who had been his pupil testifying what a good coach he had been. I see him in his dotage, beside his coal fire of an evening, living on a decent pension from the Hill-Woods. He did not return to Trinidad, or St Vincent, or Bequia; but I wonder if his heart was ever down, and his head was turning around, after leaving a little girl in Kingstown, rather than Kingston Town.

* * *

Antigua has no benefit system for the unemployed or sick. This is the rule throughout the West Indies: no safety net, unless you have a relative abroad sending remittances home. Barbados might offer a manual job, or a government department or church welfare group might catch you before you hit the pavement. Antigua is edgier. Employers, I was told, contribute to the medical insurance of their employees; and if you are unemployed and go to hospital, you will be presented with a bill, but it will be waived. Otherwise, all too often, the alternative is hustling around the harbour in St John's when cruise ships come into port.

I first went to Antigua in 1981 for its inaugural Test, which coincided with two other major events: independence and Viv Richards's marriage. The Antigua Recreation Ground is in the centre of town, and cricket then was centre stage. In *Cricket: the Game of Life* I wrote about the resentment towards the owners of the sugar plantations that built up over 300 years, and burst into a series of strikes in the 1950s when Richards was born. Even then slavery lived on to the extent that you could not move to another plantation without your owner's permission.

I visited the French island of Marie Galante and an old-style sugar plantation, with donkeys still bringing cane in carts from the fields. The machinery was all exposed: one slip and you would lose a limb. The slaves often had to work at night too, before electricity, in semi-darkness.

Popular resentment would appear to have been most intense in Antigua, more so even than Jamaica: the absence of any cane fields in Antigua by 1981, and still today, bespoke this hatred of the crop. Jane Austen's *Mansfield Park* is instructive: the landowner with a mansion in Northamptonshire, Sir Thomas Bertram, goes to visit his sugar plantation in Antigua in the company of his eldest son when the estate is not so profitable. On returning to England, Sir Thomas leaves behind an overseer – one who would have no scruples about doing everything to maximise future profits. Had he owned a plantation in Barbados, Sir Thomas would have been more likely to live there, in the right sort of society for his wife, daughters and nieces. (A fashionable magazine in 2009 invited the cricket media to a polo match in Barbados, and as everyone on a horse was white, and everyone looking after the horses was black, it was as if emancipation had yet to occur.) The presence of women and children in Barbados led, in theory, to a less inhumane environment.

Cricket, chiefly in the persons of Viv Richards and Andy Roberts, placed Antigua on the world map. The island's youth were inspired to follow in their footsteps, to play cricket for a living and proclaim their excellence to the world: mostly they became fast bowlers, the best of them Curtly Ambrose, Kenneth Benjamin, Winston Benjamin, George Ferris and Eldine Baptiste. An eighth of the island's population would pack into the ARG for a cricket match. Outside the ground people thronged, selling from their stalls, making so much music the earth vibrated. I was partly involved in one vivid example when Colin Croft, the former West Indies fast

217

bowler from Guyana, in writing a preview of the Antigua Test in his column for *The Sunday Telegraph*, said the pitch at the ARG was underprepared. After the match had proceeded for a couple of days – the pitch was on the damp, slow side but nothing dangerous – speakers inside and outside the ground blared a newly minted record, its main refrain:

> The wicket ain't bad, Colin Croft!
> The wicket ain't bad, Colin Croft!

If someone cast a slur on the Lord's pitch, I doubt whether a protest song would top the UK charts.

At the ARG Brian Lara broke the world record for the highest Test innings twice, in bore-draws against England, firstly by scoring 375 off his own bat, then 400: in the former innings a West Indian victory seemed to be slightly more of an objective. Cricket then left town. For Antigua to stage a match in the 2007 World Cup, the island had to have a ground which conformed to ICC regulations, some of them sensible, some far too finicky. The new stadium was built by the Chinese government on spare ground near the centre of the island, at North Sound: out of town, out of sight, out of mind. Antiguans ceased to watch the Leeward Islands or West Indies. The ARG was their ground, the new stadium was not.

Even the ground built by Sir Allen Stanford next to the airport for his T20 competition, much appreciated in smaller islands like Montserrat, brought in the crowds. Not a large ground, and the floodlights had to be low because they were right beside the airport, but joyful occasions nevertheless when Nevis were drawn against St Vincent, or Saint Maarten sent a team (the first T20 century in any international match was scored for them by John Eugene, originally from St Lucia). It went too far when Stanford's XI challenged England to a 20-over match for $20m, though I don't suspect that the dukes and other patrons of cricket in the Hambledon era would have objected to so large a purse. Stanford's Ponzi scheme ended in much money being lost by many people. Stanford loved to lord it, as a man who would be king.

* * *

If you were travelling through Bihar and the United Provinces of India in the late 19th or early 20th century – if not with Phileas Fogg as he attempted to go Around the World in 80 Days then as a member of an English cricket touring team, perhaps en route to play the Indigo Planters of Oudh – you might well see a certain type of man loitering on the outskirts of a town, maybe near a temple or market. He would be scanning the crowd closely: specifically he would be looking for men with chests more than 30in in circumference, hands toughened by manual labour, and – for preference – a gullible air.

When this recruiter saw a potential target, he would open a conversation and ask if the man was interested in a new job, a very well-paid job. No drawbacks at all, and this new job was located not far away, near Calcutta. The recruiter would lead his prey to a house where the rules of caste were observed and given a nice meal. What could possibly go wrong?

Hundreds of thousands of Indians were persuaded by such recruiters to sign up as bonded labourers, and they ended up in far-flung corners of the British Empire. After the abolition of slavery, manual labour was needed for sugar plantations from Fiji and Natal to Trinidad and Guyana. These men contracted to work for ten or 20 years, at the end of which they were given a piece of land and citizenship in their adopted country. Some returned home, only to find they were outcasts back in their native villages: they had lost caste by going overseas, which is why recruiters gave them the blarney about the well-paid jobs being "near Calcutta".

These bonded labourers took their cooking with them when they departed from Bombay, Madras or Calcutta, and their religion (mostly Hindu, about 13% Muslim). But as most were illiterate (otherwise most would never have appended their signature to the contract), they did not pass their native languages on to their children apart from a few words. Prime Minister Nehru declared they were no longer Indian citizens; and they were not fully fledged citizens of their adopted country either. In Fiji, although Indians became the majority, when they won a general election the result was overturned by the army so that indigenous Fijians stayed in power; in South Africa apartheid ruled until the 1990s; in Guyana the Indian leader Cheddi Jagan won the 1953 general election, but MI6 and the CIA intervened to fund strikes and depose him.

"The system [of bonded labour] never worked as it was intended," wrote K.L. Gillion in *The Fiji Indians*. "The government safeguards in India and the colonies gave way to social realities. The anticipated emigration of enterprising people anxious to improve their prospects by going to the colonies became in practice the collection by any means of stray, isolated, and credulous villagers who had not the slightest idea of what their contracts would really mean: the great distance from India, the relentless, clockwork pace of plantation work under harsh discipline, the inability to change their employer, the beatings, and the penal sanctions used to enforce their compliance and even to prolong their indentures."

These bonded labourers and their descendants were left to identify with India, if at all, through Bollywood films and music. Almost all emigrated before the First World War, when cricket was little known outside Bombay and a few Princely States; but when India's national cricket team began touring, and winning, here was another connection with the homeland. The Indians of Trinidad and Guyana flocked to Queen's Park Oval and Bourda to support India; they might even attend Tests to support other touring teams against West Indies when the home team was filled with Afro-Caribbean players. "Racial rivalries are still potent, especially between brown and black," Morris observed in Port of Spain, which "gives an extra vicious animation to the politics of the city."

Indo-Caribbeans had thus been transported by British ships into exile, much as Afro-Caribbeans had been, and into double exile if they later emigrated from the West Indies to North America or Britain. Time heals, however, and cricket is playing a part. The two most successful West Indies mystery spinners have been Indo-Caribbeans from Trinidad: Sonny Ramadhin in Tests, Sunil Narine in T20. From Port Mourant in the sugar plantations of north-east Guyana came two of the most brilliant batsmen of their age, Rohan Kanhai and Alvin Kallicharran. Bourda – rickety, old, wooden, leafy, sea-level Bourda – rocked when one of them was playing the hook shot and the trees along the dykes outside the ground swayed with their animated fruit. What the British Empire had rent asunder had been brought together, in part, by a British sport.

Hit the ball donkey, hit the ball
Cover drive him, man, make him bawl
Hook the man like Kallicharran
And put him straight in the stand.

I ask Hilary Beckles, professor of Wwst Indian history where
Britan ranked among the colonial powers. The worst were Belgium
and Portgual, he said. the best was Spain; she so loved Cuba she
founded seven universities there. Britain? Mid-table.

* * *

Tropical ports, like Port of Spain, might be more permissive than
other cities: something in the sweaty humidity at night? England
cricketers,, at any rate, have not been above carnal temptation
in Trinidad; and there are enough mixtures – of Afro-Caribbean,
Indian, Chinese, Portuguese and British – to satisfy many a taste.
Wally Hammond, according to his biographer David Foot, caught
a sexually transmitted disease on MCC's tour of 1925/26 and
almost died. Gubby Allen, captain of England's tour in 1947/48,
found two of his players emerging one morning from a brothel
in Tragarete Road outside Queen's Park Oval: one an amateur,
the other a professional, whereupon the pro was told he would
never play for England again. When England visited Trinidad in
the 1970s and 1980s, splendid parties were held by the Indian
community, who would go to the ground to support England –
such was their rivalry with the Afro-Caribbean community, which
was roughly equal in size, and stronger in political clout, but
weaker economically.

On my early tours of Trinidad, members of the media were
mugged in downtown Port of Spain, such as Henry Blofeld and
the photographer Patrick Eagar, but it was still safe enough by day
to walk across the Queen's Park Savannah. From one of the hotels
nestling beneath the Northern Range, one could walk past the
pitches graced by protagonists in *Beyond a Boundary*. Here George
John had steamed in, here Learie Constantine had learnt to field like
nobody had ever done before, and there Wilton St Hill flexed his

wrists to cut pace bowlers. C.L.R. James watched and, having tried to emulate, captured them for posterity.

In safer days, James Morris, as he was in the 1950s, walked and watched on "the piazza of Trinidad" as he called the Savannah. "Wherever you look, from the hills to the city, they are playing cricket. To be sure, they are playing the game all over the island, in numberless unmapped clearings in the bush, overhung by lugubrious banana trees or gorgeous flamboyants: but this is the very heart of Trinidadian cricket, where the game is played today with more dash and delight than anywhere else on earth. There may be thirty or forty games going on, all at the same time." An old India hand, Morris, in making this comparison, would have been fully aware of Bombay's maidans.

"Some of these sportsmen are grand and mannered, with spotless whites and rolled wickets, but they trail away through immeasurable gradations of clubmanship to the raggety small boys on the edge of the field, with an old bit of wood for a bat, and a stone for a ball, and the wicket-keeper peering with breathless excitement over a petrol can. Whatever the style, the game is pursued with panache," Morris went on. "Many a culture or tradition contributes to the texture of Port of Spain, and one of the strongest is that tough old umbilical, cricket."

Few countries flooded with oil revenue have used it to the benefit of the majority of their citizens. When Morris visited Trinidad in the 1950s, the advantages were contributing to the exuberance, but not for long. The steel band, using sawn-off oil drums, has been the one unequivocal good to have stemmed from the discovery of oil in Trinidad in the 1930s. Even cricketers on the Savannah give way to the bands that have been hammering out their compositions in the pan-yards downtown and, as Lent approaches, practise their parading.

Before steel bands, the calypso was the song of social commentary and protest. It was a step forward in the history of race relations in Britain when a MCC official at Lord's in 1950 decided to stop a policeman charging West Indian supporters who had run onto the outfield to celebrate their first Test victory in England. The Windrush generation had it hard enough without Lord Beginner being hit by truncheons.

I was amazed at the expertise of two Calypsonians at a concert one evening in Port of Spain. After one of them had picked a subject, both had to extemporise, composing verse after verse alternately. Michael Holding, then a cricketer, was in the audience and naturally made a subject. Before independence, the British authorities were so sensitive to satire that some calypsos were censored. After it Trinidad's government may have ceased to listen.

* * *

My first memory is set in the West Indies. When I was four, my father had a six-month lectureship at the University of the West Indies at the Mona Campus in Kingston, where Sir Frank Worrell was soon to be a warden, all too briefly. My father was also to write a play that was broadcast on the BBC Third Programme, as Radio 3 used to be, called *Morant Bay* – that area of eastern Jamaica which was the setting for the freedom movement in 1865 led by the Baptist minister Paul Bogle. It was savagely suppressed by Governor Eyre, and Bogle hanged.

We left Avonmouth in 1958 on a banana boat, the *Camito*. On landing in Port of Spain I came close to drinking a lot of Caribbean Sea as it was a wobbly gang-plank down which my mother carried me. That is not my memory though. The picture burned in my mind is of the beach at Port Antonio, where bananas were loaded for the voyage to Britain and we went to catch the boat home. I am looking to my left along a beach, a ship waiting offshore, but I am in no hurry to go home.

I have been back to Port Antonio, to see the track up a very steep hill to the Bonny View Hotel where we stayed before embarking. Apparently I was carried up in a basket on a donkey. Eventually I made it to Morant Bay on the south-east coast. It so happened the law court was in session, the doors and windows open to the sea breezes, so that from the street you could see venerable men in wigs, and a young man in the dock, not comprehending Latin phrases. It did not feel as though 150 years had passed since justice was meted out on Bogle.

From eastern Jamaica came two of the fastest bowlers ever, and the most intimidating: Roy Gilchrist, who dished out beamers when they were unethical but not illegal, and Patrick Patterson, who, on his Test debut at Sabina Park against England in 1985/86, was the scariest bowler I have seen – the one most liable to kill a batsman. Morant Bay was a world away from middle-class Kingston, where Michael Holding came from; a place of raw, sometimes savage, aggression.

* * *

Test-playing countries have to expand their constituency to stay strong. Just as Australia promoted Tasmania to first-class status, and England did the same to Durham, so West Indies grew when the Leeward and Windward Islands were allowed to compete alongside Barbados, Guyana, Jamaica and Trinidad from the middle of the 1960s.

The Leeward and Windward Islands were colonised by the French to grow sugar, and have a dormant or extinct volcano called La Soufrière. Then the British navy came along, especially when a certain domestic turmoil from 1789 distracted French attention, and captured these islands for the Crown. The island's capital would then be re-named Kingstown, or Charlestown, or Georgetown.

So St Vincent and St Lucia, St Kitts and Nevis, Montserrat and Dominica, dominated by their volcano, have populations living around the periphery of the island; the road connecting the settlements winds up, down and around; villages often have French or Creole names, and there is little or no flat land to spare for cricket grounds.

It is a long and sweaty climb through original rainforest to the top of La Soufrière after the road gives out. Tropical bush consists of saplings and thin trees competing for sunlight. The soil, rich in nutrients, has tangled undergrowth to trip you on a root. Once the rainforest is cut down, however, this soil is blown away by trade winds or washed away by flash floods. In a small clearing, the Rastafarian may grow his weed until the police helicopter hovers overhead.

Climbing to the top of La Soufrière is rewarded by a view into the crater: either an immensely deep lake, or more vegetation, or bubbling mud and puffs of steam. From Trinidad, the University of the West Indies monitors 19 volcanoes around the Caribbean. The biggest to erupt was Montserrat, not long after England had played there in 1981, when more than half the island was transformed from green to brown, like a Caribbean Pompeii.

Arawaks and Caribs, original inhabitants of the West Indies, repulsed Columbus when he tried to land on Dominica in 1493, but they had to withdraw in the face of British and French invaders and their slave soldiers. The last Caribs of each island must have clustered on the slopes of their Soufrière, forced ever higher until extinction. Only in Dominica have Caribs survived, a few hundred left in a reserve as their final redoubt. The pace bowler Adam Sanford, soon after the turn of this century, is their only representative to have played Test cricket.

* * *

The rivalry between St Kitts and Nevis is never more openly expressed than in sport; and in most sports, especially football, St Kitts win, fairly naturally as their population is four times greater than the 12,000 of Nevis. When it comes to the islands playing each other at cricket, however, Nevis has held the upper hand, to the chagrin of Kittitians. Nevis has produced six Test players, St Kitts none. The ferry between the islands, across "the Shallows" as they are called, has been caught in a tug-of-war when disputes have broken out on the field.

A pundit on *Gardeners' Question Time* was renowned for saying "the answer lies in the soil" but in the case of the rivalry between St Kitts and Nevis it would be more accurate to say the problem lies in the soil. Calvin Wilkin, a left-arm spinner from St Kitts who studied at Cambridge and there dismissed Geoffrey Boycott twice in a first-class match, told me the following story. The St Kitts government, sick of losing to Nevis at cricket, wanted to import some soil from their neighbour to relay the pitches at Warner Park in Basseterre which, as the name implies, had traditionally been too low and slow to produce top-class cricketers, who need pace and bounce to condition their reflexes. Nevis's soil has been true enough to produce Keith Arthurton, Runako Morton, Derick Parry, Kieran Powell, Elquemedo Willett and Stuart Williams: not bad for a community of 12,000, and enough to propel Nevis into the semi-finals of the first Stanford T20 competition in 2006.

The answer from the Nevis government was no. St Kitts could not have any of their soil for a cricket pitch. No less a person than Vance Amory said so. Amory had played for the Leeward Islands for a decade, before being the Premier of Nevis for almost 20 years.

* * *

St Lucia is another pearl, the same shape as Barbados and Sri Lanka, its size in between. Windward Islands do not have large tracts of flat and well-drained land, so their Test players have been fewer than other West Indian territories, but St Lucia emerged as a major venue because its government – recognised as one of the two most organised in the West Indies, along with Barbados – decided a new stadium for international cricket would enhance the island as a tourist destination.

St Lucia's hills have been devoted to bananas, or "green gold" as the crop was called in the 1950s and 1960s, when Britain could not get enough. Bananas have been cultivated less brutally than sugar, and St Lucia has had a kinder past than Antigua, except when wars between Britain and France raged. As a consequence of the first coloniser being French, St Lucians speak Creole among themselves, and someone thinking of going to the Gros Islet stadium will say: "Mai aller voyer de cricket" – mai being the Creole for "moi". The verbs aller and voyer are not declined.

The old ground used to be a rickety affair in Castries on the other side of the airport from the enormous cemetery which blithely stretches alongside the runway. Like most cricket pitches in the Windwards, it was soggy – so much more rainfall – and slow. Windward batsmen did not move their feet much, and they bowled finger-spin in preference to pace, before Daren Sammy became the first St Lucian to represent, and captain, West Indies. The new stadium was built in a valley in what meteorological research had indicated was the driest part of the island, and conveniently close to the tourist beaches of Rodney Bay.

One evening in St Lucia was unforgettable, and not merely because my wife was with me. We watched from our terrace on a hill overlooking the Caribbean as the sun went down, which was fine enough as it illuminated fleecy clouds. Next, after the sun had descended out of sight, came the most spectacular *son et lumière* but without a sound: for the sun, after setting, had lit up the sky from below the horizon. Not only that, the sky was so luminously red that it, in turn, lit up the sea. Above us, and below us, the West Indies glowed.

ENGLAND IN THE WEST INDIES
1929/30 — 2018/19

Overall

Played **160**   Won **51**   Lost **58**   Drawn **51**

In the West Indies

Played **71**   Won **15**   Lost **27**   Drawn **29**

In England

Played **89**   Won **36**   Lost **31**   Drawn **22**

England's record at each venue

Queen's Park Oval, Trinidad

Played **19**   Won **6**   Lost **7**   Drawn **6**

Kensington Oval, Barbados

Played **16**   Won **3**   Lost **6**   Drawn **7**

Sabina Park, Jamaica

Played **15**   Won **3**   Lost **6**   Drawn **6**

Bourda, Guyana

Played **9**   Won **1**   Lost **4**   Drawn **4**

St John's Antigua

Played **7**   Won **0**   Lost **3**   Drawn **4**

Sir Vivian Richards Stadium, Antigua

Played **3**   Won **0**   Lost **1**   Drawn **2**

Daren Sammy Stadium, St Lucia

Played **1**   Won **1**   Lost **0**   Drawn **0**

National Cricket Stadium, St George's, Grenada

Played **1**   Won **1**   Lost **0**   Drawn **0**

Series won	Captain
1959/60	Peter May
1967/68	Colin Cowdrey
2003/04	Michael Vaughan

Highest scores

325	Andrew Sandham	Kingston	1929/30
262*	Dennis Amiss	Kingston	1973/74
205*	Patsy Hendren	Port-of-Spain	1929/30
205	Len Hutton	Kingston	1953/54
182*	Joe Root	St George's	2014/15

Best bowling

8-53	Angus Fraser	Port-of-Spain	1997/98
8-75	Angus Fraser	Bridgetown	1993/94
8-86	Tony Greig	Port-of-Spain	1973/74
7-12	Steve Harmison	Kingston	2003/04
7-34	Trevor Bailey	Kingston	1953/54

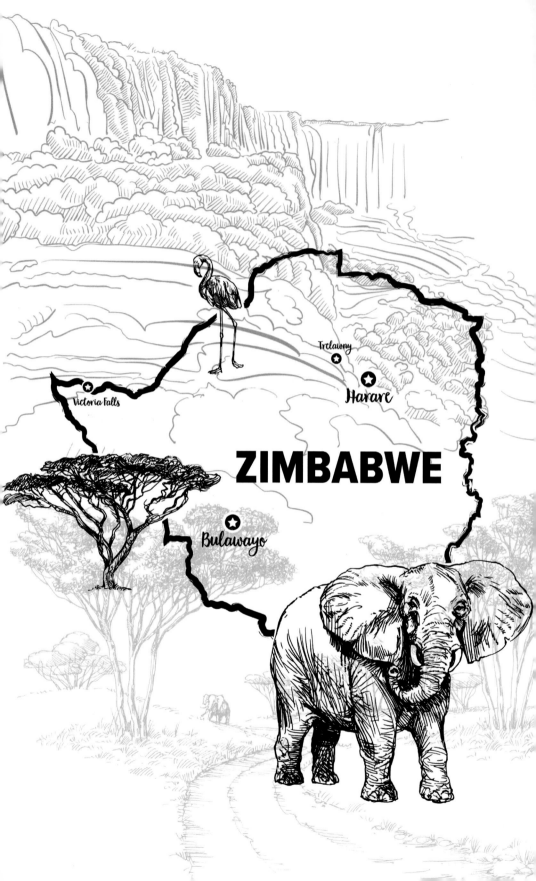

ZIMBABWE

Victoria Falls

Trelawny

Harare

Bulawayo

CHAPTER NINE

ZIMBABWE

Zimbabwe was to Britain what Algeria was to France: Paradise Colonised. In the British experience, Southern Rhodesia came closer than anywhere else to earthly perfection. Sunshine, above all, and never too intense owing to the altitude of the Highveld, and when rain fell, it was at night. Fertility, a freedom from much government, and a people who had to be paid little for their labour.

So close to perfection was Zimbabwe's climate that British settlers could grow wine like the pieds-noir in Algeria, and play cricket on the Highveld, between four and five thousand feet up, all year round, like nowhere else on earth. Parts of Queensland can compete, until the humidity overwhelms; so too some West Indian islands, until the monsoon. In Harare the league season ran from September to March, and in the rural districts from March to September.

"One realises that he is born of this country where everything is given to be taken away," wrote Albert Camus, of Algerian birth, during French colonialism. The Mediterranean Sea dominated his childhood. But substitute the setting, and what he said of his native land could be applied to Zimbabwe. "Probably one has to live in Algiers for some time in order to realise how paralysing an excess of nature's bounty can be. There is nothing here for whoever would learn, educate himself, or better himself. This country has no lessons to teach. It neither promises nor affords glimpses. It is satisfied to give, but in abundance."

Hence the pain of separation when Paradise was Lost, or Liberated, and white people lost out on "nature's bounty" in Africa. Of no country did France so reluctantly let go as Algeria; of no country did people of British stock so reluctantly let go as Southern Rhodesia. "Never in a thousand years will I agree to black majority rule," proclaimed Ian Smith, the prime minister of Southern Rhodesia and author of the Unilateral Declaration of Independence.

In the constant sunshine and nocturnal rain, the illusion had grown that African indigenes would consent to being ruled forever, and should be. Hence the pain for British and French people was all the greater, the hatred more bitter, the fighting more savage, when the time at last came for Paradise to be decolonised.

* * *

This blessed land, which contained little more than a quarter of a million white people at most, nurtured sportsmen like a latter-day Athens. Their schools had the facilities for physical development. At weekends, especially on Sundays, the whole family drove to country clubs, where females would play tennis or hockey and swim, while males played cricket or rugby. Africa's most decorated Olympian is Kirsty Coventry, a member of this community, not a runner from Kenya or Ethiopia.

When Graeme Hick promised to break all English batting records, I visited the house where he grew up, a spacious bungalow on the Trelawney Estate. It had a cricket net in the garden, where African estate workers would bowl – not at him, I think, but to him. Or, was the relationship between whites and blacks in the 1970s such that it was *for* him? I wondered, especially on hearing that when he had joined Queensland, after his prolific early summers at Worcester and even more prolific winters at Northern Districts in New Zealand, he had been shocked by the belligerence of net bowlers in Brisbane, who were supposed to be playing for his own side of Queensland. They were bowling at him.

Hick's upbringing was not confrontational; so too his nature. I observed this most vividly in a Test match in Guyana, when he walked out to face Kenny Benjamin, a recent teammate for Worcestershire. Benjamin, with a heave of his shoulders, dug one in short, angled it in and hit Hick in the ribs. It was like an antelope being shot. Hick's gentle eyes, as they dimmed, could not comprehend how the world could be so aggressive.

I visited Hick's first school at Banket, a small agricultural-service town a relatively short drive from his house. In his time all the children at Banket Junior were white – so strict were the racial divisions in the 1970s – and by 2004 every single child was black. Yet all the bats used by the previous generation of white children had been preserved in a locked cupboard: moth and dust had corrupted, the equipment was entirely useless, but thieves had not broken in and stolen it.

Hick's father John had kindly typed out a letter to me listing the first 50 centuries Graeme had scored, starting with the ones at Banket Junior School:

Year	Score	Opponents	Details
1972	105*	Mangula Junior School	6½ yrs old, 24 fours
1975	102*	Sinoia High Under-13	
1977	3 centuries	Details not to hand	
1978	100*	Prince Edward High Under-13	Out of 134/3dec
	110*	Umvukwes Junior School	Out of 125/1dec

Hitting 24 fours in one innings aged six might seem incredible, too prodigious, except that the straight boundaries of the school ground were similar to those at Clifton College in Bristol, where Arthur Collins had scored his 628. Nevertheless, a 30-yard straight boundary requires a decent hit, of at least 50 yards, by one so young. I could see the ball being driven by a boy in shorts and pads, and bobbing over the outfield in front of the classrooms to the boundary.

If most right-handed Test batsmen, perhaps since Wally Hammond's era, have favoured the leg side, Hick set up to off- and cover-drive; but that was not the main reason why only six out of his 136 first-class centuries were made in Tests. Primary, I believe, was his non-confrontational nature, which went beyond being ruffled by certain opponents: he did not stand up enough for himself in the dressing-room like more selfish batsmen did and had to do in this period before central contracts. Allan Lamb, from South Africa, wanted to bat at No.4 and refused to budge; Hick, from Zimbabwe, wanted to bat at No.3, where he could go out and bat as he liked, as unaffected as a batsman can be by the match situation. He batted at No.3 in only 20 Tests, averaging a respectable 34 against an overall Test average of 31; and at Nos.6, 7 and 8 in 24 Tests i.e. in more than one-third of his 65 Tests. Too gentle a giant for his own good.

In modern times, since Gentlemen v. Players, has there been a better amateur cricket team than Zimbabwe was – until a handful of players such as Andy and Grant Flower were paid to play and coach in schools in the early 1990s? In their first World Cup in 1983, under Duncan Fletcher's captaincy, they not only defeated Australia but reduced India, the eventual winners, to 78 for seven in their qualifying match: had the venue been more of an international stadium than Tunbridge Wells, with a short boundary on one side, Kapil Dev might not have amassed 175 off his own bat and turned the game. In the 1987 World Cup, Zimbabwe came within four runs of defeating New Zealand. In the 1992 World Cup they defeated England. So a country of amateurs was a boundary away from giant-killing in their first three World Cups.

Fielding was the forte of these amateurs, who had played multiple sports in country clubs from early childhood, and thereby learnt how to throw themselves around as well as the ball. Colin Bland, born in this environment and brought up at Queens Sports Club in Bulawayo in the 1950s, having to fetch the ball if he missed the stumps with a throw when practising, was ahead of his time. When Zimbabwe participated in the Currie Cup, they never won it – Natal and Transvaal dominated South Africa's domestic competition – but they were competitive. Mike Procter, steaming in off his angled run-up, made an inspiring sight when he moved from Natal and represented Rhodesia at the Police Ground in Salisbury. It used to be packed with several thousand spectators in makeshift stands.

League games were played on Saturdays in Harare and on a Sunday in country districts. Such fixtures, before one-day internationals were scaled back to 50 overs a side, would consist of 120 overs in a day, and start at 9am, so there was plenty of scope for a long innings. The games would be followed by barbecues and beers: the players worked hard, played hard and socialised harder. Then the hardiest souls, or those going "troppo", would go and jump in the river to wrestle with crocodiles.

This was the nursery not only of Hick, the highest first-class run-scorer born in Africa, but of Brian Davison, who blazed more than 27,000 first-class runs, and Andy Flower, who methodically worked his way to No.1 in the ICC Test rankings, and came as near as anyone of his time to mastering spin; and of two of the three most successful coaches England have had in Fletcher and Flower.

White Zimbabwean cricket was a brotherhood. Players could wind opponents up like brothers do. Members of one team would either know, or know of, or even be married to members of another. In the nature of brotherhoods, it was not easy to break into. As Henry Olonga had immigrated from Kenya, a decade passed after their inaugural Test in 1992 before a black Zimbabwean nailed down a regular Test place.

* * *

Zimbabwe's first Test captain, David Houghton, had already played international sport, and had been hailed by the captain of Pakistan's hockey team as the world's best goalkeeper. As one of the perks of independence, the new Zimbabwe could play sport against other countries, not just South Africa, as in the era of sanctions. Houghton suddenly found himself in goal against some of the world's strongest hockey teams such as Holland and Pakistan. "It was one-way traffic and the sheer volume of shots meant I saved a few," Houghton modestly remembered. Pakistan had a pair of brothers, one on each wing, who were considered the world's finest and between them had scored with 50 consecutive penalty flicks, according to Houghton; whereupon he dived the right way and saved one.

For cricketers, the fruit of independence was that English counties began to tour, starting with Middlesex. It could be argued that Zimbabwe were at their strongest in the early 1980s, before the mass emigration of players. After the 1983 World Cup, the moment was ripe, if ever it was, for Zimbabwe to be granted Test status; if so Graeme Hick, it was said, would never have left his homeland. Except that Sri Lanka had just been given Test status, and had played their inaugural Test in early 1982. The ICC, under the direction of England and Australia, cautiously waited first for Sri Lanka to justify their promotion.

Along with English counties, Pakistan International Airlines toured Zimbabwe with a strong side including Mushtaq Mohammad, and Houghton was keeping wicket when he saw a novel stroke. Hanif, Mushtaq's older brother, had introduced the reverse sweep to England in the Lord's Test of 1967, and here was Mushtaq introducing it to Zimbabwe in the mid-1980s. When Sri Lanka made their first tour of Zimbabwe in 1994, they had a young off-spinner called Muttiah Muralitharan who bowled 55 overs in one innings in the Test at Bulawayo and took one wicket. "It was turning in that game," Houghton recalled, "and he had a slip and a mid-off as his only two fielders on the offside. There was no other way to hit offside and move fielders over from the leg side, except the reverse sweep, and for two days we played cat and mouse." A lot of wristwork, developed not only in cricket but hockey and squash (in which he represented Zimbabwe at junior level), went into that innings. In Zimbabwe's ninth Test, Houghton finished with 266, still their highest individual innings.

It had been thanks to Houghton that Zimbabwe had come so close to defeating New Zealand in the 1987 World Cup, when he scored 142 off only 137 balls, a very rapid rate for those days, out of the 243 they needed. "For sheer heroism, the innings of the World Cup was David Houghton's." So *Wisden*, in its review of the competition, stated sapiently (all right, self-praise is no commendation).

To ensure Zimbabwe got over the line at least once in the next World Cup of 1992, Houghton insisted that every player who wanted to be considered for selection had to practise and play in Harare in the preceding season. Would professionals have made such sacrifices? The wicketkeeper Wayne James climbed into his car at 10am on a Friday morning in Bulawayo and belted up to Harare Sports Club in six hours to put on one kind of pads or another. He is considered to have been the best wicketkeeper Zimbabwe ever had, and set what was then a world record by making 13 dismissals in a first-class game ("all regulation catches," he told me modestly) in addition to scoring 99 and 99 not out, whereupon the bowler fired one down the leg side for byes that ended the match. Andrew ("Bundu") Waller piloted his light plane to Harare for practice, and Robin Brown drove 250kms for the Tuesday practices as well. Nobody received any mileage allowance let alone payment. "Fantastic commitment," is Houghton's fair summary.

While organising these sessions, and busy hitting catches, Houghton found he had too little time himself to practise. So he persuaded the board to employ one of the English professionals wintering in Harare, Essex's Don Topley, who fitted in so well he was offered a fee in US dollars to coach the team in the 1992 World Cup. Initially, Zimbabwe's schedule was very amenable, until South Africa were admitted at the last minute to their first global tournament. Zimbabwe's revised schedule had them criss-crossing the Tasman from Australia to New Zealand and back – and two of their games in Australia were in Tasmania. No direct flights from there to New Zealand.

Zimbabwe came close to defeating India, and would have defeated them if the rain rules before Duckworth/Lewis had not been so antiquated. But they still had not won a game before their final qualifier, when they met England at Albury, an outground whose pitch would only get worse. Still, England had not lost in the competition, and were set a target no higher than 135. Topley, having conducted the fielding warm-up, was standing beside the picket gate when Graham Gooch and Ian Botham walked out as England's openers. "Good luck, Gray!" said Topley as usual. Whereupon Gooch missed his first ball, a full toss by Eddo Brandes, who also bowled Graeme Hick for nought. Hick, a sensitive soul and naturally torn between the country of his birth and adoption, had sung both national anthems before the start.

Richie Benaud, conducting the post-match interviews with Zimbabwe's coach and England's captain, asked Topley if he was going to remind Gooch about this defeat when they played together in the next English season.

Topley: "Yes, I'm sure I'll mention it to Graham. If there are 200 days in the English season, I'll no doubt mention it to my captain 198 times."

Gooch: "No you won't, because I won't be going to watch any second-team cricket."

Throughout the 1990s, Zimbabwe were competitive in both formats. Their score against England in two Tests at home in 1996/97 was 0-0, the one in Bulawayo ending with the scores level, while Zimbabwe went 5-2 up in ODIs. Zimbabwe even won Test matches against Pakistan home and away, if in curious circumstances. Among other rumours was one that Pakistan's senior players were trying to get rid of their captain Rameez Raja. Enough money was going into the right places to shore up the batting by bringing back Murray Goodwin from Australia and Neil Johnson from South Africa to their native land. Heath Streak was a world-class leader of the pace attack, given enthusiastic if less skilled support, while Paul Strang looked as though he had a long career ahead as a leg-spinning all-rounder.

After the turn of this millennium the bottom fell out. One rift after another between the board and players left Zimbabwe with a team of unseasoned black players, after the white regulars had retired or emigrated, or been injured in Strang's case. Between 2001 and 2005 Zimbabwe won a single Test, and that at home to Bangladesh. They did not play any Tests from 2005 to 2011, owing to British boycotts and voluntary withdrawals, but the damaging effect was the same.

The embers flared up when the former Test captain Alistair Campbell was given the rein and money to introduce domestic franchises, which played all three formats. Good money went initially to Zimbabwean and overseas players, like Moeen Ali, while Jason Gillespie and Chris Silverwood cut their milk teeth as coaches. The matches were televised by SuperSport; crowds attended, and the game's base was broadened as never before. Then the money disappeared into other pockets, perhaps those of a franchise's support staff who had been appointed with no obvious purpose.

It became the same in most walks of life: where had the money gone? The country morphed into a kleptocracy. Intellectual capital drained away. Coaches of the calibre of Duncan Fletcher, both Flowers, Dave Houghton, Graeme Hick and Trevor Penney worked abroad. Whole calendar years have since passed without Zimbabwe playing a Test.

* * *

After my last tour of South Africa in 2019/20, I wanted to return to Zimbabwe because I had not visited since 2004. England had kept Zimbabwe at such an extended arm's length that the two countries had subsequently met only once, in the World T20 finals of 2007. This seemed a rather English thing to do: promote Zimbabwe to Test status in 1991, then refuse to have any contact. Like saying to someone: "Oh, you simply must come round and see us some time," which, when translated, means "do not dare to come anywhere near."

I knew times were bad, owing to the regime's corruption and the West's sanctions; but only when I landed at Joshua Nkomo International Airport in Bulawayo did I realise how bad. Arrivals were down to four planes per day, three from Johannesburg, one from Harare. The customs officer was a woman in her mid-20s. She asked me if I was bringing anything new into Zimbabwe. I said no. "I'm going to have to fine you if you say 'no' on this declaration form then I find something in your suitcase," she said. Nope, at the end of England's Test tour of South Africa nothing of mine was remotely new. So she asked me politely to open my suitcase and had a look.

"Have you got any chocolate?"

"No, sorry."

"You haven't got any chocolate? You said you were from England, haven't you got any chocolate from England?"

She was so disappointed. I think if I had brought in a suitcase of gold bullion she would have overlooked it in favour of a KitKat. A normal woman in her mid-20s, who simply wanted a very small treat, a piece of chocolate, because there wasn't any in Zimbabwe, unless you had US dollars. I wish I had not left behind on the plane a tiny carton, containing a chocolate, in the snack box dished out to passengers.

Joshua Nkomo is the most relaxed international airport I have been to, more so than those on Caribbean islands which sleep in the middle of the day. Yet every arriving passenger had his or her temperature taken: this was the end of January 2020, with Covid-19 spreading out of China, six weeks before Britain went into lockdown. During the 20-kilometre drive into Bulawayo from the airport, I saw two cars as the sum total of traffic, such was the level of economic activity. In that most African of images, a woman sat under a tree beside the road. She was waiting, waiting, for a bus that might never come. In Bulawayo, street vendors sat in the shade of buildings, and spread out their ware – singular not plural – and sat, and sat, until resigning in the evening their hope of selling one last newspaper, or bag of popcorn, or old school textbook.

Neither at the airport nor in the city of Bulawayo did I see any sign of a gun, or truncheon, or weapon of any kind. In ambience it was much like what I imagined an inland Bournemouth would have been in the 1950s. I was amazed walking round the streets at night, in semi-darkness, because only a few street lights worked. Vendors left their takings, in coins and notes, spread out on the pavement beside the goods they were selling. People milled around, to chat if not to buy, yet such was the honesty that nothing was nicked. A vast minority, perhaps majority, would have had no job and been dependent on remittances from family members, mainly in South Africa, where five million Zimbabweans were said to work (no way of counting the numbers who crossed the border). Yet the fabric of this society held true.

The Ndebele used to be a pastoral people, unlike the Shona, not martial. When Cecil Rhodes, as head of the British South Africa Company, decided he wanted all their land and their minerals for himself, and drew lines on his map, he could hardly have chosen two more different tribes to be bedfellows.

Yet this British legacy, even if the source of Zimbabwe's problems, has been lovingly preserved in Bulawayo: the Supreme Court and its dome in the city centre, the Magistrates Court and small claims court of red stone, the Custom House, the National Art Gallery, the National Museum, the railway museum where steam engines have retired, never able to run from the Cape to Cairo (if the project is completed, it will be China's government that does it). Most preserved of all, the Bulawayo Club, which now admits non-members to make ends meet, where I stayed for a couple of nights and where Jan Morris would have been in seventh heaven.

If you cannot pay the bill at the end of your visit, you can choose from dozens of pairs of horns suspended on the walls on which o impale yourself honourably. A forest of teak has been relaid to cover the floors and panel the walls. The inner courtyard is cool and remote from lorry's roar and street-vendor's cry. Many a cabinet is filled with silver trophies for rugby and rifle shooting; grand old clocks no longer tick. Cruets and cups, towels and bedsheets, some a little threadbare, have the monogram of BC, letters entwined. In my suite's bathroom, water trickled eventually out of a tap in spite of the latest drought.

Hung all over the walls were photographs, portraits and paintings of local birds, from kingfishers to hoopoes, and several landscapes of Victoria Falls, spume rising from the depths. A huge wall-mounted tapestry by the Bulawayo Quilter's Guild, dated 1894, depicted scenes of local life. On the stairs, a painting of the Abdication of Napoleon held pride of place, in another room a portrait of Queen Victoria, one of only two women depicted in the whole club – the other being Princess Elizabeth when she made her grand tour by train in 1947. But nothing, not even a sketch, of Great Zimbabwe, the ruins of which had been discovered by Europeans in the 1860s. They clearly did not fit the colonial narrative, that We bestowed civilisation on Them, albeit at the point of a gun. The stone walls and towers of Great Zimbabwe, the remains of Ming and Persian pottery, proved they had civilisation centuries before British colonisation.

I saw why the club secretary kept the key to the library: complete leatherbound sets of novelists favoured by late Victorians, from Dickens to Smollett. The set of *Punch*, from the first volume in 1841 right through until 1946, was encyclopaedic. *The Dictionary of National Biography*, in full. And a memoir by one of Cecil Rhodes's employees, not published until after his death, in which he admitted – rather sheepishly, so it sounded – that the King of Bulawayo had kept his side of the treaty, and that Rhodes's company had to conjure up a pretext to send in the troops and take over his land.

In the morning it took me ten minutes to find my way – via the Snooker Room and other rooms designed for balls, military meetings and cigar smoking – to the dining-room for breakfast. Beneath the ceiling fans and chandeliers, some of whose bulbs worked, enormous silver tureens were arrayed, but no more devilled kidneys lurked underneath. Dark-red curtains, leather-backed chairs, and a framed seating plan for a 90th Birthday Luncheon back in '77 – in 1877, of course. The one type of breakfast on offer? The Full English.

Outside the dining-room stood a gong for summoning members to dinner, above it a portrait of Captain Knapp who died in action at Spion Kop in 1900. Nearby hang photographs of the Administrators of Southern Rhodesia. Sir William Milton looks calm, composed and sensible, sitting with hands folded on his knees. He had represented South Africa in their inaugural Test, having done much as Rhodes's secretary to raise their XI and to promote the English tour.

Next to Milton, Dr Leander Starr Jameson, the Administrator from 1891 to 1896, gazes into eternity with a mad or manic look in his eye. Not the epitome of competence, either. When Jameson set off on his raid in the illegal hope of sparking an uprising by British miners in the Boer republic of Transvaal, he cut the telegraph line to Johannesburg. Only it was not the telegraph line, but an ordinary fence. The Boers, therefore, knew exactly where Jameson was, and kept in touch with each other by telegram while picking off his troops, until the defeated rabble returned home. Jameson was sentenced to 15 months in prison in London for this bungling, yet he emerged to become Prime Minister of Cape Colony, and a baronet, while Milton cleaned up the mess in Southern Rhodesia from 1896 to 1914. One of the most remarkable features of the British establishment is how nothing succeeds like failure.

Along with the Bulawayo Club and the other colonial institutions of the city centre, cricket is preserved too, just about. I went to Queens Sports Club where the 1996 Test had ended with the scores level, and where Tuskers were playing Rhinos in a four-day game which lasted little more than two because the pitch was so bad. Over the bar hung a framed copy of the front page of *The Herald* – "Zimbabwe Murder England" – as an echo of David Lloyd's famous comment when he walked round the ground after the drawn Test to be interviewed, muttering "We flippin' murdered them." The ground itself was a shell of what it had been. There had been an enormous Australian-style scoreboard with all the players' names, scores and bowling analyses: this building, of several storeys, had been reduced to a shell. Only the total and the number of wickets, and the two individual scores of the current batsmen, were posted.

As a late replacement in that Test, "Bundu" Waller flew in from his farm to make 50 on his debut, such a mature and rounded innings. Only one side had a wrist-spinner, Paul Strang. Alistair Campbell, Zimbabwe's captain, made a world-class 70 by lunch in the opening session, at No.3. England had a better, more accurate, attack but overall there had been little between the sides in Zimbabwean conditions. Bulawayo itself had been vibrant in its own quiet way, by day if not night; the future had seemed bright.

"Why hasn't the game died?" I asked Wayne James, who had shared a century stand on this ground with Houghton during his 266. "Because of the passion of these guys," James said, admiringly. "They keep going even when they don't get paid." They flung themselves around the same field where Colin Bland had raised the bar, and subsequent generations had striven to follow his example. A single player was white.

Zimbabwe's Test players, after years of corruption, were getting paid again. The other domestic cricketers were not, or only haphazardly, and then back-dated so that inflation had eroded its value by the time the money came through. James estimated that the players of the five first-class teams, outside the Test squad, subsisted on ten US dollars a day, and that was shortly before the Covid lockdown.

Zimbabwe's corruption was soon seen to extend to the top of cricket's tree and include their finest bowler. Heath Streak was banned for eight years after he accepted five charges of breaching the ICC Anti-Corruption Code while coaching Zimbabwe and several T20 franchises. I had visited Streak's family farm outside Bulawayo while he was still playing, going there in a taxi with a local journalist during one of the numerous droughts. This colleague had raised the ire of the ZANU boys on the Zimbabwe board by siding with Streak and the senior players – still mainly white – in their pay dispute. In the press box he wore a cricket shirt with Streak's name on the back.

As road signs were not abundant, we turned off the main road down the wrong track. To find the right way we stopped and talked to a family living outside what transpired to be the fence of the Streak family farm, squatter-camping with their few possessions in the little shade offered by arid bush: a strip of tarpaulin, a small fire, a pot and a pan. Had the Streak family helped them, for example by offering work, I asked, for my colleague to translate. No, they did not help neighbours like them.

When we arrived, the farmhouse was one of those mini-paradises which the British have carved out of Africa: where "everything is given", as Camus said, while you sit in an armchair in the shade. The latest drought had been damaging, but the Streaks said they had made the most of it: Heath's father Dennis – who had himself represented Rhodesia at cricket – had gone to the Bulwayo City Council and secured the contract to cut the verges alongside the main roads. Even in a drought this added up to a lot of grass, which they used to feed their cattle. Dennis had the right machinery, which was not being used on the farm. Clever business. Money goes to money. And even if we possess a thousand times more than our neighbour, some of us want more.

ENGLAND IN ZIMBABWE
1996/97

────────────── *Overall* ──────────────

Played **6**   Won **3**   Lost **0**   Drawn **3**

────────────── *In Zimbabwe* ──────────────

Played **2**   Won **0**   Lost **0**   Drawn **2**

────────────── *In England* ──────────────

Played **4**   Won **3**   Lost **0**   Drawn **1**

England's record at each venue

────────────── *Harare Sports Club* ──────────────

Played **1**   Won **0**   Lost **0**   Drawn **1**

────────────── *Queens Sports Club, Bulawayo* ──────────────

Played **1**   Won **0**   Lost **0**   Drawn **1**

Highest scores

113	Nasser Hussain	Bulawayo	1996/97
112	John Crawley	Bulawayo	1996/97
101*	Alec Stewart	Harare	1996/97

Best bowling

4-40	Darren Gough	Harare	1996/97
4-61	Phil Tufnell	Bulawayo	1996/97
3-39	Robert Croft	Harare	1996/97

Time to draw stumps

This is where I say farewell
At Terminal 3's carousel.

Been round and round, place to place,
Like that last unclaimed suitcase.

Yet, on my way home in the dark and rain,
Someone with a paper on the train,
Smiles, transported, in some small way,
To another land. Have I brightened his day?